ESSENTIAL TECHNICAL ANALYSIS

Tools and Techniques to Spot Market Trends

Wiley Trading Advantage

Option Strategies, Second Edition / Courtney Smith

Options Course / George A. Fontanills

Options Course Workbook / George A. Fontanills

Outperform the Dow / Gunter Meissner, Randall Folsom

Point and Figure Charting, Second Edition / Thomas J. Dorsey

Schwager on Futures / Jack Schwager

Seasonality / Jake Bernstein

Sniper Trading and *Sniper Trading Workbook* / George Angell

Stock Index Futures & Options / Susan Abbott Gidel

Stock Market Course and *Stock Market Course Workbook* /
    George A. Fontanills and Tom Gentile

Study Guide for Trading for a Living / Dr. Alexander Elder

Study Guide to Accompany Fundamental Analysis / Jack Schwager

Study Guide to Accompany Technical Analysis / Jack Schwager

Technical Analysis / Jack Schwager

Technical Analysis of the Options Markets / Richard Hexton

Technical Market Indicators / Richard J. Bauer, Jr. and Julie R. Dahlquist

Trader Vic II / Victor Sperandeo

Trader's Tax Solution / Ted Tesser

Trading Applications of Japanese Candlestick Charting / Gary Wagner
    and Brad Matheny

The Trading Athlete: Winning the Mental Game of Online Trading /
    Shane Murphy and Doug Hirschhorn

Trading Chaos / Bill Williams

Trading for a Living / Dr. Alexander Elder

Trading Game / Ryan Jones

Trading in the Zone / Ari Kiev, M.D.

Trading Systems & Methods, Third Edition / Perry Kaufman

Trading to Win / Ari Kiev, M.D.

Trading with Crowd Psychology / Carl Gyllenram

Trading with Oscillators / Mark Etzkorn

Trading without Fear / Richard W. Arms, Jr.

Ultimate Trading Guide / John Hill, George Pruitt, Lundy Hill

Value Investing in Commodity Futures / Hal Masover

Visual Investor / John J. Murphy

ESSENTIAL
TECHNICAL
ANALYSIS
Tools and Techniques
to Spot Market Trends

LEIGH STEVENS

JOHN WILEY & SONS, INC.

To my many former colleagues at Cantor Fitzgerald, lost so tragically in September 2001, as well as to the Cantor survivors who are carrying on so ably.

To Mark Weinstein, without whom I would not have the same understanding of how markets work.

This book is also dedicated to Oscar Ichazo, who provided the insights that so enhanced my being, living, and doing.

Published by John Wiley & Sons, Inc.
Published simultaneously in Canada.

ISBN 0-471-15279-X

Printed in the United States of America.

10 9 8 7 6 5 4 3 2 1

CONTENTS

CONTENTS

FOREWORD

Financial markets, by their very nature, attract a wealth of high-caliber individuals who are genuinely excited by their chosen profession. Their enthusiasm and their willingness to share their knowledge makes belonging to the community of traders, investors, and analysts a great privilege. It is my experience that an hour spent listening to their stories, or reading their insights, is often the equivalent to months of study in an academic environment.

Most of these individuals are successful because they recognize, in a way that academic analysis still does not, that asset price movements are not just random fluctuations driven by the rational behavior of independent traders. They recognize that human beings are, by nature, gregarious and communicative, and have an inner drive to belong to groups. Not surprisingly, therefore, group psychology provides a controlling influence over individual activity and transforms a large quantity of apparently unrelated decisions into a more certain outcome.

Importantly, this outcome reveals itself in the form of rhythmic, patterned, price movements that bear not only a natural relationship to one another but also are essentially predictable once they are understood. This is why the discipline of technical analysis—hearing the message of the market via price movements—is such an accurate tool for making profitable trading decisions.

Furthermore, since markets essentially attempt to anticipate movements in economic and social fundamentals, the accurate use of technical analysis actually implies an ability to predict those fundamentals. This is why technical analysis is such an important tool for making investment decisions.

Leigh Stevens comes from this community of enthusiastic and knowledgeable individuals. His depth of experience, acquired over very many years, has generated a deep understanding of, and commitment to, the discipline of technical analysis. Moreover, he is one of those rare individuals who have the ability to convey the essence of his ideas, not only in a wonderfully simple and straightforward way, but also charged with appropriate anecdotes and experiences. There are not many people around who can both walk their talk and talk their walk.

—Tony Plummer
Former Director of Hambros Bank Ltd and
of Hambros Fund Management PLC
Author of *Forecasting Financial Markets*

PREFACE

I've been fortunate in many respects in my life in being in the right place at the right time. I took a sabbatical from corporate life to write this book, in time to not be in my office at Cantor Fitzgerald on the 105th floor of One World Trade Center, during the tragic events on September 11, 2001. I'm immensely grateful that I was able to be here to author this book and I suppose you could say that technical analysis saved my life. Thanks also goes to my editor at John Wiley & Sons, Pamela van Giessen, who provided guidance and encouragement in the process of writing this book.

My most fortunate opportunity, in terms of technical analysis, presented itself in 1984 when Mark Weinstein, a world-class trader of stocks and index futures, began mentoring me. Mark demonstrated to me the truth of the words of legendary stock speculator Jesse Livermore, as quoted in *Barron's* in 1921, when he said that "Speculation is a business. It is neither guesswork nor a gamble. It is hard work and plenty of it."

I was at the time an investments vice president at Dean Witter, now Morgan Stanley Dean Witter. A friend, who was an active investor and sometimes speculator in bonds and index futures, came by my office to tell me of this person, Mark Weinstein, whom he had teamed up with to invest money—and that he was his wife's driving instructor. You can be sure that I did not consider that this fellow could know much about the markets, or to have been very successful in them! I then met Mark when he came by to place some orders for his new partner's account—I was his broker. Mark Weinstein turned out to be a very intense person, and the focus of that intensity was the stock and commodities markets, as well as technical analysis, the means that he used to make market decisions. He was temporarily burned out from his life as a professional speculator for the prior 10 years—and was considering buying a driving school, so he was getting a first-hand look at the basics of the business. He often said that he hoped to lead a *normal* life and that maybe some other business would allow him to do that.

Mark, I discovered, knew about all technical chart patterns, indicators and their effective use, how to interpret volume and the stock tape, going against popular market sentiment, interpreting Elliott wave patterns, and a lot more. I knew a little about technical analysis from some self-study and made some use of charts and technical indicators in my business. Mark, however, had been mentored by many top traders and analysts, such as George Lindsay. Mark would literally show up on their doorsteps and ask them if he could learn from them.

What developed over the following two years was that Mark started teaching me what he had learned about the internal dynamics of the markets. He didn't take a position in the market often, but when he did he invested heavily and called in his orders from home. Mark would, for example, take large index options positions at a market low and hold onto them for the first and strongest part of a move. He did this multiple times in this two-year period. I would know when he decided that the market had turned, as he would call me up and tell me shortly after the fact. One morning sticks out in my mind when he called and said the market had bottomed. Nothing was happening in the market either that morning or in prior weeks, as the market was in the doldrums. However, by the end of the day the market was up substantially.

Over time I spent many hours on the phone with Mark listening to him espouse his market knowledge, without arousing much notice in an office full of other brokers talking to their clients. This wasn't great for my business, but I was able to absorb a lot of what he knew. He had time on his hands then, as he was only in the market sporadically. The hundreds of hours he spent discussing his techniques and experiences were of immense value. There are rarely these opportunities to work with such highly successful speculators—these are the market professionals whose sole focus and passion is winning in the market. I sometimes didn't think that this man was real, as his knowledge was so superior to anything I had been exposed to on Wall Street up until then. The only analogy is to compare this to the prowess of a Michael Jordan or a Tiger Woods in the sports world— no doubt if you played with them, they would seem to inhabit another realm. Just as with Jordan and Woods, you won't find the world-class market pros teaching what they know—they also just do what they know. Nor do these top traders write market advice letters or sell *winning* trading systems—in fact, Weinstein often debunked this idea, saying that no one would sell a profitable system, only use it themselves to make money.

In 1986 when I was the stock index and financial futures specialist at PaineWebber, I brought Mark to the attention of Jack Schwager, then senior technical analyst there, as a candidate for his first Market Wizards book. Jack was as amazed as I was that Mark claimed he had almost no losses, in hundreds if not thousands of trades. Jack checked one of his account statements and also relied on me as judge of his trading record. I had known about dozens of Mark's transactions as they were occurring and followed the stock, option, or futures as subsequent market action unfolded. He was the real thing as far as being able to profit from his predictive abilities.

Like all the other top traders Jack Schwager wrote about in his Market Wizards book, Mark Weinstein was also intently focused on avoiding losses. He would exit a position with a small profit or with a small loss (a very rare occurrence), without hesitation, if the market did not move his way. The other very important lesson learned from this enormously successful trader was that the emotional factor makes a difference. Knowledge is important, but someone could have as much, if not more, market knowledge than Weinstein and still lose in the market because of not having the right emotional temperament and discipline it takes to be successful plus, a constant willingness to give up their current notions of market trends when wrong.

It is the emotional element that is the key to winning and losing big in the market. Part of that is waiting for the right price, the right moment, and then having the discipline to stay with your position. And to not overstay or invest too much of your capital. So while technical analysis might be the key to knowing what to buy when, there is this crucial psychological component to capitalizing on this knowledge.

At PaineWebber, I had the opportunity, besides advising the firm's brokers, to devise and run a stock index futures fund. I developed a rule-based system of market entry and exit based on technical criteria and it was these ideas that were sound. However, I found that I was one of the people who had difficulty in handling the emotional pressures of running a speculative fund. I found that I was a better *advisor*—numerous brokers at PaineWebber said they profited from my advice—than trader or fund manager. Having a natural bent toward teaching, I continue in this vein with this book.

After PaineWebber, where I ended up as senior technical analyst, I had the opportunity to combine marketing and technical analysis as the Dow Jones Telerate global product manager for technical analysis in 1993 both in New York and later in London. While still in New York, I organized the establishment and rules governing the Charles H. Dow Award, given annually by the Market Technicians Association (MTA) of which I am a member, for outstanding achievement in technical analysis work. Like the man himself, I stipulated that the Award given in Dow's name by the MTA in conjunction with Dow Jones & Co., be awarded for work that stressed the practical and involved clarity of writing that was superior. This has always been the goal of my own writing.

When I took a position at Cantor Fitzgerald, one of the largest institutional bond and equities brokers in the world, I also had the opportunity to write technical analysis columns for the *Cantor Morning News* and also for CNBC.com. This book is an outgrowth of the attention I got from publishers in 1999–2000 while I was writing these columns. I finally decided to take on the opportunity and challenge of being able to write more than 1,000 words at a time and to expand on the essential principles of technical analysis. Making this effort was very much influenced by the hundreds of e-mail inquiries I received from CNBC.com viewers and their interest in this subject, as well as the appreciation so many of them expressed of my efforts to make technical analysis interesting and useful to them. I hope that this book is the helpful introduction to technical analysis that many of them said they would like to read.

1

INTRODUCTION AND RATIONALE TO THE TECHNICAL APPROACH

METHOD AND GOALS OF THIS BOOK

The goal of this book is, like my CNBC.com technical analysis columns that came before it, to present technical analysis tools and insights that can help you make more informed, and more profitable decisions relating to trading and investing. I utilize the U.S. stock market for all examples. I also discuss some indicators and aspects that are particular to the stock market.

A major related purpose of the information and stories I present is that a process is begun whereby you start to look at markets in a different way, to see beyond the usual way that market information is presented to you or understood by you. I emphasize again my hope that you will be able to *profit* from this information. A major consideration is to discuss and demonstrate what I consider to be the more useful tools and methods from technical analysis—for example, demonstrating how to locate stocks that offer the best hope of gain at the right time, at lowest risk, and with an effective exit strategy. There are less used technical tools and analysis techniques that could be described but that might be marginal for most people, in terms of improving trading and investment decisions.

A second orientation I have is to discuss some of the pitfalls to improved trading and investing decisions, such as your *attitude* toward the market—is it gambling or is it profitable investing or trading that you can master? How much time will you invest in it and how much perseverance will you maintain? I find that a person's emotional temperament, work habits, discipline, and ability to see ahead (foresight) are as, or sometimes more, important as mastery of some of the more complex areas of technical analysis. Time spent and perseverance in understanding the most basic use of charts and technical indicators are more important to most market participants than exhaustive study of every aspect of this field. And there is a great tendency among people to think that complex ideas and techniques must be the way to approach the markets, which after all, are complex mechanisms. This is wrong, as simple is better in my experience, and I am not the only one saying this—many top advisors and money managers base their decisions on a relatively simple set of criteria.

USE OF EXAMPLES

Chart Examples

I use stock and stock averages exclusively for all examples in this book relating to demonstrating technical patterns and indicators. While I also have a background in the futures, fixed income, and foreign exchange markets, I will not provide chart examples from these markets, or discuss aspects of these markets that are unique to them—for example, describing *open interest* and how to use it in futures or the ways of constructing a *continuous contract* price series from the various futures contract–months. I do discuss some custom indicators and methods of analysis that are unique to the stock market, as I believe I have something unique to say about these things. However, again I want to emphasize that all general technical analysis principles, which comprise most of this book, are applicable to all markets.

All Markets

The popularity of technical analysis owes much to its initial widespread use in the commodities markets, especially in the 1970s, when these markets were very active, drawing in many individual futures traders. Technical analysis is very popular in the biggest single market in the world—the *interbank currency market*, usually just called the foreign exchange or FX market. Having worked in this area in Europe, I can say that I understand a major reason for this—a chart or a technical indicator is the same in any language. This said, I do not draw, for example, on FX charts of dollar–yen or of the eurodollar for my illustrations.

Further Study

I do, however, point you to other books with a more detailed and specialized orientation toward other markets or specialized fields within technical analysis that you may want to study further if you're interested—for example, on *candlestick charting* or *wave analysis*. Some of what I consider to be the best reference works on technical analysis are provided at the end of the book in a recommended reading list. Some of these books draw on more examples from the futures markets, for example.

NEED FOR TECHNICAL ANALYSIS

There are plenty, in fact a majority, of successful money managers who say they don't use technical analysis at all. There are also rich investors and speculators who rely mostly on technical analysis. It's not the method; it's the person—just as Jack Schwager found in his wonderful Market Wizard series of books.

You may not have the emotional temperament or time for short-term speculation in the market, which is my situation, but you can still vastly improve your batting average when it comes to longer-term investing, such as in stocks. You can focus on looking at long-term charts and indicators only—however, don't get married to a stock, either. Even very long-term investors decide it's time to exit a stock or stock sector and look for other situations. This group of individuals can benefit from stock market timing to find a more advantageous (cheaper) entry into a stock or mutual fund or to exit when a primary trend reverses.

WHAT IS TECHNICAL ANALYSIS?

The word *technical* comes from the Greek *technikos*, relating to art or skillful. Webster's goes on to define technical as having special and *practical* knowledge, something I want to reinforce also. *Technical analysis* is the study of any market that uses *price* and *volume* information *only* in order to forecast future price movement and trends. (Consideration of a third factor, that of *open interest*, is part of the technical approach in the futures markets only.)

Technical analysts and technically oriented investors or traders rely on historical and current price and volume information only. Some other, related, statistical information is often considered part of technical analysis. What I refer to here are *sentiment indicators*, such things as surveys of market opinion to determine whether the respondent is *bullish, bearish*, or neutral on the market. These figures are compiled as percentages of those surveyed having each type of opinion, for example, the weekly Investor's Intelligence opinion survey of market professionals or the American Association of Individual Investors (AAII) poll of its members. Studies of *short interest* in stocks or extreme readings in the Arms Index (*TRIN*) are also in this category.

A THIRD ELEMENT BESIDE PRICE AND VOLUME

The rationale for studying market opinion is the theory of *contrary opinion*. The idea of contrary opinion in market analysis is that there is value at certain times or in general of going against the predominant view of stock valuations or expected market direction. Warren Buffett, considered a master of *value investing*, looks for value in stocks that may not be perceived by the majority of fund managers. Market makers on the New York Stock Exchange (NYSE) buy when others are selling and vice versa and they make money doing it. The most knowledgeable investors and traders comprise a top tier of market participants, in terms of market knowledge. This group often profits handsomely by being contrary to the investing crowd, buying when others are fearful of a further decline and selling when the majority thinks a stock or the market will go up indefinitely.

Market psychology, sentiment, or contrary opinion, could be called a *third element* in technical analysis but is not part of the formal definition of technical analysis. My favorite sentiment *indicator* is actually a ratio of total daily equity call option volume relative to the volume of equity put options. I tend not to rely on survey type information but do place significant emphasis on whether options market participants are speculating or hedging heavily on one side of the market or the other—whether, as a group, they are betting on a rise or fall in the market. Even here I rely on volume information, which is part of technical analysis input.

TERMS

The terms applied to the use of technical analysis include technical analysis, the *technicals* or *technical factors*—not to be confused with *tech* or technology stocks or technical factors impacting a market, such as a computer failure or blizzard in causing an exchange to close early. *Technical analysis* means a set of principles and analytical tools that are used to make predictions about the market that predominantly involve the use and study of price and volume information only.

FUNDAMENTAL ANALYSIS

Fundamental analysis, rather than concentrating solely on the study of market action itself, relies on examination of the laws of supply and demand relating to a market or to individual stocks. The aim is the same, to determine where stock prices may be heading. Much of fundamental analysis revolves around one basic area—*earnings*. What is a company likely to earn in its business during the current time frame and going forward? Or what is the earnings potential of an entire group of stocks, such as the S&P 500? Relative to earnings, what *multiple* is the market likely to assign to the value of the stock or market index? Will, or should, the price of the stock trade at a value that represents 10, 15, or 50 times past and future (projected) earnings in dollar terms? Price/earnings ratios or P/E considerations form the core of fundamental analysis of stocks.

Relative to P/Es, the broad area of investor sentiment provides an area where fundamental and technical analysis overlap. Whether a stock should or will trade at a price/earnings ratio of 10, 15, or 50 is more than a matter of economic and company growth expectations, it is also a matter of investors' bullish or bearish sentiment. Market participants may decide that they will no longer reward growth stocks with a P/E ratio that is far above the average simply based on having seen a recent collapse of such ratios. Or their views of a company's or industry's growth prospects may be good, but a more cautious attitude takes hold, forcing a downward adjustment to stock prices, when even the fast growing companies with rapidly expanding earnings no longer command hefty premiums to the average stock.

TECHNICAL ANALYSIS RATIONALE

Why would someone rely on just studying charts that plot past and current price and volume information, as well as perhaps technical indicators or formulas that use the same information?

The reasons are found in observations of the stock market, as first noted by Charles Dow in this country and can be described in three ways.

1. *Efficient Market. Over time, market prices reflect everything that can be known about a stock and its future prospects.* The market as a mechanism is very efficient at discounting whatever can affect prices. Even unforeseen events, such as new competition, legal or financial problems, a company takeover, the death of a founder, and so on are quickly priced into the stock. Even unknown (not yet publicized) fundamental factors, such as a sharp earnings drop, are seldom unknown or unanticipated by everyone; those who know often act on the information, and selling volume starts to pick up on rallies. Here I am not talking necessarily about facts known only by company insiders. There are traders, investors, and analysts outside a company or an industry who see changes coming, through astute observation and sharp analysis.

2. *Trends.* The information about a company's stock and its future earnings prospects that are reflected in the stock price will also be reflected in a price *trend* or tendency to go up or down. Trends are not only up or down, but sideways as well or what is sometimes called a *trendless* pattern—I consider a sideways movement to be the third trend possibility, for example, a stock moves between 40 and 50 multiple times. A trend is the action of a body in motion staying in motion until an equal countervailing force occurs.

3. *Reoccurrence. Price trends occur and reoccur in patterns that are largely predictable.* The idea of trends reoccurring is that history repeats itself. If there was abundant stock for sale (supply) previously for sale at 50 and that selling caused a retreat in prices, it may well be the case again when the stock approaches this level again. If it doesn't, that tells you something also, as demand was this time strong enough to overcome selling.

The basic technical analysis rationale can be remembered by the ETR acronym (as in Estimated Time of Arrival). Well, you can estimate arrivals with technical analysis!

TECHNICAL *VERSUS* FUNDAMENTAL ANALYSIS

If you are reading this book, I assume you have an open mind as to the possible validity of technical analysis. I see no contradiction between these forms of analysis. I often use technical analysis as an adjunct to fundamental analysis—I may like a market sector or individual stock for fundamental reasons, for example, computer use is on a path of explosive growth. I might then use technical analysis for or because of

I Market timing—when to get in, for example, a pullback to a *trendline*
I Risk control—judging where to place protective stop (liquidating) orders, for example, on a break of a major trendline
I An end to a trend—applying criteria for when a trend may have reversed, for example, a decisive downside penetration of a stock's 200-day moving average

There are other reasons to use charts, of course, even if you don't use technical analysis techniques, such as for seeing price and price *volatility* history.

Not only do I not see the two means of analysis to be complementary, but I also consider technical analysis to be a shortcut or an efficient way to do stock market fundamental analysis! I may not be able to or want to study everything about the ongoing progress of a company whose stock I own. However, there are always an interested body of people who trade the stock and make informed investment decisions because they know the company or business quite well. I can ascertain what the informed opinion is on a stock by seeing what is going on with the price and volume patterns on the chart. I assume that the market judgment on a stock is right until proven otherwise.

CRITICISMS OF TECHNICAL ANALYSIS

I *There is no proof that technical analysis works*. Actually, there has been some relevant work done by Dr. Andrew Lo at MIT, who has answered the question of the predictive power of some technical analysis concepts. He studied a chart pattern recognized as having a predictive outcome, that of the "head and shoulders" top formation. Dr. Lo sought to determine if a subsequent price decline was in evidence after this pattern developed—compared to outcomes present without this condition. Once the pattern was defined mathematically and tested over the long-term price history of 350 stocks, it was compared to "random walk" simulations. The results confirmed that the pattern studied was in fact predictive in nature for a *subsequent* price decline.

▎ *Technical analysis works only because traders believe it works* and act accordingly, causing the action predicted, for example, traders sell when a stock falls below its 200-day moving average. While this is sometimes true, most active stocks have too much trading activity to cause me to believe in the idea of a self-fulfilling prophecy. If there was a temporary price decline due to the technical selling related to such a break, the stock would rebound if the value became too low relative to its fundamentals. Moreover, the influence of technical analysis is not that great. If you follow the market related channels like CNBC, you'll see a drumbeat of fundamental news all day long. Focus on fundamentals is the mainstream approach and the numbers of investors or traders influenced by technical analysis is small in comparison.

▎ *Price changes are random and can't be predicted.* This criticism is related to the "random walk" theory, as the idea that price history is not a reliable indicator of future price direction. Adherents of this view take a different view of the market being *efficient*. I used this term previously to mean that the market is an effective mechanism *over time*, to reflect everything that can be known about a stock and its prospects. The efficient market *theory* holds that prices fluctuate randomly around an intrinsic value. This point is actually similar to the one technical analysts make that a market price reflects everything that can be known about that item. The difference is that one school (random walk) holds that current relevant factors affecting price are discounted immediately, and the other (technical analysis) is that this *discounting* ebbs and flows, taking place over time intervals that are predictable. Random walk adherents suggest that a buy and hold strategy will offer superior returns, as it is impossible to *time* the market. More on the possibility that attempting entry and exit on intermediate price swings could increase returns, relative to a buy and hold strategy, is found in Chapter 2.

STOCK MARKET DECISION CRITERIA

Even if your primary criteria for making investment or trading decisions are fundamental ones—for example, you like a company's business, the way that company is doing that business and their growth prospects—there may be much to be learned by using a historical chart of the price and volume trends of the stock and by applying some simple rules of thumb related to technical analysis for *timing* considerations.

For example, is there some likelihood that the stock might drop back to a lower level as it's near a prior high, and previously sellers pushed it lower when it was in this price area? You could couple this information with a technical *indicator* that suggests that this stock is *overbought*. If the stock goes above its prior high, you can make a purchase at a bit higher level but with some greater degree of assurance that the stock has willing new buyers coming in.

Or you could wait until a price comes back to the old high that was exceeded, as it often does, one more time. If a stock does retreat from its first advance and you buy in a natural *support* area, you've improved your purchase price. Better entry prices over years of investing add up. Exiting soon after a major trend reversal, such as was seen in the Nasdaq in March and July–August 2000, because you had exit rules based on technical analysis criteria, could have been a major financial advantage.

BROADER APPLICATIONS FOR TECHNICAL ANALYSIS

Technical analysis can be applied to any market or any stock. Also to any market sector index by your studying the chart of that market segment, for example, the semiconductor and oil stock indexes. Or if you are ready to purchase a mutual fund, it's possible to obtain and analyze historical data on the daily closing fund values for major mutual funds. You may also evaluate the stock market as a whole in the way that Charles Dow analyzed it. Is the Dow Transportation average lagging the Dow-Jones Industrial average, suggesting a slowdown, not in manufacturing, but in shipments, a business area that experiences an economic downturn the fastest? Perhaps this observation would cause you to wait and see if the famous Dow theory barometer confirmed a continuation of a market trend, thereby avoiding a big risk by reducing your equity holdings or by waiting to put more money into stocks.

WHOM THIS BOOK IS FOR

Some of these categories of individuals overlap and one person cannot always be so easily defined, but the following are market *orientations* that are common.

- Investors in stocks and mutual funds, including those who have a buy and hold philosophy but who are open to learning the entry and exit decisions that technical analysis helps provide. Mutual funds can be charted like stocks also, and there are sources of closing prices you can download every day if you use a computer. You can chart these prices daily on graph paper also by using the financial press.

- Traders, including day traders and those who trade in and out of stocks over time as opportunities present themselves. Chart patterns and indicators work basically the same way whether seen on a 15-minute, hourly, daily, weekly, or monthly chart. Traders are going to tend to rely more on computers and Internet information.

- The average investor, who combines a bit of both investing time frames and may combine elements of fundamental and technical or chart analysis. And, by the way, it's been shown that the average holding period for stocks is now down to around 10 months.

- Someone who has no prior knowledge of technical analysis. I assume at most that you have some familiarity with stocks, the market, and have bought and sold stocks. You may not have shorted stocks previously.

- People willing to put some time into studying the market and keeping track of their stocks and mutual funds, relative to the market and its sectors. "Never stop evaluating" tends to be the motto of top money managers and traders.

- Pragmatists. Certain core technical analysis principles and precepts show useful information about market trends, but cannot always be demonstrated, proven, or even explained. The fact that they do work can be seen over and over, however. Those less interested in the theory and more interested in what works and its practical use will find technical analysis helpful.

WHOM THIS BOOK IS NOT FOR

- Someone with the expectation of averaging 10–15 percent a month, instead of annually, in stocks, may learn some things from this book, but they're also not likely to be prudent in the risks they take, which is one of my messages.

I A person who expects any system of market analysis to have all the answers all the time. You won't find that in technical analysis or elsewhere that I know of. The best traders and fund managers in the world always stand ready to admit that they are wrong, and they are the top people in making money in the market.

I Someone who will not put some minimum time into studying the market and the charts. You can only expect results from effort put into something. A few hours a week would be sufficient if you are an active market participant, less if you are not.

HOW THIS BOOK IS ORGANIZED

The chapters that follow are summarized.

Chapter 2

How we invest or trade. Investing versus trading time horizons or orientation: Choose one or both, at different times, but don't confuse the two; risk attitudes, risk control, and a trading strategy—your attitude toward risk is all-important to winning in the stock market.

Chapter 3

Charles Dow and the underlying principles of market behavior. Understanding that the internal dynamics of the market have much to do with investor attitudes or psychology. How Dow's concepts form a foundation for technical analysis and predicting future trends.

Chapter 4

Types of charts and scaling. The different ways that price and volume information are displayed.

Chapter 5

Concepts of trends, trendlines, and trading. Entering the basics of technical analysis; the trend is your friend and trendlines your best friend.

Chapter 6

Pattern analysis and recognition: price and volume. Price movement is the president or commander-in-chief; volume is the vice-president; identifying the beginning of major trends; identifying market reversals.

Chapter 7

Technical indicators. Did you need them always? The times they preserve profits or your skin; moving averages; overbought/oversold indicators; advance/decline figures and other stock market specific indicators.

Chapter 8

Confirmation and divergences. Charles Dow said it best in the West; volume divergences; not all divergences are tops but tops often have divergences.

Chapter 9

Specialized forms of analysis and trading, people, and systems. The easy Elliott wave primer; Gann principles and techniques; developing trading systems and back-testing; optimization; indicator and pattern screening techniques.

Chapter 10

Putting it all together. Developing your checklist; some fun stuff.

MORE PERSONAL HISTORY

I came to technical analysis, like many other things in my life, by the process of trial and error leading to discovery and by the fortuitous circumstances of having someone around who could help me discover how markets work. This almost always was a process of uncovering something about the inner workings of the market as a dynamic process of individuals interacting with each other and with outside forces. In the early stages of my learning about technical analysis, it was usually not about the *obvious*. I think Joe Granville said that "if it's obvious, it's obviously wrong." Various events and experiences I had taught me that there was something beyond the obvious.

THE 1970S—MY FIRST *BUBBLE* AND PIGS IN A POKE

In the 1970s there was a speculative *bubble* in the commodities markets, especially in the gold and silver markets. You may be of an age to remember people melting down their heirloom silverware to sell it when prices went from $3 to $30 an ounce and higher. There is no precise definition for a bubble, but generally it's a rise so steep in the market that it's a very rare event. This was a decade of inflation, and tangible assets like real estate and commodities were seen as safe havens, whose price appreciation would stay ahead of rising prices.

I fled to it myself and decided to become a commodity futures broker at Merrill Lynch where they had offices specializing in this type of brokerage. One of my early clients, someone who knew the commodities markets firsthand as the president of Continental Grain Company, was an active trader of the live hogs contract. This contract called for future delivery of the porkers in the pens, before they got cut up into bacon (pork bellies). Merrill Lynch's livestock analyst at the time was an old pro. Growing up in Michigan, I happened to have heard this analyst at times on a farmer-oriented radio show hosted by a neighbor. This expert had a calm voice of authority and his manner gave no doubt that he knew this market and what was going on.

Many years later in the late 1970s in the Merrill Lynch commodities office on Fifth Avenue where I worked, it happened that this same expert was our livestock analyst. He would attempt to predict where prices were likely to be headed in the coming season based on all the known factors of supply and demand. I emphasize *known* here, as another study of the obvious. Based on his own and my firm's experienced market analyst, my client bought a sizable number of hog futures contracts—maybe 50 contracts, which is a lot—a dime change in the price per pound for hogs was worth $15,000. Then prices started falling. My firm's expert was saying, "Don't worry; it's a temporary downturn and not justified by the fundamentals."

You can guess the rest of the story. As prices sank so did my spirits. My client was a very knowledgeable man in the commodities markets and I had the advice of the best fundamental analyst out there, but we were stumped by what was happening. I remember my client ended up selling most, if not all, of his position at a substantial loss. It was a shock to me, as

I didn't know what else to rely on but the kind of analysis related to supply and demand projections I was getting. I don't remember what reason came out finally to explain the substantial price drop. I became very interested in how I could be forewarned about price reversals in the future.

An old friend and a commodities broker himself, Jeff Elliott, told me about using something called an *oscillator* and that this indicator could give me an idea when a market was *overbought*. This was a term in technical analysis suggesting a price rise that was so steep as to be unsustainable—and a situation that would most likely be relieved by prices dropping back to a level where supply and demand equilibrium would be more in balance. The suggestion was that I should not rely just on fundamental analysis and our expert's interpretation of the price influencing factors. I could also rely on price action itself to see if a market might be vulnerable to a substantial price trend reversal.

I THOUGHT I KNEW SOMETHING UNTIL I HEARD GEORGE LINDSAY

In early 1982, with inflation under control and a prospective investing shift to financial assets, I was in the process of becoming a registered stockbroker. In February 1982, George Lindsay, a technical analyst with the institutional and specialist firm Ernest & Company, appeared on the PBS television program *Wall Street Week*. Interestingly, through subsequent years I met many people that also saw that broadcast and remembered it quite well. George Lindsay, by then in the late stages of his career and an unimposing figure, spoke softly and often referred to a small piece of paper. At this time, stocks had been underperforming every other asset class for many years and stockbrokers were becoming real estate brokers. Lindsay stated flatly on the program, that in August, some six months away, a stock market rally of monster proportions would begin. In the prior 20 years the S&P Index had gained only 55 percent.

Figure 1.1 tells the story for the market after August 1982, using the S&P 500 Index, which comprises the stocks forming the core mutual fund holdings in the United States. From mid-February, around the time of Lindsay's public prediction, the market declined approximately 8 percent from the mid-February peak into mid-August. In August a broad advance got underway and in the next 18 years, the S&P gained nearly 1,400% as measured to the weekly closing high in March 2000—using the March 2001 close, the gain is more than 1,000%.

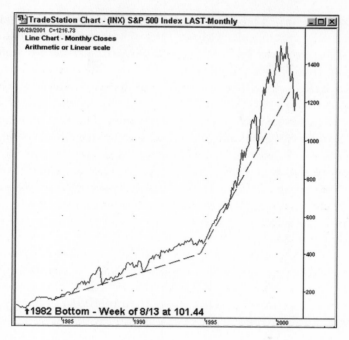

Figure 1.1

Of course, anyone can have a lucky guess. But doing some research on Lindsay, I found other even more startling predictions, including a documented political one from 1939, that Russia would experience a severe collapse and a prolonged period of hard times 50 years hence—1989, of course, corresponded to the fall of the Berlin Wall and ushered in hard times in the U.S.S.R. No, Lindsay wasn't another Nostradamus, just a master of *cycles*. The importance to me of George Lindsay's predictive abilities at the time was the possibility that someone really could know where the market was heading and that I could learn some of this or similar methods.

At the time, in February 1982, I had no frame of reference for any kind of basis or validity to this kind of prediction, even though by then I was studying chart patterns, using some technical indicators and was learning to read the stock tape. To predict market turning points so far ahead of time was a curious novelty at best with the possibility of its being a lucky guess. However, like many others I was struck by Lindsay's confident air of authority when he talked about what the market was going to do well in advance—it was like he was reading the road map ahead on that little piece of paper.

Lindsay, it turned out, had a reputation in professional market circles of being so accurate in his forecasts for market trends, that some traders were said to go away on lengthy vacations if the market wasn't doing much and come back weeks later to buy heavily when he indicated an uptrend was due. Lucky guesses—I suppose he made a lot of them! The other question is whether his forecasts were self-fulfilling prophecies, because he had a sizable professional following. It's doubtful that he or anyone else ever had or will have that kind of influence, as the U.S. stock market is just too huge for it. Years later, someone who had studied with him told me that Lindsay had discovered 12 master cycles to the stock market that had predictable patterns in the way they unfolded—once he identified which one (of the 12) we were in, he could forecast things like "the market will experience a moderate uptrend for three months and then move down sharply beginning in December."

No one whom I know of has been able to continue Lindsay's work, at least with the accuracy and authority he had. His methods, which he kept quite private, may have died with him. Or it may be that the market doesn't conform to such analysis anymore. But he was an inspiration for learning more about the predictive power of the forms of technical analysis that I could learn.

FAST FORWARD TO 2000

Events I describe leading to my wanting to learn more about how markets work, are similar to the shock many investors had in the collapse of the stock market in 2000—after a multitude of Wall Street analysts continued as cheerleaders for stocks at the time of the hyperinflated values of early 2000. During the months following its March peak and while the market sank to its worst performance in many years, most of the technology and Internet stock analysts kept their buy recommendations intact. At one point, when the Nasdaq Composite Index was down 60 percent from its top, less than 1 percent of analysts' recommendations were to sell.

It may well be that this same event led you to consider other ways to analyze the markets that will not only get you in the market, but tell you when it's time to *exit* also. The bursting Nasdaq bubble is our most recent lesson to look beyond the obvious—up until March 2000, as Nasdaq stock values rose to astronomical heights, the *obvious* accepted truth was that the new Information and Internet Age was going to change everything. We no longer had to use the old valuation models that defined normal price to earnings ratios. I heard from many people via my CNBC.com technical analysis columns who held on during the steep downturn—not many said they blamed the analysts and market commentators who gave only buy recommendations. However, if the analyst community can't do better, then investors need to themselves. One way is to gain some practical basic knowledge of technical analysis, as it will provide a means to evaluate when market trends are overdone.

SUMMARY

Tools and techniques to spot market trends is the theme of this book. I assume people are looking for some guidance on this and the subject of technical analysis in general. I hope to save you time and loss by pointing you toward what I've found are the most effective ways to employ technical analysis. I invested the time and took the losses to get to this point. Not to say that you don't need to have your own experiences in using technical analysis—experience is the best teacher. But this book will also guide you in certain directions, and I don't see all techniques and tools as having equal value.

It's my expectation from this book alone that you can learn to spot emerging new trends developing and also see that a trend is ending. However, it's also my hope that this book will also stimulate your interest enough for you to continue to perhaps read other books in this field. Most importantly, start to look at charts—as many of them as you can. And make notes, mental or otherwise, of how you think the trend is unfolding and how it might end. As time goes on, see where you were on or off the mark—if events surprised you, see if there was some other way of seeing the situation that you overlooked.

2

OUR TRADING OR INVESTING GAME PLAN

INTRODUCTION

This book is designed to explain and demonstrate the technical analysis methods to both shorter-term traders and to investors. You may wonder why I am first discussing the topic of our style of market participation and tactical things like a market game plan. It is because as a veteran trader, investor, analyst, and market advisor I have seen all the pitfalls of trying to make money using technical analysis principles and tools. And these pitfalls often have little to do with technical analysis per se, which actually works quite well. The shortcomings are more due to our inability to see and apply these methods objectively or artfully, due to the difficulties of overcoming our market biases, impatience, and fears.

The biggest obstacle to making money in the market is our own self. We know the saying well, that we are our own worst enemy. It is even more true in the market because it is a game where we are pitted against some of the smartest professionals on the planet. The person who is learning the investing game in a more volatile time of fast moving markets may not have a long time to decide about whether to stay in or exit a losing position before facing a big loss—and we can be locked into losses for a long time if we don't have a game plan and exit strategy. Increasingly, when market participants are disappointed with a stock, there is less inclination to be patient and wait for the situation to get better. As our attitudes are the foundation for our ability to *use* technical analysis effectively, this chapter examines the attitudinal and market strategy questions that relate to:

I The temperament needed for market success

I A trading versus investing orientation

I Trading can be tempting

I Our attitude toward risk and willingness to take a loss

I Use of stop orders

I Shorting the market

TRADING AND TRADERS

Traders range from people who buy and sell stocks looking to profit from price swings as short as hourly and who probably consider themselves to be mostly or exclusively *day traders*, to those who are in a stock for a defined price objective only. This latter group, comprising a larger number of individuals than day traders, might think a stock is undervalued and due for a bounce. They may exit a stock if it goes up or down a few dollars. Traders may be in a stock for a few days or a few weeks. The term *profit taking* applies to this group's activities if they have profits to be taken.

There is an old trader saying to "take quick profits." That is, if there is a sudden run up on speculation of a takeover or sale of a company, an impending piece of business or just some piece of news that reflects favorably on a company's sales and profit outlook, it is tempting to book the gain.

There is a tendency for investors to think that the highest high for a stock was a profit they had, and then lost, if the stock comes back down substantially. It is important to remember that all profits are *unrealized* gains until you sell what you bought or buy back what you sold short. Market participants who have a trading orientation and style are less likely to think this way. They tend to be more quick, often too quick, to exit if they have a small profit. This group may not have been nimble enough to exit on a good-sized upswing if they were not watching closely enough or expected more upside. However, when the stock heads back down toward their entry price, they are quick to exit while they still have any, or a small, profit.

A *trading* versus *investing* orientation is more than a matter of the time horizon, but that is a big part of it. The trader is concerned with what Charles Dow called the day-to-day fluctuations of the market and of individual stocks, or the *secondary* movement of the market, which he defined as any substantial rallies in a primary bear market or *reactions* (downswings) in a primary bull market that take place over a few weeks.

More on these terms later, but these are the time frames. Keep in mind that the average time that a stock is owned is down to 10 months, shorter than what Charles Dow defined as the duration of a *primary* market trend of a year or more. Of course, this average holding period is skewed by the large number of market participants attempting to trade shorter-term price swings.

INVESTORS

The investor is, or should be, primarily concerned with what Dow called the primary movement in the market, which tends to run over a period of at least a year and sometimes over periods of multiple years. A drop could occur in just a few months, such as in 1987, but be so steep that it is considered a *primary* bear trend. A decline can be this short, but not in an advance considered to be a primary bull market. An old market saying is that "they slide faster than they glide"—markets go down faster than they go up.

Jesse Livermore, one of the legendary stock speculators in his day (the 1920s), used to say that there are always lots of early bulls in a bull market, or early bears in a bear market. But he made most of his money by "sitting." He stated that these early bulls or bears lose their conviction. The market as a mechanism is almost guaranteed to shake you out of your conviction as the news is still quite bearish in early rally stages and quite bullish in the early beginnings of a decline.

THE TEMPTATION TO TRADE

An example of some stock charts with some intermediate price swings both up and down, within a primary trend and that have already been completed—giving the benefit of hindsight—will demonstrate the attraction or temptation to trade in and out of a stock to increase the possible return. Some people can do this, of course—many others will not have the temperament, trading discipline, or focus on watching the stock closely enough to do this.

Figure 2.1 shows the chart and assumes we take an investing approach and purchase Alcoa in the beginning of 1999, at $20.72. This was in the early stages of a rise that took the stock above its prior year's trading range—a good technical signal for entry. Assume also that the stock was sold in June 2001, after a sizable run up in the preceding 8 months and after the stock started to sink and fell first under its 50-day moving average and then to below its up trendline. Our hypothetical investor then decides that there was not much further upside potential with the stock, as the trendline break was an exit indication, and got out at the closing price on that same day, 6/14/01. The liquidation sell price was $39.22. The increase over the 30 months of holding the stock netted a gain of $18.50 or a very respectable 89.2 percent return. On an annual basis, the return on the money invested is approximately 36 percent, which was outstanding given that the S&P 500 Index was down about 4 percent during the same period. The entry and exit points for our investing approach are seen in the *weekly* chart of Figure 2.1.

Taking a trading approach, where there is purchase and sale every time there appears to be an opportunity for profit, we'll assume the same initial

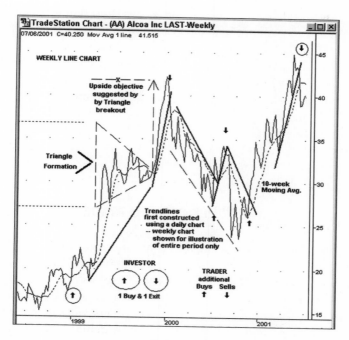

Figure 2.1

entry point at $20.72. However, over the same time period the stock was bought and sold 5 times, based on technical criteria using *trendline* analysis—trendlines will be discussed in a later chapter. Substantial assistance in plotting strategy was provided when, over the course of March–November 1999, Alcoa's stock formed a large *triangle* pattern, which provided an upside objective for the subsequent rally after November when the stock moved sharply higher—more on triangles later, but this pattern is traced out anyway on Figure 2.1.

The five trades' entry and exit points are noted by up and down arrows both in Figure 2.1 and Figure 2.2, a chart of the *daily* closes, providing a more close up view of some of the price swings of the stock and the relevant trendlines. It is assumed that our hypothetical *trader* was always in the market. After selling to liquidate a long position, a short position was also established and vice versa—after a purchase to offset a short position, a long position was also established by purchasing double the amount of stock that was held short. Our trader entered or exited only if there was a favorable penetration of the trendline on a closing basis.

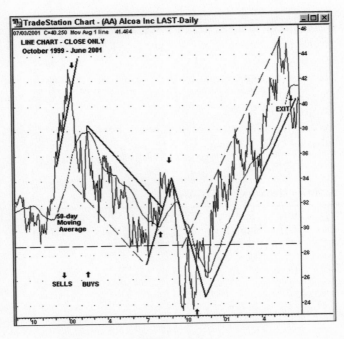

Figure 2.2

An assumption was also made that our hypothetical trader was able to monitor the close and place an order near the close of a trading session, on the few occasions where prices were near enough to the trendline being monitored that it might be penetrated. To make the example as simple as possible and to determine the entry price more exactly (the close), it's assumed that only a close above or below a trendline determined a new trade. A short sale is assumed at the same price as a sell, but this is an approximation only due to having to short on an *up tick*—more on this later also.

The 5 trades are detailed in Table 2.1. In our hypothetical trading scenario outlined in the table, there is a perfect record of wins and no instance of where the person misinterpreted how the trendlines were unfolding. By unfolding I mean the necessity to periodically redraw trendlines due to market action and with the hope they are drawn correctly, such that a shift above or below will in fact highlight a reversal in the trend.

Of course, I have the benefit of hindsight to figure out how the trendlines were best constructed. Nevertheless, this stock provided a good example of how a person with a good aptitude for trading coupled with a good trading strategy, could greatly increase profits by trading in and out of a stock. In this case the effective trading strategy made very expert use of a major technical analysis tool, trendlines. The gross trade profits—versus *net* profits after commissions—jumped to a whopping 200 percent because the stock traded had some wide-ranging and well-defined price swings. I emphasize that the real world of trading is different from a hypothetical example like this, when you can't practice rear view analysis and your emotions are let loose.

Figure 2.3 provides another example to demonstrate the allure of in-and-out trading. The increase of trading activity of recent years is facili-

Table 2.1   (AA) Alcoa Inc. LAST—Weekly

Trade Entry Date	Buy (B)	Selling Short(SH)	Entry Price	Exit Price	Gain (Loss)	Date of Exit
1/8/99	B		20.72	40.00	$19.28	1/14/00
1/14/00		SH	40.00	32.38	7.62	8/7/00
8/7/00	B		32.38	32.63	.25	8/29/00
8/7/00		SH	32.63	28.25	4.38	10/30/00
10/30/00	B		28.18	39.22	11.04	6/1/01
Total					$42.57	

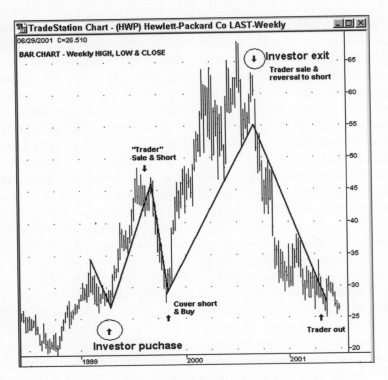

Figure 2.3

tated by better information and the ease of online trading—but also from people looking at charts like those I have just shown you and calculating their own "what if" scenarios. And turnover has increased dramatically as the average holding period for stocks had shrunk to about 10 months by 2000, from a multiyear time period a decade before. More on the pitfalls of trying to profit from all possible intermediate price swings later.

Figure 2.3 consists of a weekly bar chart of the high, low, and close for Hewlett-Packard (HWP) for the 1999 period into mid-2001. For an investor who thought HWP had some promise, and decided to use some basic technical criteria as to the right time to purchase the stock, they might have bought it at $28.55 the week of 4/9/99, when the stock closed above its down trendline. Chances are they then rode the stock up in 1999 and back down into 2000. This time, when the stock had an even bigger advance in 2000, our wiser investor decided to exit the stock if it closed under the weekly uptrend line. The criteria of a weekly close below the steep up trendline triggered their exit during the week of 9/15/00—assuming the trade was closed out at the close at $51.50, there was an 80 percent profit or $23. Thank you very much, stock market!

Our nimble trader could reasonably have had four trades executed, two purchases and offsetting sales and two short sales, with offsetting purchases, and they are also noted on Figure 2.3. The last profitable exit was in March 2001 for a profit on the short side of $19.80—the first three of our hypothetical gains were $14.45 (purchase and sale), $11.17 (short sale and then buy back), and $19.67 (buy and sell), for a total gross profit of $65. Relative to the first purchase price of $28.55, same as our investors, there was a profit of some 288 percent. Even if we assumed that no trades were taken on the short side, only two purchases and sales based on the trendline criteria, the profit on the two long side transactions increased roughly 40 percent. There could be many other entry and exit rules and refinements, but this one has the benefit of simplicity and ease of demonstration.

The trading examples particularly present a best-case trading strategy. In the real world of the market and with participation by someone following this and other stocks on a part-time basis, it is not likely that the outcome would be as profitable as the one presented. Nevertheless, someone with the necessary temperament for trading the market and who works at it consistently could achieve a greater return than the person following a buy and hold strategy *if* there are two-sided trading swings of sufficient size. In a major stock bull market or bear market, especially in the steepest part of the trend, a strategy of just holding a stock, not trading, is usually what garners the best return. However, technical analysis used properly could also tell you that this was the type of market cycle that existed.

Many individuals will not maintain the necessary attention to detail or have the time consistently to devote to trading. Even though the transactions were relatively few in number in our examples, it meant fairly frequent monitoring of the charts and multiple decisions regarding re-drawn trendlines, continuing evaluation of the chart and the overall market patterns as they change, and possibly some attention to *technical indicators*. And multiple instances of calculating the right levels, then canceling old exiting stop orders and re-entering new ones. Use of preset stop orders that are always in place is my preferred trading strategy and the one designed to prevent the all-too-common big loss. However good your trading strategy and considering the time and potential stress involved, our would-be trader might quickly become an investor again.

HOW TRADERS BECOME INVESTORS BY GETTING STUCK

Many stock traders inadvertently become *investors* and I know from personal experience one major way that this transformation occurs—investors also get stuck in stocks with bad performance in the same way. That way is the lack of risk control or predefined risk points, especially through always having a *stop order* for every stock owned or held short, where a stock ends up being held at a substantial loss, for a prolonged period, relative to the purchase price.

ATTITUDE TOWARD THE MARKET AND RISK CONTROL

Before I mention a few details of stop orders and short selling, I'll first discuss *risk*. You may wonder why an introductory book on technical analysis first talks about your trading philosophy and strategy as it relates to losing money. You probably got this book to find out how to *make* money. The reason why I go over the topic of risk and always having an exit strategy is that *not* controlling losses is a killer of consistent profits in the market, regardless of how skillful you become in your use of technical analysis. My goal in using technical analysis is not only to be right in the market, but also to profit from being right. And then to keep the lion's share or as much as possible of any prior realized, or current unrealized, gains and not give them back due to market fluctuations.

If your attitude is that the market is a gamble and you are just rolling the dice, you begin at a major disadvantage to the multitude of market professionals who are in the market every day. It is true that the market is more speculative than, say, the fixed income market and certainly more so than money market instruments like U.S. Treasury bills. Market professionals do a better job of getting out of losing trades and investments or they won't last long in the profession—they, by necessity, have to minimize the chance that their most precious commodity will be wiped out, which is their trading or investing capital. There is an old market saying that the small loss is the easy one. Here are seven trading rules related to how you manage your trading strategy, capital, and risk.

1. **Right entry**—Buy early in a trend when a stock or index has initial technical signals suggesting a trend is beginning, and don't wait. Or buy or sell short after a setback (*reaction*) to the trend that is underway, for example, when a stock comes back to natural technical

support or resistance points. Waiting and patience are the greatest virtues in the market.

2. **Determine an objective** when you are thinking of buying or shorting a stock. This is important because (and it may seem strange) it's necessary to change your focus from how much you can make to how much you are willing to *lose*. Set profit objectives—how much we're willing to risk or lose is defined in relation to how much we think the item could move in our favor, based on technical analysis criteria, of course!

3. **Do the math**—If you set a stop (your risk point) equal to one-half or one-third of what you hope to make, here is the calculation: On a 2:1 reward to risk—we calculate entry only when we could make $2 for every $1 risked—you could be stopped out or exited on one-half of your trades and still make a substantial gain, minus commissions, as long as the other transactions achieve your profit objectives on average.

    In 10 transactions on a 2:1 risk/reward basis and where a loss is taken 5 times and a gain 5 times, but the average profit is double the average loss, the net result is that total profits are double total losses. However, then also assume that 1 or 2 losses get away from us. We decide to watch and see what happens—it's not apparent why the stock, for example, is not performing. We hope the setback is temporary—but the stock ends up losing *more* than several earlier winning transactions. This then upsets the profit equation and we quickly are at break even or down substantially from where we started.

4. **Physically place the stop**—Many investors don't actually enter stops, preferring to take a wait and see attitude. After all, they are in this for the long haul. But think of all the surprises that occur in companies and their competitive positions in the marketplace. Traders are afraid of stops being *hit* or activated, only to see the stock go back up. The underlying problem with both of these attitudes is related to stock trading tip number 1: Select an entry at an optimal point, where there is an effective place (either under *support* or above *resistance*) to place a liquidating stop order that is both not likely to get hit and is relatively small in relation to your entry price. With mutual funds, it's suggested you set *mental* stops, however wide, and adhere to them by liquidation when the loss point is exceeded.

5. **Use trailing stops**—Sell stops protect a *long* position or initial purchase and buy stop orders protect a *short* position. Canceling and re-establishing stop orders as needed so that they *trail* along with the ongoing price trend requires some work and diligence as you need to periodically raise or lower your stop orders. This insures that your stops can reflect what is a moving target—the point at which a trend *reversal* has begun. As things move in your favor, this process first gets your liquidating stop order to a break-even point, where you would have no loss if you exit. Assuming a further favorable trend, you can next begin to lock in some of that profit you had projected.

   For example, when you are in a stock that reaches your price target, the question arises whether to sell at your preset objective—a question without a set answer. If a price objective is based on the fulfillment of an objective implied by a chart *pattern*, then completion of the objective may remove the reason you had to take the trade. In other instances, I view initial projections as *minimum* hoped-for objectives within a trend. I also like to stay with, and in, a favorable trend. Once the price has passed a hoped-for objective, simply be vigilant to the trend reversing and protect as much profit, by use of a stop, as is warranted by technical considerations, as we are going to study in the chapters ahead.

6. **Be willing to get out or get back in**—As soon as the reasons for being in a position or in a trade are no longer present, it is best to exit. You may have bought a stock because it was in a strong uptrend. You purchased it right, the stock went up, and now you have a probable break-even situation due to moving a stop up to your entry point. However, the stock then goes into a sideways trend and basically moves laterally for many weeks. If you got into the stock because of its having a strong uptrend or the expectation of one, now may be the time to exit. The reasons you bought the stock are no longer present, particularly if the overall market continues to trend higher.

   Let's examine further the case of a stock that goes against you. The object is to never let a loss get out of control, not to forget about or get negative on the stock(s) in which you were and may still be, interested in. If you get stopped out of such a stock and the countertrend runs its course, with the stock then resuming its prior trend, a repurchase may be warranted. But again, use favorable risk-to-reward criteria: If you risk to a point where liquidation would result in losing 10 percent of the money invested, but upside potential is calculated for at least 20 percent or more, and enough of these transactions average out this way over time, the result is a substantial overall profit.

7. **Stick to your game plan or strategy and to sound money management rules**—If you are successful in business or whatever profession you are in, you have probably had a particular plan or methodology you adhered to. You didn't change the plan when it didn't produce results right away or even for a prolonged period, assuming you were following time-tested practices. Setbacks are part of this and of stock market investing. Time and patience are required. You can't force a business, or the market, to do what you want it to.

   You have to be sufficiently capitalized also. In investing or trading, just like in business, you need to have sufficient reserves to stay in business. In the same way, don't commit all of your investment or trading money to the market. I suggest keeping one-third to one-half in reserve, the larger figure when you're in more speculative markets or stocks. If your losses are more than you anticipate as you gain experience, that experience you gain will be of no use to you if you are out of the market due to lack of money to invest. As well, some people will get very aggressive and not only be 100 percent invested but buy on *margin* or borrowed money. I have seen many people lose considerable amounts in the end, even after having substantial profits at one time, because they were on margin and didn't having staying power because of it—this is the well-known forced margin selling situation. The market might come back in your favor, but you can no longer profit from it.

   I also suggest reducing the size of your position if the market turns difficult and gets into turmoil. It would be best to not be in only one or two sectors of the market. I love tech stocks myself, but also find a lot to like in health care and drug stocks, for example, as they reflect another dominant and earnings-favorable investment theme, that of an aging population. If you like a stock, you don't have to buy all that you would hope to buy initially. See how it behaves. If it looks good, buy some more after the first setback, and see how it behaves after that. If the item resists going down further, an eventual rally may develop.

There was the story told by Jesse Livermore of a great stock tip he gave to a veteran stock investor. Instead of doing what Livermore expected, this man promptly sold some of the stock and Livermore protested that this was hardly what he expected from this gift of information. The potential investor calmly watched the stock tape for a time. Finally, he began buying a substantial amount of the stock, saying to the young Jesse Livermore that he had first wanted to see how the stock behaved when he sold some. If it was being accumulated by a well-funded group of investors, any selling would be absorbed easily, and it was. His test was how the stock did when there was some selling against it. This is a good lesson, and also reflects going against the obvious and expected behavior.

Jack Schwager, in the Wizard Lessons summary chapter from his book, *Stock Market Wizards,* found many common traits in his group of supersuccessful money mangers and speculators. I'll mention some of these lessons that reinforce what my own experience has shown. A universal trait, regardless of the method used to select stocks, was that individuals in this group had effective trading strategies and stuck to a game plan that accounted for all possibilities. They would assume that everything that could go wrong would go wrong—it's all downhill after that. Great traders and money managers are marked by their flexibility. They were willing to see their pet ideas and theories proven wrong and change accordingly. This includes never falling in love with a stock. Save that for your spouse. It also takes time to become successful. Don't give up.

Something I've discussed and Jack puts very well about his supersuccessful market professionals, is the role of hard work. Ironically, many people are drawn to the markets because it seems like an easy way to make a lot of money. Wrong! This group is, as was my own market wizard mentor, Mark Weinstein, extremely hard working—he, like most other big market winners, has a major passion for the market. Have a *little* passion and carve out a few hours a week from your busy lives, if you want a moderate success potential!

Last, all the very successful market participants that I've known are constantly, and I do mean constantly, concerned with avoiding loss and with how they manage their trading capital. The professionals believe that one of the most common mistakes made by novices is to expend great energy on finding the big potential winning stocks and a good entry price. They spend comparatively little time on preventing and controlling losses as time goes on. This point also goes back to the work ethic that is required, to frequently assess and reassess your strategy and assumptions you may have made that could be wrong. Think about when to get out and keep thinking about it until you are out.

I have congratulated myself many times on getting in at the right time on a stock, for example, only to go to sleep, so to speak, and miss seeing the point at which upward or downward momentum slowed and then stopped. By the time the reversal was well underway, I was still hanging on because of having suspended my ongoing evaluation. I then missed the profit potential that was to be had. I expended good effort to research and find the trade but then wanted the work part to be over. This is a common fallacy and situation. I can only suggest that you remember when this happens to you so that you can correct it once experience has shown you this lesson.

All the above lessons and points have the common ground of being led astray by the great dual enemies of fear and greed. Greed is what drives many of the initial mistakes. We don't expect to get rich quickly in most businesses and professions. Yet somehow when we see a stock make a huge move, we start to imagine finding just that kind of stock next. This tends to lead to haste in selection, or bad timing because we don't wait for those special situations, as well as overcommitment of capital to the big hoped-for winner. Fear comes mostly from letting losses get out of control and overtrading. There used to be a saying among traders to "sell down to a sleeping level." If you are so worried about your losses, actual or imagined, then reduce the size of your holding. I have sold stocks that I was sitting with at a loss, thinking I had no choice but to hope for the stock price to rebound. But by taking the loss and then being careful to select and closely monitor some other stock or stocks that looked promising, I started increasing the value of my portfolio again. And perhaps as important, I found a renewed interest in the market. And renewed commitment to not make the same mistake or mistakes I made before.

STOP ORDERS

A stop order is a *suspended* market order (to sell at the best price at that moment) that is triggered when the stock or other item trades at or *through* that price. For example, a market closed at 10.5, but opens at 9, and our stop is at 10—the item will be sold at 9 or the best price that can be obtained. A sell stop order, which is the most common stop, is placed *under* the current market price. A buy stop order is the reverse of the sell stop, in that it is a suspended buy order that is placed *above* the current market price. Its purpose is usually to cover or offset a short position. However, the buy stop order can also be used to initiate a new long position.

Such an order might be part of a technical trading strategy, because you wish to buy if the price exceeds the high end of a recent trading range or the stock breaks out above a trendline. A sell stop order would not be used to initiate a new short position in stocks because of the rule allowing a short position only on an *up tick*, whereas it could be used in the futures markets.

Good Til Canceled (GTC) stop orders are not always actually *until* canceled in practice. Most brokers will have a time limit in which the order is effective, for example, a couple of months, which they inform you of. In an active market, you may have canceled and replaced the order one or more times during this period, but otherwise it's important to keep track not only of what stop orders you have in place, but of how long they are effective.

SHORT SELLING

Selling short is a very underused trading strategy by the investing and trading public. Keeping aside the tax consideration that any resulting profit will never be long term in nature, shorting is something you may want to consider as part of your market strategy. One reason is that half of all possible trading opportunities in an average year, are the result of price declines or downswings. The other very good reason is that profits can come very quickly, due to the fact that when support for a stock or other market crumbles, the imbalance of selling drives the item down with little resistance.

Short selling in stocks means simply that you are borrowing the particular stock from your broker, which is owned by someone else. Chances are the broker has the stock in house, being held by someone in their account. Or the broker will borrow the stock from another institution, for a small fee, in order to lend it to you in a short sale. You *owe* the broker the stock and you anticipate or hope to buy it back at a lower price and thereby offset your obligation to replace the stock. The gain or loss is calculated like a purchase and sale, as the difference between the two prices. If you sell XYZ short at $25 and buy it back the following month at $20, your net gain is $5. If you buy it back at $30, you will have a loss of $5.

In stocks, you must sell short on an up tick—the stock can only be shorted if the traded price represents a value that is above the immediately preceding transaction in the stock. You must also have a margin account, as opposed to a *cash* account, in order to affect a short sale. Other than these considerations, the short sale is a relatively easy transaction to make, especially in actively traded stocks where the stock can be readily borrowed from your brokerage firm. In futures and some other markets, there is no rule to prevent selling short when prices are declining. This fact alone tends to make these markets more volatile.

Stocks and many other markets fall generally much faster than they rise. When fear sets in, the resulting worry and panic causes action on a much-compressed timescale, whereas buying may have occurred over a long period. By and large, most institutional holders of stocks representing you and me in our mutual fund holdings, as well as you and me as individual investors, are *long*, or owners of stocks. So there is a mountain of selling that can occur when a company is adversely affected in its earnings or by other news. You can see how relatively easy it could be to go with this avalanche and profit from the fall. Back in Figure 2.3, a weekly chart of Intel Corporation (INTC), the fluctuations in the stock are seen from late 1998 into early 2001. The stock took 23 months to go from just under $19, in early September 1998, to its closing peak at $74.87 in late August 2000. After that, a steep break in the stock down to the $23 area occurred over just 7 months—during that timeframe, the stock dropped approximately $40 in one 27-day trading period!

SUMMARY

Technical analysis is an outcome of attempts to better understand the dynamics of market movements and trends. Its overarching purpose has been to enable more accurate investment decisions and investment advice. However, making profitable use of this form of analysis has proven to require something that comes *before and along with* mere accuracy in identifying the dominant trend in effect, movements within that trend, and prediction of trend reversals. The other major component to success with technical analysis involves other elements—in the broadest sense, profiting from technical analysis also requires (1) adopting a style of investing or trading that best suits the individual's temperament and abilities and (2) effective risk management.

1. Adopting a style of investing and trading that best suits the individual means determining and defining such things as how much to commit to the market, whether the objective is long-term capital appreciation or shorter-term speculation, and so on. Whether committing for the long term or shorter term, it's crucial to have patience

and not exit just because there is no immediate success. Under-staying can be as much of a problem as over-staying. Let your liquidating stop take you out of the market or item in question—otherwise, there can be many occasions when you see your price objectives met, but without your participation. Don't do short-term trading unless you have a definite ability to be successful in it, as proven by your profit and loss statement—otherwise, be an investor.

2. Effective risk management means determining risk-to-reward parameters, investing or trading only amounts of money that are appropriate to the total you have to work with and, most importantly, using stop orders that are in place at the outset and kept in place. This area of focus also includes being willing to exit the market if, and as soon as, you determine that a market position is no longer valid. Flexibility is a key ingredient of ultimate success.

We could add that ongoing assessment of your portfolio or trading is important. For example, you buy in a strong bull market, the trend continues, and everything goes well. However, every entry decision also means being alert about when to exit if you want to retain the maximum extent of the gains that a market has given you. And, as the old saying goes, "Never confuse brains with a bull market."

In the following chapter we look at origins, and hence some of the rationale, of technical analysis. We begin with Charles Dow, the creator not only of the Dow averages, but of the very idea of a market average.

3

CHARLES DOW AND THE UNDERLYING PRINCIPLES OF MARKET BEHAVIOR

INTRODUCTION

There is a tendency to think that every important bull market is driven by some new dynamic, and that perhaps *this* latest megabull market is immune to the cyclical nature of financial markets. It is true that technology continues to compress time, so to speak, and provides more goods and services faster than ever before. However, human nature has not changed nor have the workings of human behavior across markets. Nowhere is this clearer than in the fact that the work of the pioneers of technical analysis date to the 1700s and 1800s and remain foundations of accurate market predictions in the new millennium. In the 1800s this was the seminal work of Charles Dow in this country and, in the 1700s, the observations of one of the greatest of Japanese rice traders, Munehisa Homma, who formulated the rules that govern the use of candlestick charts, now in widespread use in the West.

CHARLES DOW

In this country, the originator of what became technical analysis is Charles H. Dow, the late 1880s cofounder of Dow Jones & Co. and its flagship newspaper, the *Wall Street Journal*. Charles Dow was born in 1851 in Connecticut and had the image of what is sometimes associated with a New England type of personality—sober, industrious, and rather serious minded. He was a reporter and editor most of his life, which ended in 1902. In his starting out years he worked for the famous newspaper man Samuel Bowles, who had the distinction of demanding that a reporter put it all in the first sentence of a news story—who, what, when, where, and why—a widely used practice today in journalism, including Internet news stories.

Charles Dow's market observations, as presented in a series of *Wall Street Journal* editorials, were highly original and insightful. I find them a worthwhile inclusion even in this introductory book on technical analysis, because it helps understand the practical underlying rationale for technical analysis—a descriptive term unknown in Dow's day.

Also occurring in the 1880s and 1890s was Charles Dow's formulation of the first stock market averages, which became, over time, the Dow Jones 30 Industrial, 20 Transportation and 15 Utility stock averages known today. I tend to call the 30 Dow *Industrial* stocks, the *Dow 30* as these stocks have become more technological, manufacturing, and service oriented and less industrial, unlike the case of the heavy industry stocks like U.S. Steel that were part of the early Dow Industrial average. Today, common parlance is the *Dow*, the *Dow Jones* or the *Dow 30* stock average. This average of 30 stocks is not capitalization weighted, as is the case of the Standard & Poor's 500 or Nasdaq Composite indexes. Dow stocks of companies that have become price laggards, even if they're much smaller than, for example, General Electric, will have a dragging effect in the equal weighted Dow 30 average, unlike indexes that give more weight to larger companies—by the way, only GE was an original member of this average and still is.

Only the Dow Industrials and Dow Transportation (then a group of railroad stocks) averages are used in what became known as "Dow theory." Charles Dow never called the market principles he wrote about "a theory," only observations on how the economy and the market functioned. Charles Dow's principles were later discussed in a book by the *Wall Street Journal* editor succeeding Dow, William Hamilton, that was called *The Wall Street Barometer*. Robert Rhea is credited with distilling the ideas of Dow further and wrote a book in the early 1930s called *Dow Theory*.

This background given, I will describe the basic tenets of Charles Dow and discuss their continued present-day relevance. Robert Edwards and John Magee, who wrote what many consider to be the bible of technical analysis, *The Technical Analysis of Stock Trends*, popularized the description and analogy of market trends to "tides, waves, and ripples," although these terms did not originate with them.

THE MARKET DISCOUNTS EVERYTHING

Dow determined which stocks, using them to make up his averages, best represented the overall market. He believed that every possible fact and factor relating to the price of a stock within his averages was quickly priced into the current traded price of that stock and hence into the averages. Down saw that the traded price reflected all knowledge that existed about a company and its current and future prospects, in terms of its earnings power. Even so-called *insider* information will show up in the price and volume patterns that can be seen by astute observers of the trading in that stock. This group will in turn act on that information and that activity will become apparent to an ever-widening group. This principle is even truer today, given the extremely rapid and widespread distribution of information that occurs on the financial channels and on the Internet.

CYCLES OF BULL AND BEAR MARKETS HAVE THE SAME REOCCURRING PHASES

The point to emphasize here is that the phases of both bull and bear markets, while different depending on whether it's a bull market or a bear market, are similar in terms of two factors:

- I Relative knowledge about the market
- I Investor *sentiment* (attitude) about the market that ranges from disinterested to indifferent to interested, with varying degrees of intensity within disinterested and interested

Bull Markets

A bull market, named for the animal that charges ahead, comes after a lengthy and substantial decline in stock values that comes about due to a downturn in the economy or a recession. Major market advances are usually, but not always, divided into three phases. These phases are marked by who participates in them and what they are doing in each phase.

1. *Accumulation Phase*. In the first phase of a bull market, there is *accumulation* of stocks or buying over a period of time, during which very knowledgeable investors with good foresight about a coming business upturn, begin buying stocks offered by pessimistic sellers who want out. This group of knowledgeable buyers will also start to pay higher prices as the willing sellers exit. The economy and business conditions are still often quite negative. The public, and this is mirrored by the financial press, is quite disinterested in the market, to the point of where owning stocks is very unattractive to them and they are out of the market. The people who lost money in the last bear market are actively disgusted with the market. Market activity is modest at best but is picking up a bit on rallies, but this is mostly only noticed, if at all, by professional market participants.

2. *A Steady Climb*. The second phase is one of a fairly steady advance, but one that is not dramatic. There is a pickup in business and encouraging economic reports as an improving economy leads to a pickup in corporate earnings. This phase is also a period where money can be made relatively safely, as technical indicators turn positive and there is an absence of volatile trading swings.

3. *Main Street Adopts Wall Street*. The third phase, which at one and the same time can be both highly profitable and ultimately risky, is marked by heavy public interest and participation in the market. The economic news is good during this period, and suddenly, front pages of magazines have articles heralding the new bull market. The new stock issue market gets going as the public now has an appetite for new companies. This is the phase where you will hear banter at parties about the stock market, how well so-and-so is doing in stocks and where, today, market-related Internet chat rooms are quite active. Price advances can be huge and volume is equally large. The more speculative stocks continue to advance but it is here that the blue chip stocks of the most established big-name companies start to lag the overall market. Some sharp downswings occur among stocks that fall out of favor. Speculation is intense as seen in increased option activity, the first-day closes of hot new issues and in the level of buying stocks on margin. The end of this phase is always the same, varying degrees of collapse. This can come after a year or two or even after several years have passed from the beginning phase.

Bear Markets

This animal analogy is quite apt, as the bear can be both very fierce and unforgiving or can just go to sleep for a long period. Bear markets can usually also be divided into three phases. That this does not always occur is seen in the 1987 bear market that was sharp and steep, but with the decline only lasting two months. After that, there was a slow gradual process of advancing prices during which there remained significant bearish sentiment and the public tended to stay out of the market. This phase didn't reach the typical bearish price extremes, however, as within 7–10 months the Dow had recovered nearly half of its October–November decline.

1. *Distribution Phase.* The first phase of a primary bear market tends to be a period of *distribution* of stocks. This period begins in the final phases of the bull market. It is the phase where selling begins with the same type of experienced investors that didn't get overly swept up in the extremes in emotion and paying high prices. This group has sufficient market knowledge to understand that company earnings and profits have probably reached their peak and that the price multiples paid (the P/E ratios) for those earnings are also at extreme levels. They begin to sell or *distribute* stocks to the still eager and willing buyers. Volume of trading begins to slow. The public is still in the market heavily but begins getting frustrated as the rate of price increase slows down and not all stocks participate in rallies.

   The distribution phase is also one where people who are not usually in the market become buyers of stocks. A friend of mine who had always invested only in real estate told me near the 2000 market top, that he had decided to buy some stocks, but had modest expectations as he "only" expected or wanted to make 20 percent on his money. This kind of expectation for stocks that historically return 10 percent on average and had already been going up sharply for months, was the final telling event that got me out of the market. I had noticed the froth, that the volume was slipping and profits harder to come by, but my friend's actions and comment was my *shoe shine boy* event—referring to the famous story of Bernard Baruch, who one day got a stock tip from the fellow who shined his shoes. After this, Baruch went and sold his holdings, saying that when shoe shine boys give *him* stock tips, this was the time to sell. I was struck by a similar occurrence in 2000 at Cantor Fitzgerald, a large institutional broker, where I was working at the time. I overheard one of the security guards on the telephone discussing his trading and going on about this and that stock just like one of our floor traders.

The *distribution* phase I already knew well, having been through two earlier such periods. The first such event was in the silver and gold bull market *bubble* of the mid- to late 1970s. In the final phase of it, I finally succumbed to the siren call of this market and made an impulse buy of some precious metals. At least I can re-plate my silverware with the silver bars I bought. In the late summer of 1987 I was the manager of a leveraged stock index program at PaineWebber and had the sense to sell my positions on Black Monday, but not the conviction to be short, where fortunes were made over a couple of days. Actually the distribution phase had been over by the preceding Friday and we were about to enter a *panic*. Of course, the other side of my missed profit opportunity (from not being short) was that a lot of losses were incurred when investors panicked and sold or traders had to sell to meet margin calls and didn't hang on for the ensuing months of recovery.

2. **Panic Selling Phase.** Panic is a major characteristic of the second phase of a bear market. Buyers become scarce, bids fall sharply, and sellers become desperate to get out. The downward acceleration becomes extreme and a near vertical drop can ensue, as was the case during *Black Monday* in 1987. The market action after March 2000 in the Nasdaq stocks that had the steepest declines, occurred over weeks and months, but there were some very sharp down weeks, especially in the beginning. The decline goes on longer when there is very strong conviction about the continuation of the bull market that has ended already—the investing public, in general, does *believe* in the market by now. The handmaiden of fear, here, is hope. There is a reluctance to take a loss in stocks, especially a sizable one. Better to hope for a recovery. This is the phase where people will make a point of telling you that they are *long-term* investors. Investors here have become conditioned to stocks going up and will maintain their faith in a market rebound for longer than is warranted by facts.

3. **Discouragement Phase.** After the worst part of the decline or where prices are not dropping so steeply and that can be at the point where the economy has stabilized, there often comes a gradual market recovery and a rebound in prices of the stocks of the strongest

companies. Or this may be a long period where the market trends sideways. This third phase is marked by discouraged sellers, perhaps those who didn't sell in the panic atmosphere that had prevailed earlier. Or selling may be coming from those investors and traders who bought during and after the steepest declines, as they thought stocks looked cheap relative to the inflated values of the late bull market stage. What causes this discouraged selling is that the rallies aren't sustained and prices tend to sink again after rallies. There's an old analogy about the erosion of a bear market being like a dripping faucet. Such slow steady loss, over time, becomes buckets. Business conditions at this stage may deteriorate further. Certainly there is an absence of good news with corporate earnings as the economy slides further. The stocks that were very speculative, in terms of their potential to make money, may lose most of the rest of their value in this phase. There were many Nasdaq stocks that lost 80 percent to 90 percent of what they had gained in the prior bull market, in the 12 months after the March 2000 top. Blue chip stocks tend to decline more slowly because investors hold on to them the longest.

A bear market ends when all the possible bad news has been discounted. And after it ends, there is usually more negative news that keeps coming. Keep in mind that the *discounting* mechanism of stocks is always also an attempt to look ahead, so stock values will reflect the expectations of what earnings could be when business conditions improve such as six months ahead. It also should be noted that no two bear markets are exactly alike. The 1987 bear market was amazingly short in duration and was measured in weeks, although the price declines were quite severe. Some bear markets skip the panic stage and others end with it as in 1987. Bear markets go on for quite different time and price durations. Of the 13 years with significant declines in the 40 years preceding the March 2000–March 2001 market drop, 6 have had steeper selloffs in percentage terms as measured by the S&P 500 Index. If we measure by the Nasdaq market, the drop from the peak to a low was 68 percent, relative to 1987's loss of 37 percent.

However lengthy the phases are, such as the long and spectacular bull market runup into 2000, knowledge of the characteristics of each phase will help you keep a level head. You know what is coming when the phase you are in ends and you can prepare for it. Keep in mind also that these original bull and bear market descriptions were made more than 100 years ago. I have added more up to date examples, but the nature of them remains *human* nature. Human nature is what you have to deal with in the stock market, and it benefits you greatly when you can see the human dynamics of each market phase.

TRENDS ARE OF THREE TYPES

Just as the market tends to have three phases related to mood or market *sentiment*, market trends can be divided into three types. The most important to *investors*, those who look to buy and hold stocks for as long as a stock is tending to command an increasing price over time—is the *primary* or major trend. The primary trend is one lasting a year or more, up to several years. There are countertrend movements in the direction of the major trend, and these trends Dow called *secondary* price movements. As we have seen, bullish or bearish expectations for the market get overly one-sided and *ahead* of the fundamentals related to earnings prospects. Eventually a reaction develops that causes prices to correct back to a more realistic price level. *Reactions* or *corrections* are price swings that are in the opposite direction of the main or major trend. Once these run their course, the primary trend resumes. The segments that make up the price swings both in and against the direction of the primary trend can also be referred to as *intermediate* price swings or moves and last a few weeks to a few months only. Within these intermediate price moves are day-to-day price fluctuations that Dow called *minor* trends. These can be a few hours to a day or a few days—they're most often contained within a one-to-two-week period. Both intermediate and minor trends are of importance to traders primarily—minor trends are all that concern a day trader who will likely complete every trade within the same day. Intermediate trends are of some importance to investors when they are looking for the best point to enter the primary trend or to add to their position(s) in a stock or the market.

The Primary Trend

The *primary* or major trend is a price movement that usually lasts for a year or more. The exceptions to this time duration do exist and I pointed out the very short duration of the 1987 decline. It's considered to be a major trend because of the percentage decline involved and by the prior intermediate lows it exceeded, as can be seen in Figure 3.1. One widely accepted measure of what constitutes a bear market is when there is a de-

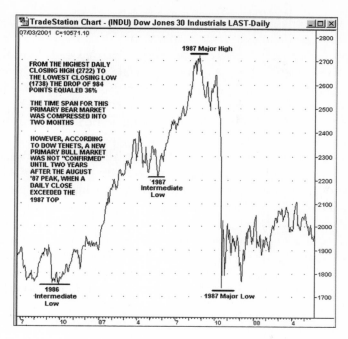

Figure 3.1

cline that takes prices more than 20 percent below the high point reached in the prior advance. Dow didn't have a rule or guideline on this subject.

The primary trend is composed of smaller movements of an intermediate duration of a few weeks to a few months. Some of these *intermediate* trends run in the same direction as the primary trend and occur after a market move that runs in either the opposite direction or sideways. These are also called *secondary* trends and will be discussed in the following section. There are often, not always, three intermediate movements or *waves* in the same direction as the primary trend, as will be discussed in a later chapter that has a description of *Elliott wave* theory.

An essential guideline as to a trend being a primary bull market is that each advance within the advancing trend should reach a higher level than the rally that preceded it. And each secondary reaction or countertrend move should stop at a level that is above the prior decline. The reverse movement occurs in a primary bear market trend as prices fall to lower and lower secondary laws. An analogy to the primary trend is that it is like the tide of the ocean. In the rising tide, each wave comes in to a higher and higher point. And just as the rising tide lifts all the boats, a bull market takes all stocks higher. The waves in an outgoing tide gradually recede from a high point and everything falls with it.

A primary up trend is considered to be a *bull* market and a primary down trend, a *bear* market. If you are an investor in terms of your time horizon and investment goals, you should attempt to buy stocks as soon as possible after a bull market has begun. An example is shown in Figure 3.2, taken from the 1990–1991 period, showing both a primary down trend or bear market and the primary up trend or bull market that developed following it.

You have noticed from this and the other earlier bear market example from 1987, that the duration of primary bear market trends can be relatively short, compared to the duration of primary uptrends. On average this has been true since the 1950s due to the longer periods of economic expansion and shorter periods of recession, as there is more urgency to end a recession. It also relates to the fact that investors tend to stagger their purchases over the duration of bull markets, providing ongoing buying power, whereas selling out is often a one time decision and would be buyers stay away and don't support the market on the declines, especially in a panic phase.

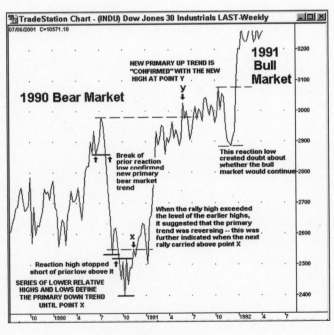

Figure 3.2

Secondary Trends

Secondary trends are of a shorter duration—typically, three weeks to three months—and interrupt the major direction of stock prices with a countertrend movement. Such moves are also called *corrections* in a bull market as they *correct* the situation where prices have risen too far, too fast. Secondary rallies are also called *recovery* rallies in a bear market. Frequently, these secondary countertrends retrace anywhere from a little more than a third to as much as two-thirds of the prior advance or decline. Very common is to see *retracements* of 50 percent of the prior price swing in the direction of the primary trend. It is not always easy to decide when and if a secondary trend is underway, but there are technical analysis measurements that will help us tell, which we will be examining in later chapters.

To continue the ocean analogy, the secondary trend is like the waves of the ocean. They can be big and they can knock you over, but they will come in and go out within the bigger movement of the tide—the primary trend.

Minor Trends

The minor trends are the price fluctuations that occur from day to day and week to week, although a minor trend will rarely last more than two to three weeks. In terms of the overall market trend these are just *noise* and relatively unimportant. They can be compared to mere ripples on a wave. Together, however, the minor trends make up the intermediate trends. According to the *wave* theory devised by R.N. Elliott, who was influenced by Rhea's Dow theory work of the 1930s, there are usually three distinct minor movements in the same direction as the secondary trend. Elliott wave theory also recognizes the importance of the three phases of a bull or bear market, as we discuss later also. Last, we could say that the minor trend could be one that is set off by the actions or words of an individual—for example, the chairman of the U.S. Federal Reserve Bank when that individual makes a statement hinting at the direction of Fed policy regarding interest rates. Or the precipitating action might be a statement from a key company in a key industry about their actual or expected earnings or profit trends.

PRINCIPLE OF CONFIRMATION AND DIVERGENCE

One of Charles Dow's most important contributions was the idea that *confirmation* of the primary trend must exist by the actions of both the Industrial and Transportation averages. A related aspect to this, really the flip side of it so to speak, is the concept of *divergence*. Dow spoke mostly about confirmation. Concepts of divergences between averages, between prices and volume, and between price action and *indicators* are mostly contributions made by technical analysis in the past 50 years.

What Charles Dow said was that if the Industrials moved to a new closing high or low, without the Transportation average following suit—confirming it—or vice versa, with the Transports going to a new peak or bottom, without the same action in the Industrials, no change in the primary trend was signaled. He was attempting to define the situation where there is a potential *reversal* in the primary trend. To suggest such a change, the averages must be in synch.

Now, the reasons why the two averages highlight economic reversals are simple, but accounted for a very astute observation on Dow's part. Industrial or manufacturing activity could continue to be very strong for a period of time while orders for those goods were slowing. This would result in the buildup of inventories. Where such a slowdown would show up, however, is in Transportation orders and activity. Slowing orders in the Transportation sector, as fewer goods were shipped, would result in a fall off of transportation company revenues. Astute followers of these companies would notice this and selling would start to show up in these stocks, either keeping a lid on their stock prices or actually driving them lower. Therefore, a new high in the Industrial average, not confirmed by the Transportation average, is suspect and may indicate that the same slowing of earnings and hence stock prices will show up later on in the Dow Industrials due to a developing economic slowdown.

The reverse situation occurs in a new primary bear market low in the Industrial average, not confirmed by a similar new low in the Transportation stocks. It may be that shipments of goods has started to rebound and has shown up in a slowing of the decline of the Transportation stocks or in an actual upturn in their prices, whereas Industrial companies are just shipping, and working off, built-up inventories, and a rebound in their earnings still lies ahead. There is lag time for the two averages, so it's important not to jump to such conclusions too quickly as one average may just be lagging the other and in a month or two or three, there will be a similar new high or low and confirmation will occur.

Sometimes more can be made of the *divergences* between the two averages than the confirmations. If the economy is slowing, it will tend to show up in the Transportation sector first. If the economy is rebounding, the Transportation stocks will tend to pick up sooner than the Manufacturing sector although there are exceptions—if Manufacturing inventories are low, a pickup in orders could mean that the Dow Industrial average recovers ahead of the Transports. The important thing is to use this information of one average moving contrary to the other to be right on a trend reversal early on.

An article in the *New York Times* on January 16, 2001 called "Seeing Hardship Through a Truck Windshield," described truckers being idle and waiting for orders to show up. The point was made that the trucking industry (our *rails* of today) is one of the first to notice the signs when the U.S. economy is retreating. A transportation analyst in that article was quoted as saying he had known the economy was in trouble six months earlier. As 80 percent of all goods move by truck in the United States, if you want an indication of where the economy is going, you need only count trucks on the highway.

In Figure 3.3, showing a weekly line (close-only) chart of the two averages during 1994–1997, you'll see that the Industrials failed to confirm the primary trend reversal that was taking the Dow Transportation average to lower and lower levels in 1994. Therefore, the primary trend for the market as a whole was still considered to be up. You can see what happened over the following three years as very strong rallies developed in both averages.

In Figure 3.4, depicting the 1998–2000 period, it is striking how failure to confirm new relative highs in the Dow Industrials in both 1998 and again in 1999, by a similar move in the Dow Transportation average, preceded major downside reversals in the Industrials within a few weeks to months. The 1999 example is very striking. As the Industrial average was going to greater and greater highs, the Transportation stocks were moving to ever-lower lows. Eventually, there was a sharp decline in the Industrials in late 1999 into early 2000, followed by a lengthy sideways trend with no further new highs. The flip side of a lack of confirmation is the warning signs posted by such pronounced *divergences*.

Recapping the Dow theory primary trend analysis for the chart shown in Figure 3.4: In 1998, the Transports did not confirm the new high in the Industrials and eventually both averages fell to new lows signaling a primary trend reversal from up to down. In the following year, 1999, both averages went to new closing highs signaling a new bull market trend. However, the Dow Transportation average only made a slight new high and then failed to confirm all subsequent new highs in the Industrials. Eventually the Industrials made a significant new low halfway into 1999, signaling a primary down trend, which is then in effect for the entire period

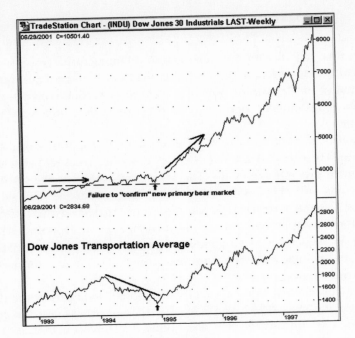

Figure 3.3

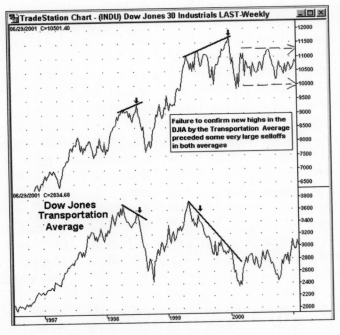

Figure 3.4

shown, even though the trend was sideways throughout 2000. In line with the slowing economy idea reflected in the extreme divergence of the Transportation sector, I took this as an indication to sell rallies—or watch for other technical signs of the Industrials breaking support and selling stocks at that point.

Figure 3.5 carries us into the 2001 period and shows again how the failure of the Dow Transportation average to confirm a new high could have kept the astute investor out of stocks (or more lightly committed) and prevented some potential losses. The same analysis might have led a trader to be on the outlook for when the market would again turn down and to anticipate that that downturn would be a good shorting opportunity.

All in all, one or two of these major forewarnings, compliments of Charles Dow's market observations of the century before last, fuels the wish that the money saved could fund a time machine to go back to say thank-you to our Connecticut Yankee.

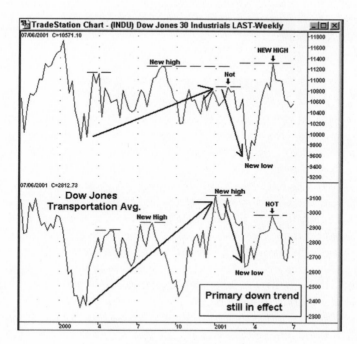

Figure 3.5

CRITERIA FOR A TREND REVERSAL

Just as a statement in physics says that a body in motion will tend to stay in motion until impacted by a countervailing force strong enough to divert its direction, a primary trend is assumed to continue in effect until a reversal is definitely indicated. A primary trend reversal, according to Dow, must be confirmed by the actions of both averages. It is not enough for the averages to *diverge* for a time—each must establish an intermediate low or high that is clearly under or above as the case may be, the point where the prior intermediate trend stopped. Dow did allow that the longer a bear or bull market goes on, the probabilities of a reversal increases. But because he felt that you could not know how long the trend would last, an end to it should not be anticipated until definitely signaled—meanwhile, hold your position.

I tend to be more ready to take market action on extreme *divergences* such as seen in Figure 3.4 for 1999, perhaps not waiting for confirmation. However, this steps outside the bounds of Dow theory and in another similar situation I might be premature in assuming an end to the primary trend. Also, the 1999 circumstances were unusual; the Industrials did eventually confirm a downside primary trend reversal and the next rally in the Industrials after that was a high-potential shoring opportunity within the tenets of Dow theory.

VOLUME CONSIDERATIONS

An important advantage that exists in stocks is that volume information is readily available. One of the great lost arts is that of *tape reading*. When brokerage offices made widespread use of the big running tapes, it was very clear when a rally or decline was significant—you could easily see the blocks of stock being traded, indicating big institutional activity. Volume should go in the direction of the trend and expand as prices moved that way. Dow related this to the rule that volume will increase in the direction of the primary trend. However, the same rule is often true for intermediate trends. It is likely that volume will ratchet up even more in the direction of the primary or major trend. We are talking here about the volume trend over time. I especially like to watch *upside* volume activity. It should increase as the market moves up and decline as prices fall. Upside volume is the sum of transactions done on up ticks. A true test of buying interest or strength is the willingness to pay up for stocks. However, this is an aside from Charles Dow's writings on volume.

The corollary of volume increasing in the direction of the primary trend is that volume will tend to subside on price swings counter to the direction of this trend. In general, volume will expand on a move with the trend and contract on a move against the prevailing trend. Volume is however, secondary to price in terms of forming conclusive evidence of a trend or trend reversal. Price is king in terms of studying market trends and volume is like the prince of it.

LINE FORMATIONS

Dow described a sideways price movement in one or both of the averages, lasting anywhere from a week or two up to a few months, as a *line*. This would typically be where prices fluctuate within a relatively narrow price range, such as within a few percentage points of the high or low that preceded the line formation. The line can *substitute* for a secondary up or down trend. Such a sideways trend—I consider a sideways movement to be a third type of *trend*, whereas many analysts consider trends to define only an up or down direction—indicates that buying and selling are in relative balance. Eventually, buyers are willing to pay more or sellers take less and this moves the market back into an up or down trend. A penetration of the upper or lower part of the line formation usually signals the direction of the next intermediate price swing.

Usually, the longer that these sideways trends go on, the more significant is the next move in the average. There is often a direct correlation between the time duration and the extent of the next price move above or below the line. The sideways move in the Dow Industrials, seen in Figure 3.4 from 2000 on, while more on the order of a 10 percent fluctuation (between approximately 11,500 and 10,000), shows a duration of more than two years. The number of tops and bottoms made within the same price-area, forming well-defined upper and lower boundaries, define this pattern as a line. These well-defined boundaries are more important than the fact that the price range lacked the more typical narrowness between the highs and lows. The line formation today is more often called a *rectangle* pattern, especially as it relates to individual stocks.

Lines mostly form as a pause in the trend or a period of price consolidation of the averages. The line in this situation is part of the formation of the major trend and can take the place of an up or down secondary move. Sometimes a line forms after a lengthy bull or bear market. Some technical analysts assume that a major line formation is a *distribution* top if the trend was up preceding it and an *accumulation* bottom if the prior trend was down. Dow himself did not indicate that the direction of the next price move after a line pattern ends could be forecast.

USE OF CLOSING PRICES

Dow theory does not take into account intraday highs or lows in terms of determining a change in trend. Only a new closing high or low is considered. There has been discussion in the past by interpreters of Dow theory as to whether the averages should simply clear an old high or low by any amount or whether they should be by some point margin or even some percentage amount. I would look at the circumstances and tend to look for some degree of separation. If the new high or low is very close to the other, this second high or low could qualify as a double top or bottom, if prices then reversed from there.

SUMMARY

An early key observation by Charles Dow was the interconnectedness of production and distribution in the economy, as reflected by his Industrial and Transportation averages. Both economic aspects had to be healthy for the overall market to go up—if this was the case, the averages would move in tandem or confirm each other's trend. If this was not the case there was a lack of confirmation or divergence between the two averages, signaling an upcoming downturn in the economy and in stock market prices, which reflect the economy. From this concept, other ideas emerged later that tied *confirmation* and *divergence* not only to each other but to various technical indicators, a key concept of technical analysis today.

Dow also was one of the first to describe the *cyclical* nature of market cycles, with their reccurring patterns of accumulation and distribution of stocks, which was in turn associated to varying degrees of public enthusiasm or avoidance of stocks. He saw these patterns repeating over and over, which is a foundation of technical analysis and its rationale.

Dow was one of the first to describe the workings of human psychology and behavior as it applied to the stock market. As a student of human nature Dow always allowed for surprises, and history has borne him out. A reversal in the market's trend can occur any time after that trend has been confirmed by the other average. Even if you are concerned only with the major or primary trend and take an attitude that you are in the market for the long haul, it's also true that a major bull market can deteriorate or end relatively suddenly and shake up this thinking. Therefore, Dow's practical and hardheaded advice is not to get complacent and to continue to monitor and pay attention to how the averages are behaving. This advice is as valuable in 2000 as it was in 1900.

Dow made use only of closing prices as the only price history he considered important to study and keep—of course, daily price fluctuations were generally narrow during this era. However, another important method of charting prices had already evolved before him in Japan (candlestick charts) that also attached significant importance on opening prices, and still other forms of plotting price activity came into use after Dow. These other means of displaying and analyzing price activity are considered next.

4

PRICE AND VOLUME BASICS: CHART TYPES AND PRICE SCALES

INTRODUCTION

One foundation of technical analysis is the use of charts that graphically show a price history, for some specific duration, of a stock or any financial instrument that fluctuates in price. Charts can depict prices in a variety of ways. For example, as with Charles Dow's method, we can plot only closing prices. We can also make use of the open, high, low, and closing prices in different ways for any time period, such as a day or week that we want to measure. *Point and figure* charting graphs price changes only when there is a new high or low of a preset amount, but the trading period when this occurs, is ignored. For all other chart types, there is a choice of a time duration for the type of price information we desire such as weekly and monthly, which best depicts the primary trend. How prices are calculated varies as well. A price *scale* can not only be calculated to make each price interval equal, but price changes can also be marked off on a scale where only equal *percentage* changes are an equal distance. Volume is important information also and there are different ways to display volume—in this chapter, there is also an analysis of the role of volume in technical analysis.

BAR CHARTS

A *bar* refers to a vertical line on a graph, the bottom of which is drawn at the point that represents the low price of a trading period and the top of which is drawn at a point that represents the highest price for the same period, relative to a price on a right-hand vertical price *scale*. A price *chart* consists, with one chart-type exception, of a left-to-right horizontal scale on the bottom that measures how much time has passed—the *time scale*—and a vertical, up and down scale on the right that measures prices—the *price* scale. The horizontal and vertical scales, you may recall from geometry, are also named the *x* and *y* axis, respectively.

A bar can have another mark like a hyphen (-) on the point on the left side of the high-low price range that represents the opening price and always has another on the point of the right side of the bar that represents the level on the price scale where the item closed. If all four of the price possibilities—Open, High, Low, and Close—are shown, you may also see it referred to as an *OHLC* chart. If the bar omits the opening price and shows just the High, Low, and Close, it may be called a *HLC* chart. The OHLC and HLC references show up as choices on some charting software.

Another aspect that we want to know about a bar is the time *period* that the bar measures for its open, high, low, and close. A bar can represent trading for 15, 30, or 60 minutes, a day, a week, a month, or a quarter. Other time periods are possible as well if you have the data for it and the software that will display it. I do not utilize period intervals of less than a day in this book. Not that they are not important, but they are important mostly to either day traders or short-term traders who might trade the two to three day price swings that develop, especially when using *hourly* charts.

Hourly closes for the Dow Jones averages are recapped in the *Wall Street Journal* and in *Barron's*, which are important to some traders and analysts. I may use an hourly chart over a 10-day period at times when looking at hourly *bars* might better pinpoint areas from which prices either are rebounding from or are unable to penetrate. You can call up hourly charts, as well as other intraday periods like 15 or 30 minutes, for 10-day periods typically, on Internet sites like *bigcharts.com*, a favorite site of mine in terms of all the charting options it provides.

An example of both a *daily* and *weekly* bar chart for the same stock, is shown in Figure 4.1. The weekly bar, which completes itself when the last trading day of the week ends, is constructed from the daily price history for the trading days in that week and takes its date from the last day of the

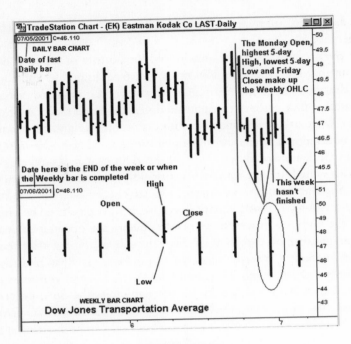

Figure 4.1

week whether that day had trading or not (if a holiday)—a weekly bar chart viewed on Monday will be labeled with Friday's date, which is when the weekly *bar* completes itself. The opening price on the first trading session of the week becomes the weekly *open*. The highest high made during the week is the weekly *high*, the lowest low becomes the weekly *low*, and the close of the last trading session becomes the weekly *close*.

A *monthly* bar chart is constructed in the same manner as the weekly bar chart and also uses daily OHLC values—it's not constructed from the weekly bars. A monthly chart *open* is the same value as the open of the first trading day of that calendar month, the highest daily high in the month becomes the monthly high, the lowest daily low is the monthly low, and the daily close of the last trading day of the month becomes the monthly close.

CHARTING PERIODS

For evaluation of the primary or major trend, the weekly or monthly charts are the most important. I tend to review the weekly and monthly charts less often, but they are my starting point. These long-term charts are very decisive in determining the major trend. You want to understand the bigger picture and the environment we're in, just as Dow did. Surprises will tend to come with moves in the same direction as the primary trend. When the major trend has been going on a very long time and recent weeks and months have seen an accelerated uptrend or downtrend with a steep rate of change, it's important to be looking on the daily charts for any indication of a secondary trend reversal, which could also be the start of a reversal in the major trend.

I know professional traders who do only very short-term trading but find it useful to remind themselves of this big picture often, as it can impact their strategy—for example, they may trade a greater number of shares when that transaction would profit from a move in the same direction as the primary trend. At a minimum, a review of at least the weekly chart is a good idea after the close for the week is known. If you look only at the daily chart in order to make a decision on purchases, you may be surprised when you look at the weekly chart, as it may present a quite different picture. One example is shown in Figures 4.2 and 4.3. In Figure 4.2, if you got

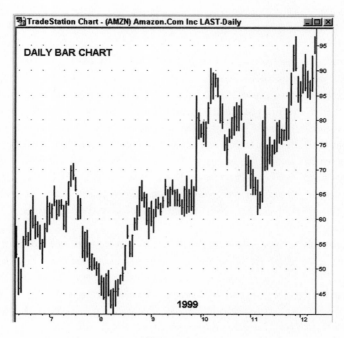

Figure 4.2

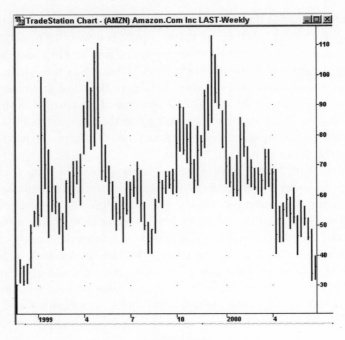

Figure 4.3

too focused on just the months shown on the daily chart, you would miss a lot—once the stock rallied to above the prior $90 high in November 1999, you might focus solely on its further upside potential, as clearing an old high is bullish. While you could look at more history on the daily chart, it's usually easier, and only a click of a mouse button, to switch to the larger time frame of the weekly chart as shown in Figure 4.3, which brings a longer-term historical perspective. In Figure 4.3, it's quickly seen that rallies to above 90 had reversed twice before and very steep declines followed, which is not promising for new purchases. Checking the weekly chart could have gotten you prepared to take profits on any signs that the trend was faltering.

A daily chart typically will show at most 2–3 years of price history and more often, somewhere between 6–18 months. Otherwise, on a computer screen at least, the bars get quite compressed and it's impossible to make out details. Figures 4.4 and 4.5 provide examples where some prior relevant chart history is far enough back in time that it wouldn't show up well without the use of a long-term chart—this leads to another point about the significance of prior highs and lows. Figure 4.4 is a chart of International

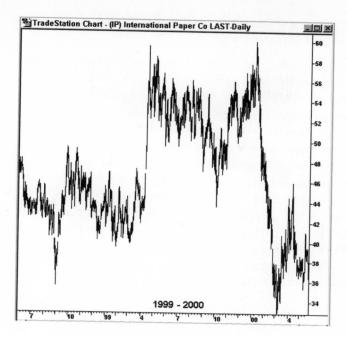

Figure 4.4

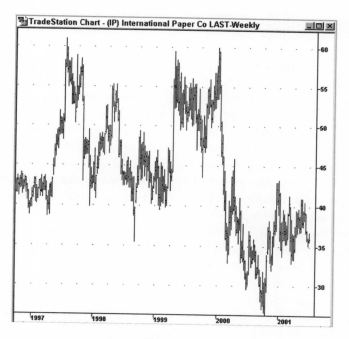

Figure 4.5

Paper (IP) for the 1999–2000 period—you'll notice the problem of bar charts with this much *compression* of the bars, which could be helped by use of a chart that plots only the close as we'll see next. Some forewarning was provided, by examining this amount of price history shown on Figure 4.4, that another advance to the $57–$59 price zone might offer some trouble for the stock—six months earlier, selling developed after a move to this area and prices reversed and then went substantially lower. Nevertheless, it might be easy to believe that this time would be different—however, not if the weekly chart was examined as shown in Figure 4.5. The longer time frame of the weekly chart here would offer a more compelling view that there could be a significant supply of stock for sale in this area of the high $50 range—enough to overwhelm buying interest.

Areas of anticipated *resistance* (expected selling pressure) is another way of saying that some particular price point or zone, based on historical precedent, is a likely area of *supply* or ample stock that may be for sale at or above a certain price area. The related point about prior lows or highs is that there is a greater likelihood that a long prior area of price *support* or price resistance will be significant once this area is reached again—for example, a high made two years ago may assume more significance than a high made two months ago. This was seen to some extent in Figure 4.3—the first two occasions when prices approached or surpassed $100 were separated by about four months—however, it wasn't until the stock got over $100 again after a year, that prices dropped very sharply.

The idea that the more time that passes from a prior major low or high makes such a price point more significant tends to stem from two factors: Long-term holders of the stock who bought before near a major top or sold near a major bottom, see their opportunity to exit (or get back in) at a price that is compelling. Let's take the case of the potential buyers. There are often plenty of buyers near a top as enthusiasm for the stock runs high. However, it is rare that these same investors have an exit plan and will ride the stock back down! But when the opportunity comes again to sell at a price that allows a small profit or is a break-even situation—the resulting selling can be the catalyst for a sales avalanche. The other reason for strong buying or selling at major prior lows or highs is that investors, especially professional money managers, look at charts. And they will tend to do at least some exploratory selling at a high that hasn't been seen in some time, or conversely will make an initial purchase to test the waters, at a low that is the cheapest price at which the stock has been offered since a prior major bottom.

LINE CHARTS

Line charts, or as they're sometimes called close-only charts, are as the names imply, constructed with a line that connects closing prices for whatever period is being studied; for example, hourly, daily, weekly, monthly. Charles Dow, as we have seen, was only interested in the close, the moment of *truth*, so to speak. The close determines each day's unrealized profit or loss. Dow felt, as do other investors and traders today, that plotting a record of the intraday (or intraweek) highs and lows tends to obscure the real value of the stock, which is settled only by the close. Some institutional fund managers buy or sell only on the close.

Figure 4.6 shows a line chart with a bar chart above it of the same stock, so you can easily compare the two types. The stock shown, Amgen (AMGN), had some extreme intraday price swings that resulted in lows well under the close. The bar chart is useful for showing the occasional bouts of volatility that appear part of this stock's pattern—useful information if you were attempting a purchase of this stock and especially useful for setting a sell stop

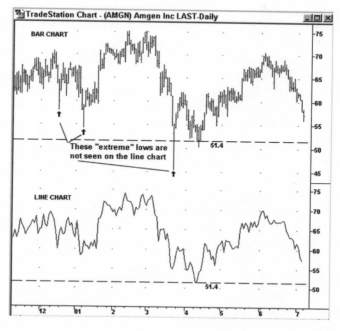

Figure 4.6

order below your purchase price. It was easier to see on the line chart that the stock closed at the same level two to three times in February/early March and it could be determined more quickly with this chart type that this was a likely top. Interestingly, both bar and line charts had well defined *trendlines* that could be drawn through the December/early January lows allowing an accurate determination of the final low—both intraday and the close—in March. I use this chart again later on in a demonstration of trendlines.

I don't find the question of bar versus line charts an either/or situation. I like to look at both, and as we will see, sometimes a better idea of support or resistance can be seen from one or the other chart type—sometimes in the same stock only at different periods. A line chart will also let you take in more history for the same screen space. I encourage the habit of looking at every market of interest, from both the perspective of a close-only line chart and the perspective of also viewing the highs and lows or the open, high, and low of a bar chart. I make an effort to not habitually look only at one type of chart type because of the number of times I've gotten a more complete idea of the trend by looking at both types.

Once when I was going to be on CNBC, the producer of my segment was reviewing with me the type of charts I would use on air. This person indicated that they only used line charts, because when the viewers were presented with a bar chart, it had more detail than they could take in quickly and confused the audience. I suppose if you have seconds to take in the data and if you're never given the opportunity to see bar charts, this is true or is going to remain true.

I use both types of charts in this book, but you may notice that bar charts, which show the highs and lows, are more numerous. This is because many technical analysis techniques make use of the highs and lows. Again, in technical analysis, price and volume information are all we have to work with so the more price information, the better!

CANDLESTICK CHARTS

I mentioned previously, in the chapter on Charles Dow, Munehisa Homma, a famous and very successful Japanese rice trader active in the mid-1700s, whose trading principles evolved into the *candlestick* method of charting and pattern recognition. Drawing the chart requires the high and low for the period, the same as in a bar chart, but the open is *always* part of a candlestick chart, whereas a bar chart can have it either way. In the Japanese candlestick method how a chart is drawn is a function of the relationship of the close to the open. Steve Nison, who wrote the book *Japanese Candlestick Charting Techniques*, which helped popularize this charting form in the U.S., mentions the Japanese proverb that says, "The first hour of the morning is the rudder of the day." The opening level is where all overnight news and expectations for the day ahead is translated into an actual starting value for a market. As to the relative importance of the close, we've seen that Charles Dow considered this value only when determining trend direction.

Figure 4.7 is a candlestick chart expanded to show more detail for a short time span on the daily chart of General Electric (GE). The thick part of the candlestick is called the *real body* and represents the price span between the opening and closing prices. Any real body that is not filled in (hollow) indicates that the close was higher than the open. When the close is below the opening price, that candlestick has a real body that is filled in (black). So solid is down and white is up, in terms of the close relative to the open. The thin lines are called the *shadows* and the topmost point of the upper one marks the high and the lowermost point on the lower line represents the low for the period being measured. In at least two of the

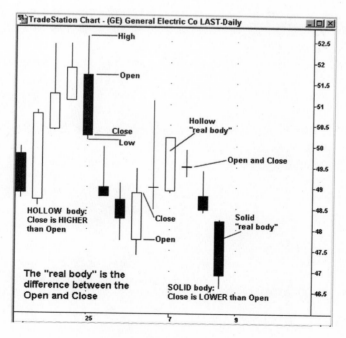

Figure 4.7

candlesticks seen in Figure 4.7—both with hollow, thick (real) bodies—you'll note one daily candlestick figure that has no thin (shadow) line above and one with no thin line below. This is because the high was the same as the close in one instance and the low was equal to the open in the other.

Figure 4.8 shows the same daily stock chart again (GE) with more days shown but also includes a bar chart for comparison. If you study the two different chart types, you'll note that the candlestick figures immediately highlight the days when the close fell below the open and vice versa. For the most part the hollow or white, thick (real) bodies are up days and the solid or filled in, real (thick) bodies are down days relative to the prior close. When the real bodies are *short* because there is a relatively narrow difference between the open and close or when the open and close are the same (no thick body at all), this quickly points to indecision or a temporary balance between buyers and sellers. The candlestick depiction of open, high, low, and close allows an immediate grasp of more information visually. For this reason, candlesticks have become quite popular in the West.

There is another important aspect to candlestick charting that involves interpretations of what may be developing in the trend—for ex-

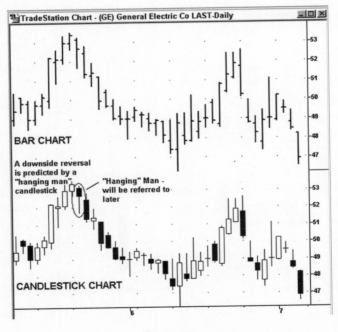

Figure 4.8

ample, a possible reversal of the most recent trend—when candlesticks take a certain form or make a certain *pattern*. For example, certain types of candlesticks, even a single one, are said to predict reversals of the current trend. Bar charts have certain predictive patterns from one day's price action also, but they don't always hold a candle, pun intended, to this chart type.

I do not enter into a description of all candlestick patterns that are thought significant and their colorful names, as that is a specialized study. However, some examples of common candlestick types, with the related explanation of what they mean, demonstrate the method and provide a flavor of the richness of this Eastern tradition—part of the most global form of market analysis. I mentioned before that the use of technical analysis is very widespread in the worldwide foreign exchange market, as the visual interpretations involved transcend languages.

The Hammer and the Hanging Man

The *hanging man*, as the name implies, suggests that a market is at the end of its rope, so to speak and looks a bit like that unfortunate figure. You can go back to Figure 4.8 to see an example of the hanging man. The three criteria to indicate this candlestick type are:

1. The (thick) real body is at the upper end of the recent price range—whether it is solid or hollow is unimportant.
2. A long, lower shadow (thin line) should be twice the height of the real body.
3. It should have no upper shadow or a very short one.

The longer the lower shadow and the smaller the real body, the more predictive it is for an imminent reversal of the trend that has preceded the hanging man candlestick. While the thick body can be either solid or hollow, it's a slightly stronger indication if a real body is solid, which depicts a close that is down from the opening, as in Figure 4.8.

The *hammer* seen in Figure 4.9 has the same look as the hanging man but this candlestick occurs at or near the end of a downtrend and takes its name from the saying that the market is *hammering* out a bottom or base. The same criteria apply except for number one: The (thick) real body is at the *lower* end of the recent price trend. The hammer seen at the end of a steep downtrend in Boeing (BA) has a solid real body, indicating that this

Figure 4.9

candlestick does not have to show an up close to suggest an upside reversal. However, note the long *shadow* (the thin line) that comprises the lower portion of this candlestick, as this is meaningful and adds to the bullish impact.

Candlesticks Summary

This very brief look at a couple of candlestick patterns suggesting reversal formations barely touches on the field of candlestick charting interpretations. But it should serve to give you an idea that these patterns can help identify new and emerging market trends, which is what this book is all about. There is nothing to be lost in using only the more common bar or line charts, as a skillful eye will show you all the same information and possible outcomes. However, there may be something to be gained if you are made surer of the current trend or see a reversal coming, because you also checked a candlestick chart. This assumes you have the ability to examine a candlestick chart and there are fewer possibilities to do so unless you have your own charting software, as most of them plot this chart type. And the Internet web sites that offer charting may be providing this option more in the future.

POINT AND FIGURE CHARTS

Point and figure (P&F) charting is an old technique also—not as old as candlestick charts—but it was around in Dow's day and appears to have predated bar charts. *Figure* charts were made by recording each price (figure) change on paper as prices changed. Later, Xs, referred to as "points," were inserted in the place of prices—this technique later became known as the "point and figure" method of charting. As with candlestick charting, an introductory technical analysis book such as this one cannot cover this topic in full. However, you may become a fan of this technique if you develop an interest in it after being exposed to it—and have or acquire the charting software that will allow you to display price data with this chart type. There is also at least one charting service that I know of, Chartcraft, which sends updated P&F chart books to subscribers using the "3-point" reversal standard.

Point and figure charts essentially view all trading as a single stream of prices and ignores the time duration it takes to get from price point A to point B. You can also apply to point and figure charts many of the technical analysis techniques that relate to chart *patterns* in general and chart *markings* like trendlines, which we'll explore further on. However, many analysis techniques cannot be used as they require session information, for example, *moving averages*. Also volume (of trading) is never accounted for, either. On the other hand there are some techniques of projecting future price movements that are unique to P&F charting. These I also cover briefly.

Construction of a Point and Figure Chart

A point and figure chart is constructed by a series of Xs and Os as can be seen in Figure 4.10. Each X or O represents a price move of some amount, for example, 1, as in the chart of GE shown in the figure—this amount is called the *box* size. On the chart, every X or O is equal to a price move of $1—an X is an advance of this amount, an O is a decline of this magnitude. As long as prices continue to advance by $1 or more, an X is added above the box containing an X in the same column. Boxes do not get filled in partially, but new Xs or Os keep getting filled in as long as any *new* high or low is equal to or more than the *box size*. The chart in Figure 4.10

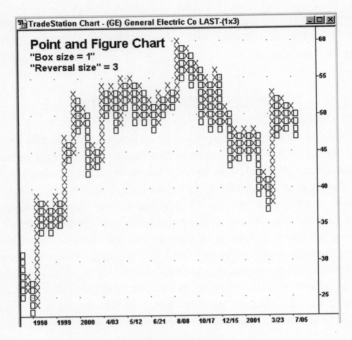

Figure 4.10

reflects price changes that occur in a day's trading. If you have the data for it, you could also specify that the box size apply to prices registered in a period less than a day, for example, on an hourly basis.

The second key element besides the *box size* is the *reversal* amount, which is quoted as a multiple of the box size amount—for example, 3, as is the case in Figure 4.10. This means that when the market is advancing and there is a price decline equal to $3 or more below the value represented by the highest high and the topmost X, a new column of at least 3 Os is made and recorded in the next column to the right in a *descending* manner. The reverse is true of new advances—a rally from the lowest box with an O, of $3 or more (or whatever is the reversal amount) will result in a new column to the right with 3 or more *ascending* Xs . You may notice that the X and O columns always begin one box up or down from the end of the prior column—it's a convention of P&F charting to start the new column this way. The box size and reversal size in Figure 4.10 is described as 1 by 3 ("1 X 3") as noted above the chart. The first number is always the box size, and the second, the reversal amount. The reversal Xs or (number of) Os will have to equal at least 3 always, before a new column is begun.

You'll note that there is a reference to dates on the bottom, on the time (horizontal) axis. This is not a time scale in the sense in which it is normally used—one that marks regular increments of time, say days or weeks. Rather, the dates noted to the right of the little slash marks represent when a new column began. A P&F chart might have no dates noted at all, but a time reference is useful and no doubt a feature requested by the users of my charting application.

A box size could be greater than or less than 1. An example of a box size of .25, allowing you to record the smaller price moves implied, is shown in Figure 4.11, which is the same stock as shown in Figure 4.10. Here, each X or O denotes a quarter point price change. The *reversal* size remains the same—therefore, it takes a reversal in price of .75 to cause another column shift to the right and a change to the opposite figure; for example, from Xs to Os. The result of this is that we now see a more detailed view of the price changes that occurred in the same stock. For example in Figure 4.11, the March 2001 bottom in GE is shown in much greater detail than in Figure 4.10—this period now appears as price action that traced

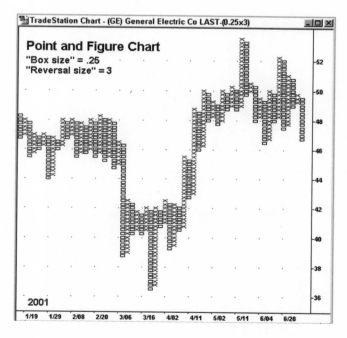

Figure 4.11

out a fairly broad *base*, as seen by the width of the columns from when the stock traded between 37 and 42.

Variation of the reversal size will also make a significant difference and a large reversal amount can encompass many years of trading as can be seen in Figure 4.12. This chart of IBM has a box size of 1, but a reversal size of 10 and displays nearly 15 years of price history on the same size chart as the earlier examples. Much of the detail is lost and we see only the bigger trend changes. For an investor with a long-term horizon a larger reversal amount is going to be preferred. For comparison purposes, a monthly line chart of the closes each month for most of the same time period is shown in Figure 4.13. Relative to this line chart, you can see in greater detail in the P&F chart of Figure 4.12, the back and forth price action between 90 and 130 that occurred since 1999. This additional detail is valuable information— for example, it leads to an evaluation that the stock is having a lot of difficulty overcoming selling in the 120–130 price zone. This information could, for example, suggest to a long-term holder of the stock that profited from the 1995–1999 price increase, to replace it with a technology stock that might have greater upside potential in the next few years.

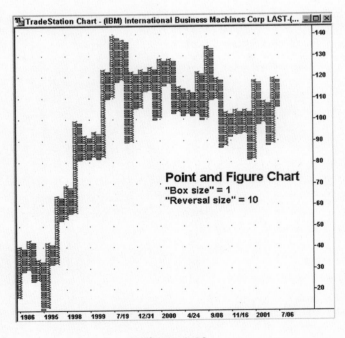

Figure 4.12

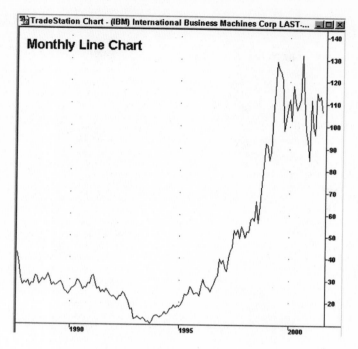

Figure 4.13

Point and Figure Chart Advantages

1. **Finding support and resistance areas.** I touched on this aspect previously. A striking feature of point and figure charts is that they highlight and define areas of price *resistance*, where there is more stock for sale than buyers can absorb and areas of price *support*, where buyers will purchase as much stock as sellers will offer—these, of course, being the areas where P&F reversals occur. Figure 4.12 provided a reasonably good example of this, as it relates to highlighting a major overhead resistance zone in IBM at 120–130 and significant support in the mid-80 area. Figure 4.14 also provides an example of how point and figure information can quickly pinpoint both support and resistance areas. It is readily apparent on this P&F chart that a substantial supply overhang (resistance) exists in Home Depot (HD) at $68 and, conversely, that the stock has been a buy, and has reversed, each time prices fell into the $36 to $40 price zone. While this same information can also be determined from a close study of the bar chart in the lower portion of Figure 4.14, the

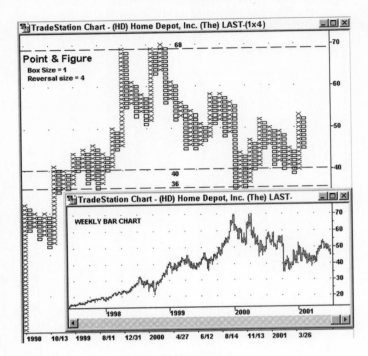

Figure 4.14

information stands out visually when you look at the point and figure chart.

2. **Measuring upside and downside potential.** Point and figure charts allow horizontal measurement across the chart to determine upside or downside price targets. This is mostly unique to P&F charts. The premise here is that there is a direct relationship between the *width* of a sideways (horizontal) trend—how long it goes on—and the subsequent price swing up or down, when prices begin their next advance or decline. An equal measurement to width is made on the vertical price scale. To relate this to market psychology and dynamics, the longer the tug of war goes on between buyers and sellers, buying or selling interest will often be more pronounced when it ends—we all know what happens when you let go of the rope in a tug of war game. An example is provided in Figure 4.15. A count of the number of boxes in different columns is made across the middle of an area where prices are trending sideways—also called a (price) *congestion* area. We determine which horizontal line has the most

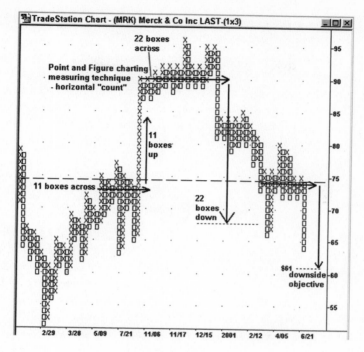

Figure 4.15

number of Xs and Os filled in, then count the total number of boxes across, whether filled or empty. When there is a rally or decline taking prices above or below this line, count the same number of boxes on the vertical price scale, to arrive at a *minimum* price objective. The projected price target arrived at by this method is equaled or exceeded more often than not in my experience. This is not all there is to possible *measuring* techniques in P&F charts, but it is the most important in my estimation.

3. **Generation of trading signals.** Such *signals* are generated when a column of Xs rises one box higher than the highest X of the prior X column. Trading sell signals are generated when a column of Os declines one box below the lowest O of the prior O column. As implied, this is a technique of more use for shorter-term traders except when the *breakout* move is from a long sideways movement. Since the reversal size is defined, the point where a new X would be added is known and a buy–stop order can be placed just above that price. If the aforementioned stop were triggered due to an advance,

it would initiate a new long position. You can use Figure 4.15 to see examples of where these conditions are met.

4. **Confirming or refining interpretations of chart patterns.** Price objectives implied by chart patterns on bar or line charts can sometimes be seen more clearly using a point and figure chart. When I discuss the measuring implications of chart patterns, I provide examples of this point and some occasions where some aspects of a bar (or line) chart pattern were clearer by using a point and figure chart.

P&F Charting Summary

The foregoing is by necessity a brief overview of point and figure charting. I find that the most value from this charting technique is offered by its potential usefulness in (1) finding support and resistance areas and (2) measuring upside and downside potential on a breakout. There are additional refinements and aspects in this charting method best left to further specialized study. It's possible to construct these charts yourself on graph paper, by obtaining a P&F chart service, or by utilizing a charting/technical analysis software application on a personal computer—of the three choices, use of a charting application will be the most flexible and least time consuming to employ for the markets or individual items like stocks that you are interested in.

SCALING CHOICES FOR CHARTS

In all but P&F charts, there are two scales: a horizontal time scale along the bottom of the chart and a vertical price scale going up the side of the chart. There are also two methods in use to measure or *scale* prices for bar, line, and candlestick charts.

An *arithmetic* or *linear* scale is the most common way that prices are displayed and is constructed such that each price *unit* is exactly equal—any equal point price move measures the same distance on this scale. Sometimes, linear is used as the term of choice on web sites and the like. *Linear*, relating to a graph that is a line or straight line is not quite as accurate a term as the term arithmetic for what it describes, but linear is in common usage. On an arithmetic or linear scale, going from 5 to 15 is the same distance on the price scale as an advance from 50 to 60.

There is a limitation inherent in the arithmetic scale. Using the example of a low- and a high-priced stock and the percentage return for each on an equal dollar increase, there is a much greater return based on the money invested, in owning 1,000 shares of stock bought at $5 and sold at $15 (a 200 percent gain), than from owning 1,000 shares of a stock that advances from $50 to $60 (a 20 percent increase). To account for this relative difference, a type of *logarithmic* scaling called "semi-logarithmic," or *semi-log* (*log* for short), has been used widely. On the semi-log chart, distances on the vertical price scale, between the price notations in Figure 4.16, represent equal *percentage* changes. This means of displaying price changes is especially useful on longer-term charts where a stock or an index makes an enormous gain. To keep the more recent increases in perspective after a long runup, and as we'll see later, to aid in *trendline* analysis, log scaling is quite valuable.

Figure 4.16 is of a long-term Nasdaq Composite chart, with the upper weekly chart having a linear scale and the lower weekly chart, for the same 1998–2000 period, with a log scale. Use of the log scale immediately shows that the steep drop shown has put the Nasdaq back in a price zone

Figure 4.16

where the percentage gains and losses are of a much greater magnitude than when the index was in the 4,000–5,000 zone and has become more like owning the Composite in 1998. Comparisons like these are greatly facilitated when you use the semi-log scale.

Arithmetic and Logarithmic Scaling Summary

For the most part, on daily charts going back a year or two, unless there was an enormous price change in this time span, use of a linear or arithmetic scale will be adequate for technical analysis purposes. I tend to use an arithmetic scale on long-term charts as well, but also refer to long-term weekly and monthly charts with a log scale for the major indices—especially when I want to see how long-term trendlines might vary, but there will be more on this later. In general, make use of logarithmic scaling to keep major price changes in perspective. If you have major gains in stocks, use of the log or semi-log scale will be particularly helpful in seeing which stocks have achieved the greatest returns.

DATA CONSIDERATIONS

It is important to keep in mind that technical analysis does not work in isolation. These analytical tools depend on accurate data. When a bar chart appears with a low or high that is significantly above or below the ones around it, you should be aware that this might be a distortion due to a bad *tick* or reported price. This happens more often in the futures markets, where the stream of price changes are monitored from "open outcry" trading in a ring or "pit." There is also the "crowd" (of floor traders and brokers) in front of the different stock specialists stands on the New York Stock Exchange (NYSE) floor, and trading can get hectic. However, the NYSE system is not open outcry, as trade goes through the specialists and a portion of the order flow is electronically matched these days. The Nasdaq market transactions are all electronic, of course. But given the volume of trading in this era in general and how active the markets can get on those wild days that do come along, there is always a possibility that a bad price will get into the system one way or another. This, in turn, creates the problem of price *spikes* on intraday and daily charts and by extension to weekly and monthly charts if the bad tick doesn't get corrected in the daily record.

Look at the stock chart in Figure 4.17, that of Amgen (AMGN). Are those spike lows that are circled, the real intraday lows, or are they bad ticks or prices that were reported incorrectly? They are the correct lows, at least based on my checking of other database sources than the one I use. I check other sources when possible if I see a high or low that seems out of the ordinary, because I have seen many bad ticks and resulting spike highs and lows over the years, even from the best data services. Fortunately, bad ticks are often obvious as they are so extreme, but not always. They came about for various reasons—some recent spikes on my charts came from some power outage problems that were not corrected entirely by my data service.

A price *spike* could give you a false idea about a market that influences a buy or sell that otherwise might not have happened—for example, you think that a stock just shot up above a prior peak and you decide to buy based on that false impression. Your analysis can be only as good as your input— "garbage in, garbage out," as is said. Correcting bad ticks is not always given the highest priority by the exchanges or the data services, as real-time traders and money managers see a next price on the stock that IS correct.

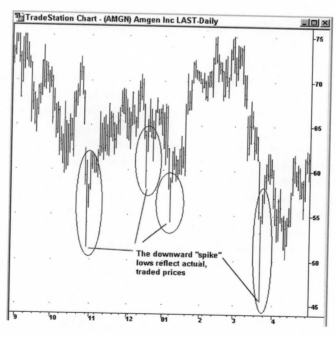

Figure 4.17

Having worked for a data service vendor, I speak from some experience. Some charting services are better than others in *cleaning* or removing the bad price within a day or two, at least from daily charts. A reputation for data integrity, or lack thereof, for a charting service or site can be as important as providing a lot of options in how data can be charted and manipulated.

Phantom Prices

This is an attention-getting way of saying that the further back you go on a chart, prices may not be *real* in a historical sense. In stocks, prices from several years ago may be sharply under actual trading at the time, as they were adjusted downward to account for stock splits that have occurred since this period. The standard treatment of stock splits, so as to not cause a big price change from the split itself, is to adjust all past prices proportionately. If the stock split is 3 to 1 (3:1) and the stock involved closes at $90 on the day of the split, the next day's adjusted price will be one-third of this price and the record of past prices is also divided by 3 (the split *ratio*).

Therefore, the past record reflects phantom prices in that trading never actually occurred at the levels indicated by this new price history. While these adjustments should not alter price *patterns* they may lead to confusion when you rely on the historical price record only and not also on the record of splits, to tell you where a stock actually changed hands on a given day in the past.

This backward adjustment of prices based on splits is important in back testing technical trading *systems*—such testing is done by a scan backward to test the results of a trading rule, for example, buy when a stock crosses above its 200-day moving average, sell when it crosses below the same average. To account for stock splits, a fixed dollar amount is typically used instead of a fixed number of shares when testing trading systems.

In the futures markets, the *continuous* future prices series has similar phantom price phenomena due to the downward, backward (sometimes upward) adjustment of prices in order to remove price *gaps* that exist between contract months. While the resulting price *trends* remain accurate, actual trades will not have occurred at those prices.

VOLUME ANALYSIS

Figure 4.18, a daily bar chart of Cisco Systems (CSCO), shows the usual method of displaying daily trading volume along the bottom. Each day's

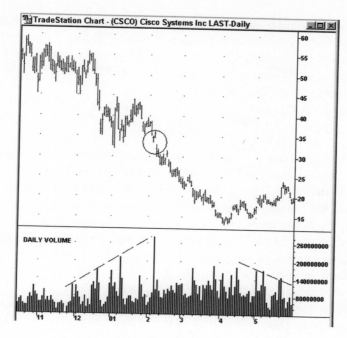

Figure 4.18

volume figure is directly under the bar, line (close), or candlestick that represents the same day's price history. The display of *volume bars*, a type of histogram, is such that the top edge represents and is drawn at the level where that day's total shares fall on the right-hand volume scale. Weekly volume is the cumulative total for the week, as opposed to the closing price, which is the Friday close only.

Remember the discussion on Dow's observation that volume *expands* in the *direction* of the trend? The use of an upward sloping line on the bottom left in Figure 4.18 shows the tendency for volume to increase or to hit higher and higher daily totals at successive points during a strong (downward in the example) price trend. Not surprisingly, the biggest volume day was recorded on a sharp decline from one day to the next. In this instance of high volume, the next day's open was well under the prior day's low—see the circled area—and related to some news that impacted the company's share price after the close.

To demonstrate a shrinking daily volume trend in a rally phase for prices, you'll note on the chart in Figure 4.18 a downward sloping line at bottom right that is drawn above daily volume figures to demonstrate, that on balance, volume peaks were lower than the one preceding it. If volume will normally expand in the direction of the trend, it may also *contract* in a *countertrend* price move. If the advance seen in the chart in Figure 4.18 during the May to June period was the start of a new uptrend, we would expect to see volume increasing.

There is another theory about volume, one drilled into my head by my market mentor, an extremely successful private stock trader, that *volume precedes price*. This might be more accurately stated as volume changes tend to precede price trends. This goes back to what Charles Dow talked about when some group with good insight into the probable end of a bull or bear market starts doing the opposite of the crowd. This *smart money* group will do enough buying or selling (trading activity) to cause prices to move up or down accordingly. As volume picks up, this activity attracts more interest and attention, and the resulting shift in the trend brings in more players and more volume. In this sense, volume precedes price.

Volume is a secondary confirming indicator to price. Volume should *confirm* the direction of the price trend by bigger volume days on upswings in a bull (up) market and larger volume totals in a bear (down) market— Dow considered this rule to apply to the *primary* or major trends only and also indicated that volume does not *have* to confirm price activity, as price is the chief determinant of *trend*. I find some validity in the rule of thumb about volume expansion as applied to *intermediate* or *secondary* trends also, but agree that the biggest volume will be in the direction of the primary trend. Moreover, I have found in many instances that a diverging volume tends to often offer a good indication that a current trend may not have staying power or may be subject to reversing. But it was a refinement to the standard way of displaying each day's volume that led to even more predictive volume information.

On Balance Volume (OBV)

On balance volume or *OBV* is a technical *indicator*. An indicator is a mathematical calculation that is applied to a financial instrument's price and/or volume information. OBV uses daily stock trading volume in its construction and was devised by Joe Granville, a legendary market analyst who was especially well known in the 1960s through the 1980s. He was also a very colorful person who, at times, seemed to be more of a showman than an analyst and market advisor. However, his market knowledge was thorough and his insights often profound. One such insight furthered Dow's concept that volume should increase in the direction of the dominant trend. On balance volume provided some further assessment of this principle and enhanced volume analysis.

To construct the OBV indicator, a running total of volume is kept. Assume we started with a stock that traded 1 million shares on day 1. This is a neutral starting point, as we have to start somewhere. If the stock closes higher the next day and 750,000 shares are traded, day 2's volume figure is added to the first day and assigned a *positive* number, as our running total is so far a positive number, with OBV on day 2 at +1,750,000. [*Note:* OBV would be a *negative* number, if our example stock closed lower on day 2, on 1,500,000 shares: OBV would be –500,000.] On day 3 the stock closes lower on 500,000 shares and we subtract that day's volume from our *cumulative* OBV total: On day 3, OBV is +1,250,000. When the stock is unchanged in price on day 4, we leave OBV unchanged at +1,250,000. This continues on into the future. If we graph the points, the resulting line will start moving upward or downward following the direction of the price trend of the stock for which OBV is being calculated.

An example of OBV is provided in Figure 4.19, which shows a daily chart of VeriSign Inc. (VRSN), with its corresponding on balance volume indicator.

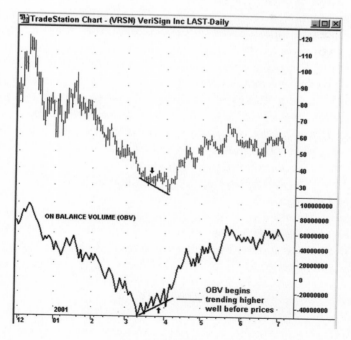

Figure 4.19

This example is useful in that it shows OBV when its cumulative total is both a negative and a positive number. However, we are primarily concerned with the *direction* of OBV and whether the line is moving up or down.

If the direction is up, the OBV line is bullish, as there is more volume on up days than on days when the stock price is down. A falling on balance volume line is bearish, as more stock is being traded on down days than on up days. If both price and OBV are moving up together, it is a bullish sign portending higher prices. If both price and OBV are moving down together, this is a bearish indication for still lower prices ahead. However, if prices move higher during a period of time when OBV lags or moves lower, this is a bearish *divergence* indicating diminishing buying activity and warns of a possible top or trend reversal.

A *divergence*, in technical analysis, is what occurs when one aspect or way of studying market activity goes in one direction and another related aspect goes in an opposite direction. The first example of a "divergence" was Dow's example of one of his averages going to a new high or low when the other did not. This last example relating to price and volume is another type of divergence—that of price going in one direction and an indicator, based on a calculation involving price or volume, going in an opposite direction.

An opposite, bullish divergence occurs in a down trend if OBV starts trending higher—the sellers would now appear to be less active and this divergence suggests being alert to an end to the down trend. This concept goes back to the idea that volume activity can *precede* a change in price direction. Now, the foregoing is not to suggest taking action *before* price activity confirms what OBV and volume activity have suggested. But if this does occur, you can be ready to take appropriate action. An example is noted in Figure 4.19 of an upturn in OBV *preceding* a reversal of a down trend in VeriSign during the period shown. To date on this chart, the up trend looks to be a secondary up trend, within a primary down trend. The OBV/price divergence information could have prompted a profitable trade in the stock. It could also be the beginning of a reversal in the primary trend but, for the price history shown, it is too soon to predict that. We would need to see another upswing exceed the prior high, and so on.

SUMMARY

Chart and scaling choices, as we have seen, are not unlimited. However, people new to technical analysis sometimes wonder why there is not one standardized way to work with price and volume data. We need only remember that technical analysis works primarily with price and volume information only. Therefore, in a sense this is *all* technical analysis has to work with, so there is a natural tendency to study price and volume history in different ways.

There are different ideas and theories about what is more or less important in price activity. Studying different aspects of price can provide complementary but different information, just as mastering tennis might break down into several different components—there is the short and long game or the net strategy versus playing back, the serve, and so on. The different means of recording market prices and the resulting price trend need to be understood so we know what tools we have to work with in technical analysis.

The importance of checking daily and weekly volume numbers, along with price activity, cannot be overestimated. On balance volume or OBV is also useful as a related standard study, along with price and daily volume bars. Volume is especially valuable to confirm any apparent price reversals. While volume, as a confirming indicator or as a diverging one, is discussed in this chapter, more examples will be found in a later chapter on confirmation and divergence and in putting it all together at the end. Next will be a further exploration of price *trend* and *trendline* concepts as we build an ability to use technical analysis.

5

CONCEPTS OF TREND AND RETRACEMENTS AND CONSTRUCTING TRENDLINES

INTRODUCTION

I assume you came to this book thinking there may be some better ways to manage your investing or trading activities, and technical analysis might be one such approach. We can now start to build a method of examining markets using technical analysis. Although my examples are drawn from the U.S. stock market, except for a few specialized indicators related to equities, the basics of technical analysis are the same whether applied to stocks, futures, cash commodities, bonds, or the foreign exchange (FX) markets.

Central to the validity of technical analysis theory is the concept that markets have predictable trends and that such price changes are not random. Moreover, this view suggests that it is quite possible to forecast the expected further duration of a trend based on past and *current* price and volume activity. However, this is not a universal view. Understanding the arguments on this subject is relevant to a basic understanding of technical analysis. It is also relevant to look at enough charts and unfolding market moves to gain experience in seeing the various ways those trends develop. This leads to a greater conviction that trends unfold in predictable ways and boosts confidence in staying with the trend—success in this area is not just about *techniques*.

84

Another central idea of this chapter relates to identifying trends during their emergence, due to the benefit of being in a new trend early. Getting in early in an emerging trend allows establishing an exiting stop order that is not far above or below our entry price, resulting in high profit potential relative to risk. A new trend implies that an old trend ended or reversed direction. A primary tool to define when a trend has reversed is by constructing *trendlines*. We will study the techniques for drawing trendlines and related trend *channels* and look at the ways that penetrations of trendlines are indications of trend reversals. Trends also are subject to countertrend moves where prices retrace some portion of a prior price swing—there are reoccurring and common retracement percentages, which is a related topic in this chapter.

RANDOM WALK VERSUS TREND FORECASTING CONCEPTS

Charles Dow's ideas about how markets trend and Dow theory predictions related to *forecasting* trends are not accepted as having been proved in terms of modern economic theory. There has been a long-standing debate as to whether continuing trends in individual stocks or other financial instruments are predictable, or whether a *buy and hold* strategy is a must because of the inability to know when market moves will begin, continue, or end—therefore, one cannot *beat* the market by being in it sometimes and out of it during other periods. You may say: But I know that markets *trend* because they have trended against *me*! However, in the academic world, a debated question in modern finance revolves around whether financial asset price changes can be forecast. Some confusion revolves around the *random walk* concept, which is based on studies of historical stock price data.

RECENT ACADEMIC RESEARCH
RELATING TO TREND FORECASTING

Dr. Andrew Lo, director of the MIT Laboratory for Financial Engineering at the MIT Sloan School of Management is someone who has done research on the question of randomness in stock price fluctuations. Dr. Lo directed research at MIT that showed that price changes in a NYSE equal-weighted portfolio "exhibit a striking relation from one week to the next." In other words a statistically significant amount of the price variability of next week's return is explained by *this* week's return. These findings actually surprised many economists because his findings would imply that price changes could be forecast to some degree. You may be experiencing some degree of a "what else is new" attitude toward this finding! However, Lo's work also held that forecasts of price changes are *also* subject to random fluctuations, so that having a degree of predictability does not imply that there are *riskless* profit opportunities.

Origins of the *random walk* theory, like many other economic ideas, are traceable to Paul Samuelson, the famous economist. Back in 1965 he wrote that in an "informationally efficient" market, price changes must not be capable of being forecast if they are properly anticipated—in other words, *if* they fully incorporate the expectations and information of all market participants. Here lies the crux of the issue—we have efficient markets to some degree, but how long does it take to incorporate the expectations and information of *all* market participants in the light of Dow's description of the time it takes to get all investors on board in the typical three phases of a primary trend? And, as Dr. Lo wrote, the concept of informational efficiency has "a wonderfully counterintuitive and Zen-like quality to it: The more efficient the market, the more random are price changes." His view is that randomness in financial markets is not like physical and biological systems, but is rather the outcome of many active market participants attempting to profit from their information. The idea that this process is instantaneous, so to speak, does not account for human nature. In fact, only if a security's price changes are predictable to some degree does it supply the reward potential relative to the *risk* involved.

Technical analysis, sometimes called *chart* analysis, is primarily something we take into our brains by way of visual images. It is a well-known fact that the mind can take in the most information visually. For this reason it employs the tools of geometry and *pattern recognition*. Perhaps this is part of its long-lasting appeal, as people are quite visually oriented. Moreover, pattern recognition is one in which computers do not have a flat-out advantage over the human eye and brain. In fact Dr. Lo indicates they studied the predictive effectiveness of some of the most widely used technical patterns in technical analysis, such as the *head and shoulders* pattern. To obtain statistical proof for the ability of this chart pattern to predict future events—and it won't take you as long to figure out this pattern when we get to it—took three months of intensive processing time on MIT computers.

TREND CHARACTERISTICS

The basic rationale or underpinning of technical analysis is that we can identify trends and to some extent the duration of trends. As discussed already, Dow defined a trend as a series of higher (upswing) highs and correction lows in an uptrend and lower downswing lows and correction highs in a downtrend. For this reason, most definitions of *trend*, as used in technical analysis, are that a trend is either up or down. A sideways or lateral trend is typically defined as a *nontrending* market. However, because trend also implies the direction in which a market is moving and one direction could be *sideways* on all chart types we've seen, I view sideways movements of price as a third type of trend. Anyone who has been in a stock that stays in the same narrow price range for months, probably feels that they are caught in a market movement or *direction* that they would rather not be going in—not as painful as having mounting losses, but wearing nevertheless. However, I should point out that the formal definition of *trend* in technical analysis is usually reserved for price movements that over time keep making new relative highs or lows. *Relative* refers to within a particular trend—as opposed to an *absolute* new high or low, such as for an all-time historical high or low for a stock.

A sideways trend is most often a secondary trend that is a consolidation of a previous uptrend or downtrend. *Consolidations* are movements where prices fluctuate in a relatively narrow range in a sideways direction, in comparison to the move made in a prior uptrend or downtrend. In a consolidation, buyers and sellers adjust to the change brought on by the prior trend. In a trend *correction*, prices make a definite *countertrend* move and retrace some part of the distance traveled in the previous trend, up or down. Price movements that are corrections to the dominant trend can also be called *reaction* moves within a trend—hence the term *reaction lows or highs*, referring to the maximum extent of a countertrend price swing. You may remember this term from the physics proposition that for every action there is a reaction.

In Figure 5.1, that of a daily chart of Alcoa (AA) during September 1998 to early May 2001, the chart begins with the stock in a downtrend. This is followed by a couple of months of a sideways consolidation where the October low was made in the area of the September low—you often hear the term that some market or stock *held* the low or its prior low—then began to rally. The subsequent rally peak, after these two lows, was no higher than the prior early-October top. What do we know at this

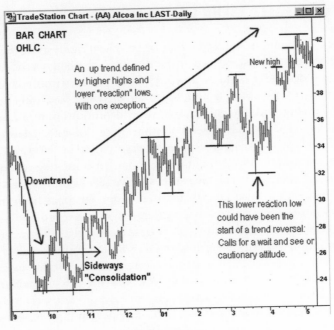

Figure 5.1

point: both nothing and something. We know *nothing* in that we have no evidence that the down trend could be reversing, as no higher high developed. On the other hand, we also know *something*, in that the low held the area of the prior low, so circumstances may be changing in the outlook for the stock. The definitive price action was when, in early December, the prior two tops were exceeded. Prices continued to make higher highs and lower reaction lows, until late April when a prior low was exceeded on the downside. Does this change the trend? There is no definite rule on this, only differing opinions. Mainly, technicians would probably concur that this action is a warning that the trend may be reversing. We need to wait for confirmation of a trend reversal or a trend *continuation*—continuation being a term applied to a resumption of a prior trend—in this case, buyers would have to push prices up to a new relative high, which is what happened. Those long the stock could have placed exiting stop orders under the January reaction low, which is one low before the one that was exceeded, as breaking of a second prior low would be conclusive for a reversal of the trend that we are examining.

Now here comes another important real-world question: Do we use a bar (or candlestick) chart that shows the intraday highs or lows, or should we be taking our visual clues from a line chart reflecting the close? Charles Dow would have no trouble answering that we should use closes only. However, intraday lows are important, too, especially in helping determine *stop* or exit points. My answer is to use both. You can better see the closes on a line chart and the intraday or intraweek fluctuations on bar charts. In some cases what was a higher high or low on the bar chart, when we consider the intraday price extremes, was not seen in the line chart shown in Figure 5.2 of Alcoa, for the same time period as in Figure 5.1.

You'll note that the same horizontal lines that previously marked (intraday) highs and lows on the bar chart in Figure 5.1 remain. Note the quite different look of the chart, however. The closes are, for the most part, some distance away from the lines that represent the intraday lows. Now, does a different depiction of prices change anything relating to defining the trend? No is the answer in this case. There are only some different nuances that show up in the use of the bar chart versus the line chart—if you look at the series of highs made in early November, use of a line chart made it

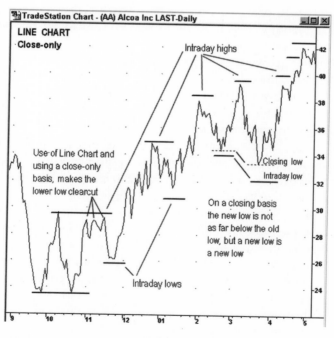

Figure 5.2

clearer that the series of highs that occurred, when considered on a closing basis, were somewhat below the prior closing high.

The lower low seen in the line chart in Figure 5.2, noted with a dashed line, does not exceed the prior closing low by as much, if measured on a closing basis. Does it matter? No. Unless you apply a *filter* or rule that says that a new high or low must exceed the old high/low by at least 1–5 percent, then it doesn't matter. I don't recommend the use of such a filter, but it can be a valid strategy if it is applied consistently. Remember that what the amateur tends not to have versus the professional trader or money manager is a *consistent* way of deciding his or her entry and exit rules.

The rule that I apply is that an uptrend is considered to be intact until there is a lower closing low relative to the previous closing *swing* low—if the context is known, we can dispense with the added description of whether the prior price swing or movement was up or down. Conversely, a downtrend should be assumed to be intact unless there is a closing high that exceeds the previous closing swing high. The first close above or below the prior swing high or low can also be considered a *warning* of a trend reversal, which sometimes calls for a brief wait to see if the subsequent market action continues to move further in the same direction.

Something else we can consider is the lower low that is seen both intraday and on a closing basis in April, in Figures 5.1 and 5.2 that injected a warning note about a possible end of the uptrend. There is something discussed already that would help us make an informed guess as to whether the lower relative low is going to lead to further weakness, or a reversal of the prior trend. Examining volume, the handmaiden to *price*, can help here, especially with trade strategy—a *definite* judgment will have to wait for a still lower low or a renewed high. If we had some valid reason to suspect that the new low was not the start of a new trend, we might, for example, want to give more latitude to a trailing stop–loss order by placing it under the downswing low that occurred *before* the low that was exceeded. A valid reason would be a lack of follow-through in the direction of the trend reversal.

What we are most concerned about in our discussion of determining whether the trend has reversed is the period of time outlined with a box in Figure 5.3, when the stock had closed under the prior low. Did volume also confirm a new trend with a jump in volume at the same time as prices slipped under that prior low? No volume confirmation was indicated, as both the daily volume as represented by the volume bars at the bottom of Figure 5.3 and the on balance volume (OBV) indicator, which is the line overlaid on the volume bars, actually showed a contraction of volume at

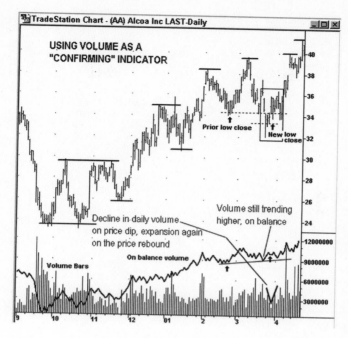

Figure 5.3

the new low. Volume would normally *expand* if a new (down) trend was underway, due to the increased activity of more sellers. The lowermost numeric scale to the right on the graph in Figure 5.3 reflects only the daily volume bars, not the OBV, the level of which is unimportant as we are interested in the relative direction of the line, not the absolute numbers. My suggestion is to always also examine what volume is doing if price action has suggested a change in trend. Price is the ultimate determinant of the trend, but volume activity can provide important additional information.

Also, in relation to Figures 5.1 and 5.2, there is one more related point that could be considered when we analyze a trend. We can't really be certain if the uptrend we are looking at for September 2000–May 2001 is also within a primary or major uptrend for the stock. We would have to look at Alcoa's long-term chart, as shown in Figure 5.4, to determine if what we are seeing on the daily charts is also the major trend. In fact, the intermediate (less than a year) uptrend dating from the September low, became part of a new primary up trend when the major high made in the prior year was exceeded. The way of defining a trend—higher highs and lower lows—is the same regardless of the charting period, for example, hourly, daily, weekly,

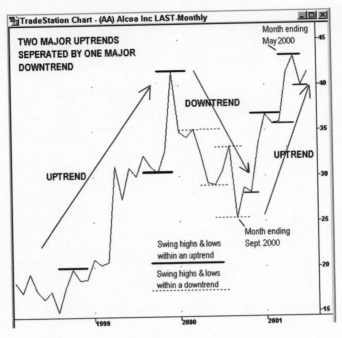

Figure 5.4

or monthly. The sole difference is that in Figure 5.4 we are going back over a multiyear period and looking at prior monthly highs.

Figure 5.5 is a chart with a well-defined down trend that developed also after a period of a sideways trend that could have been either a consolidation of the prior up trend (not shown) or what Dow called a line formation or sideways move, that could precede either an up or down trend. Some technicians assume that a sideways trend like this, with an upper and lower line that touches multiple highs and lows, is assumed to be a *top* if the trend that preceded it was up, and a *bottom* if the trend that preceded it was down. This is often true but not always. The important thing is to wait for the higher upswing high or downswing low relative to prior high or low. This will tell the story as far as defining the trend.

Big price breaks, as seen in Figure 5.6, are different in terms of defining a trend reversal, only in that there is not a series of tops and bottoms or *peaks* and *troughs* that form before the price is already sharply lower.

In Figure 5.7 there is both a major sideways movement suggested by the upper and lower parallel lines, but also by our foregoing rules of defining a trend, a warning of the reversal of the prior uptrend. This broad

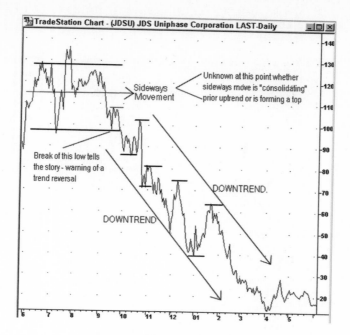

Figure 5.5

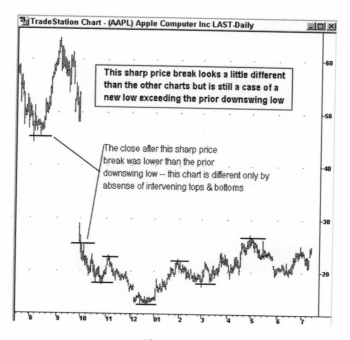

Figure 5.6

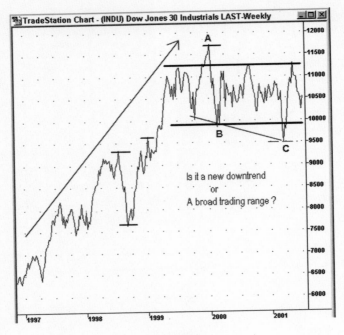

Figure 5.7

lateral or sideways movement in the Dow Jones Industrial average has a duration on the weekly chart of 2.5 years. There is one extreme high and one extreme low that is above and below upper and lower horizontal lines shown. Those extremes are where we find the warning of a trend reversal. Point A, the highest high, has not been exceeded. Point B was a lower low than the prior bottom. And point C was lower than point B. So, by our strict definition of trend, the point C low especially has *confirmed* a down-trend. However, with the failure of prices to continue lower and the con-tinued rally tendency up to the upper horizontal line, this chart pattern looks like a broad sideways trend. We are about to go more into the world of theory on one hand, versus the more sloppy world of the mar-kets, driven by human behavior.

TIME DURATIONS OF TRENDS

There are many terms related to technical analysis that are very vague in the way they are used by the financial press. For example, it is a bullish or *good-looking* chart. What is so bullish about it or *good* about it is not defined. Another set of terms relates to "short-term" and "long-term." As explained in the section on Dow theory, there are definitions of trend durations, but "short-term" and "long-term" are a bit vague in order for us to better pinpoint what time frame is being talked about. I'll quickly review the time durations and then, more importantly, break down some charts into the differing trends.

Short-term should refer to the *minor* trend of a few hours up to, at most, three to four weeks. The minor trend either is going in the same direction as the larger trend of which it is a part; is a *correction*—correcting or going in the opposite direction of the larger intermediate trend of which it is a part; or is a *consolidation*—price action that is consolidating the prior gains, or basically a sideways price movement. The minor trend is mostly of concern to traders.

The *intermediate* or secondary trend is between short-term and long-term, meaning a few weeks to several months, up to at most six to eight months. This trend is composed of minor trends and also either moves in the same direction, is a consolidation, or is a correction (countertrend move) to the larger price movement of which it is a part—the major or primary trend. The intermediate or secondary trend is of concern to traders, but is also of interest to investors if they are looking for the end of a correction to the major trend, and for a price are to then enter the market.

The major, or what Dow called the *primary*, trend should be what is referred to as "long-term" and has a duration of at least six to eight months—usually closer to a year—to as much as several years. This trend is comprised of various intermediate or secondary trends, with some of these secondary movements going in the same direction as the major trend, some going sideways (*consolidations*), and some going against the dominant trend director or *corrections* within the primary trend—occasionally, a secondary reversal becomes the start of a new primary trend in the reversal direction. The major trend is of concern to investors. Generally it seems, those looking to be short stocks for the duration of a primary downtrend aren't considered *investors*, but whatever you call them, short-sellers with a long view can also be primarily focused on the major trend.

Figures 5.8 and 5.9 illustrate intermediate and secondary trends within primary or major trends. All short-term price swings within the secondary trends, whether up, down, or sideways, are minor trends. Many times people think technicians are simply hedging their predictions of market direction, when in fact they are simply unsure of which trend is predominating at the moment or are not sure of which trend

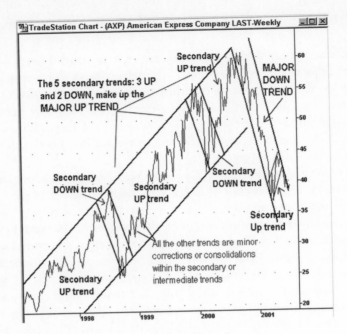

Figure 5.8

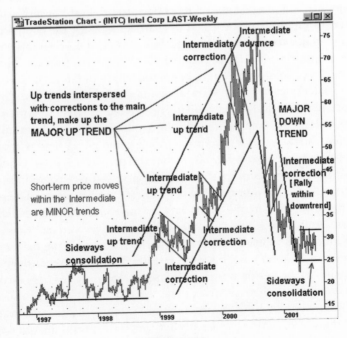

Figure 5.9

96

(minor, intermediate, or major) you are asking about. Also, many of their predictions are *conditional,* for example, the trend is up as long as the low at X is not exceeded. However, technical analysis is like a journey that is completed safely using the multiple signposts along the way—where each turn is known only at the time the road sign appears.

HIGHS AND LOWS DEFINE TRENDS AND SUPPORT AND RESISTANCE

The question often comes up as to why prior highs and lows, or peaks and troughs, are so important. Prior highs and lows largely define or allow us to make an educated guess at, *support* and *resistance* levels or areas. A low becomes a low because buying becomes strong enough at that point to start pushing prices back up. "Support" often refers to a prior low and is a price point or area where there is anticipated buying interest based on what happened in the past. We continually rely on what happened in the past in technical analysis because we see that the market patterns and interests repeat and repeat. This is no more than a reflection of human nature and the analysis we make of relative values, which we tend to stick to until we're forced to make an adjustment—by the actions of others, in this case via the market. Support could be just prices digging in where there is buying interest and may not be in the area of a prior low—in that instance we would just take note that this new low was above the prior low. Support is a price level at or below the current level of an index, stock, or other financial instrument.

You hear that a market index or stock "finds" support—meaning buyers started purchasing in a certain price area. You also hear that prices "bounced from" support—this is often referring to a prior low or series of lows—or that prices "held" support. When support is "broken" it refers to prices exceeding a prior low or series of lows—there is a downside penetration of the support area as willing buyers withdraw, and/or sellers offer more than all buyers want, so prices fall if the sellers persist. A *test* of support is that prices go back to a prior low. A successful or failed test of support is determined by whether buyers again come in to buy and prices rebound from the support area or not. Support is always an *implied* aspect to price levels.

"Resistance" is just what is implied by the word, a price area where sufficient selling develops to push prices lower and to *resist* the buying pressure. Resistance is a price level at or above the current level of an index, stock, or other financial instrument. Resistance is often a prior upswing high or series of highs. Prices also "bounce off from" resistance or are deflected by, or "turned back" and "fall back" from it. A common statement is that a rally "failed" at resistance, or an advance failed to "take out" resistance—meaning that prices fell once they got into the area of a prior high. These are some of the terms that are bandied about.

The important thing to remember about resistance is that it was an area where holders of the stock or other financial instrument found it attractive to sell previously—enough so that their selling overwhelmed willing buyers, so to speak. If it was attractive once to sell in this area, it may well be again. A push through resistance is where prices rise above the prior low or series of lows. You also hear for example, that a stock "overcame" resistance in a certain price area.

Areas of stock support indicate a price(s) where a stock is being accumulated by buyers, hence the term *accumulation* to refer to this process. A particular price support area may be said to be an area of long-term accumulation. Areas of accumulation are areas of support, as there is buying interest there. Stock market bottoms occur when some savvy buyers begin to *accumulate* stocks, anticipating an end to the decline.

Areas of stock resistance indicate a price(s) where a stock is being "distributed" (sold) to other willing buyers, hence the term *distribution* for this process. Areas of distribution are areas where previous owners of a stock are willing sellers. Stock market tops tend to begin forming when some of the more savvy holders of stock begin to sell their holdings. You may hear terms like "distribution tops" to describe this process.

TIME CONSIDERATIONS OF SUPPORT AND RESISTANCE POINT

The further back in time, from the present, that a support or resistance area was established, the more important it tends to be. With a support or resistance area that has "held" or turned back repated price moves to it, the more importance this area assumes. You might hear that a stock went to a new three-year high, which means that an old high was in place for that long a period. In Figure 5.10 the inability in late 2000 of Johnson & Johnson's (JNJ) stock to advance above the high of a year earlier preceded a significant decline. The most recent advance shown on this chart brings prices once again in this resistance area. If this upswing culminates in a move above resistance this time, the probability for a further good-sized advance should be significant.

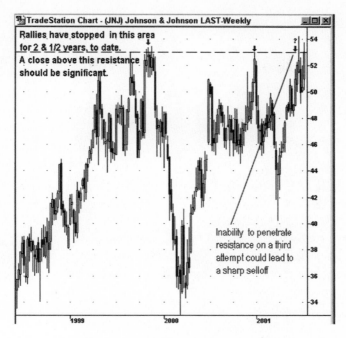

Figure 5.10

Figure 5.11 contains an example that is often cited to illustrate the importance of the time duration separating prior lows. The two closing lows in IBM in the 10.5 area, on a (price) split-adjusted basis, were some 20 years apart. The second low marked the beginning of a 6-year advance that took the stock 1,300 percent higher. This example also reinforces the point of looking back on long-term charts to gain a complete perspective of all significant price points.

Another aspect related to the importance of time duration relative to support and resistance areas, is that the longer that rallies or declines cannot penetrate the same price area, the more significant is that support or resistance. Figure 5.12 shows widely dispersed and multiple rallies for International Paper (IP) that stopped in the same price zone. The last rally failure led to a huge decline relative to any prior downswing. An example is also pointed out in Figure 5.12 of a break of support from a few months prior that led to a limited decline, but not a major one. The significance might have been far greater if the prior low that was exceeded was from a few years before rather than a few months. In Figure 5.13, as noted by the arrows on the monthly chart of Eastman Kodak (EK), there were lows in

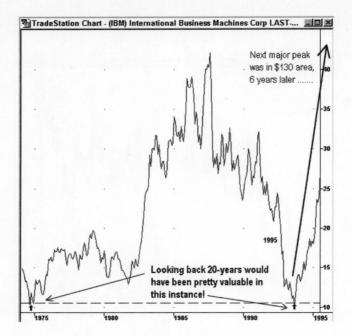

Figure 5.11

Figure 5.12

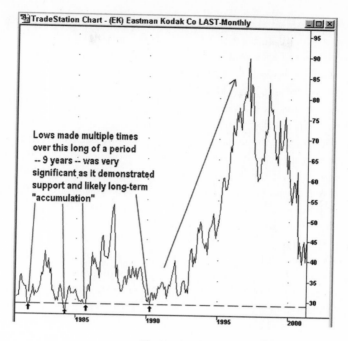

Figure 5.13

1981, 1985, and 1990 that were all in the $29 area. One low, in 1984, was lower, but within $2 of the others. An enormous rally in the stock followed these series of multiyear lows in the same area.

Time considerations are not only something to consider on an absolute basis, but relative to the time frame of the chart you are looking at. If a major price advance stops at a prior high from five years ago, that is usually quite significant. If you are looking at daily charts for a year period and on three occasions over that year, there were lows at $20, that is also significant. It is also suggested however to look back even further to see if the same low was also a significant bottom during the prior several years or prior decade.

There are multiple reasons why longer time frames assume more significance in terms of support and resistance. A prior high or low that has been in place for several years becomes a sort of "benchmark," especially for professional money managers—often they use a prior high or low as suggesting a present value, or overvaluation, and decide to do some buying or selling, on a return to the same area. In this sense, heavy selling or buying at a prior high or low may be something of a self-fulfilling prophecy in terms of establishing these price areas as important support or resistance. However, if an inflated value (or an attractive value) is not perceived in these areas, prior highs and lows, just because they are there, will not be enough to start a buying or selling wave.

Another dynamic, per Dow's observations, is that prior highs and lows mark emotional high points of bull and bear markets—there are always significant market purchases and sales near these extremes and by some of the more unsophisticated investors. Those buying near a significant top often end up holding the stock through major subsequent declines, as per the common investment advice to "buy and hold." I wish I had a dollar for every time I've heard someone say about a stock they own that "I can't sell now; it's down too far." This group will want to be sellers—they'll decide they just want out—when the same stock comes back into the area where they can exit at a face-saving price, at or near their break-even point. Of course, *break-even* never accounts for the *opportunity* cost of tying up money in an investment that doesn't return a profit, versus the possibility of putting that same money to work elsewhere profitably.

The reverse situation is true at a prior major low, as this was likely an end stage of the panic selling described in the earlier discussion of the *phases* of bull and bear market trends. The sellers near the bottom remember quite well the area they sold in—now *wiser*, they tend to view a subsequent return to this same price area as a buying opportunity. Professional money managers will also be inclined to view this area as a benchmark area of probable value.

A last example of the significance placed on new highs or lows of some duration is the daily and weekly compilation that can be found in some of the financial media, of the new high/low list for both the Nasdaq and NYSE markets. These are new 52-week highs and lows. Keeping track of the difference by subtracting new lows from new highs—the numbers, whether positive or negative and whether increasing or reversing in one direction or the other—will provide a good confirming indicator of the current trend or an emerging new trend. I'll have more on possible uses of the new highs/new lows daily figures in my indicator section.

An advance through an old resistance area (or any prior resistance) or a decline through a prior support point, does not guarantee anything. As I stated before and coming from Charles Dow originally, bull and bear market price swings can reverse at any time. This would be the ideal time to inject something about either rally or downswing failures—sometimes called, failure *swings*.

NEW HIGHS AND LOWS THAT ARE
FOLLOWED BY TREND REVERSALS

I may have heard the term elsewhere, but technical analyst Jack Schwager, during the time that we worked together at PaineWebber especially, drummed into me the terms bull and bear *traps*—describing, in the case of a *bull trap*, a rally that goes to a new high after which the advance then collapses. A *bear trap* is the reverse situation where a decline exceeds (*takes out*) a prior low, and then is followed by a strong rebound in prices.

These reversals differ somewhat from what are called *key reversals*, the definition of which is an occurrence of a new low (or high), followed by a close above (below) the prior bar's high (low)—this applies to any period the bar measures, for example, hourly, daily, weekly, and so on. There will be more on key reversals in the section on chart patterns. The main point is just to note that with a key reversal, the new low or high is in relationship to the prior bar or two (e.g., day or week) and not necessarily to the preceding price swing.

In a bull trap reversal, the rally that takes out a prior high tends to bring in new buying because this often signals a new up *leg*—another wave or price movement of intermediate proportions. Otherwise, the new high serves to convince those *long* a stock or other security that they are on the right side of the market. If this rally then fails, by reversing to the downside, it has the effect of *trapping* the bulls or those with the conviction that prices will keep rising—hence the term "bull trap" or "bull trap reversal." An example is shown in Figure 5.14 of a weekly chart of McDonald's Corporation (MCD).

An example of a bear trap reversal is shown back in Figure 5.11, as the weekly chart of International Paper (IP) also provides an example of a bear trap as noted in the lower right. After a prolonged downtrend, there is yet another in a series of new lows and it exceeds the prior low by a comfortable margin—however, this time the lower low was followed by a rapid and good-sized advance. Renewed selling had no doubt come in as the old low was exceeded. Sellers, or buyers who had finally liquidated their positions, would have had expectations of another downswing or another down leg. The bears instead were *trapped* by the rapid reversal. Of course, they are only trapped as long as they don't cover (buy back) their short positions, but as I said before, there is often a considerable period of disbelief that a trend *reversal* is occurring. Remember that prices have to exceed the prior upswing high to confirm a new trend, and prices may have to travel some distance before this occurs.

Figure 5.14

There are implications of the trend reversals of the type described here as bull and bear traps, that go beyond the significance of affirming that market trends can reverse suddenly, even after exceeding prior lows and highs. Very often, such trend failures and reversals after a lengthy trend, offer excellent opportunities to take a position in the direction of the new trend, as it may be very powerful. Price moves often reach a point of *exhaustion*, where the forces driving prices in the direction of the trend become spent or come to a conclusion. After almost everyone who is a potential buyer, or potential seller as the case may be, has bought or sold, there are few left to keep the trend going. When there are few or no sellers left, only a modest amount of buying can drive prices back up sharply. When there are few or no buyers left, a modest amount of selling can drive prices sharply lower. This is what is meant in the saying that "bull markets die of their own *weight*"—a market that has no group of substantial buyers left, will fall simply due to the removal of new buying and only a modest amount of selling.

As seen in the two examples provided, and you can find more, these price swing *failures* or reversals have a record of offering some major profit opportunities. Going back to Figure 5.9, the last high made by the stock can also be viewed as a bull trap reversal. There was a new high, *relative* to the trend that was ongoing, followed by a sharp and very steep price collapse. If you don't want to *reverse* positions, at least consider exiting at a point just beyond a prior significant high or low recently exceeded if the move doesn't last. For example, if a significant prior high is penetrated, followed by a close *under* this area, get out. I take this and every opportunity to caution against the *intent* or a *plan* to exit versus actually having a liquidating stop order in with your broker. When you have these big price swings the effect can be like the deer caught in the headlights—paralysis— I've been in that position enough times to know.

SUPPORT BECOMES RESISTANCE AND VICE VERSA

There will be more on this topic relating to trendlines, but the starting point is how a prior high, or what was formerly resistance, later can *become* support and vice versa—a prior low, or what was formerly support, later becomes resistance. This is an important concept and when you start looking at charts with this awareness, you will see many examples such as shown in Figures 5.15, 5.16, and 5.17.

Why this phenomenon exists, like most other market dynamics, is a function of what happened to investors at those prior lows and highs and their later attitude when prices return to the same areas. When a significant high is reached in a stock, particularly an intermediate top, it is also a high point in terms of bullish *sentiment*—relating to the degree of emotional conviction that prices will go still higher—and there are buyers who are even showing up for the first time. If there is then a *correction* to the uptrend and prices fall substantially, there will be many buyers, especially those who bought near the peak, who sell at a loss. If the stock subsequently rallies back above the prior top, those former sellers are often either not watching the stock then or take a wait and see attitude about it. Later, many notice that the stock is back into an uptrend. If the stock then drops back to near where they bought before (at the old high), many of the former owners become willing buyers again—if they liked the stock earlier they may even like it more now as they chide themselves for having not stayed long and become intent to make up their initial loss. This dynamic results in a built in source of buyers at a price that is at or near a prior top(s) and what was resistance has *become* support.

At a significant low, particularly at the end of an intermediate or secondary downswing, there are many buyers who see this as only a correction

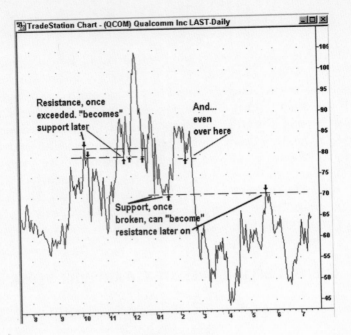

Figure 5.15

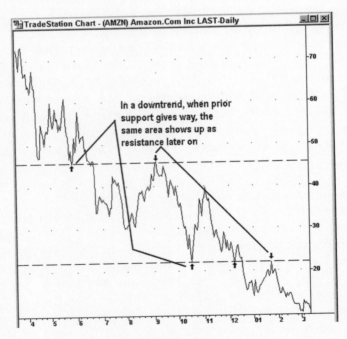

Figure 5.16

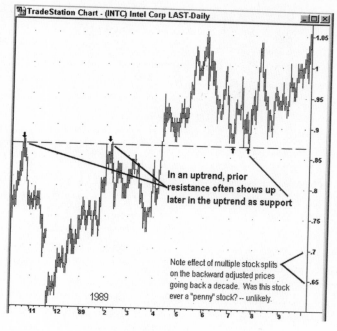

Figure 5.17

to the major trend and buy. Their buying interest creates a bottom and the stock or other financial instrument rebounds—this area is pegged as a support area or level. Later, prices break this support but the buy and hold investors are still long. However, bullish convictions or sentiment wanes with the market trend sooner or later and eventually more investors want to get out. If they then see prices come back to the area of the last bottom, many of these investors take advantage of the return of prices to their breakeven point (or close to it) and they sell. This selling creates a secondary top and becomes defined as a new resistance area—and (prior) support *becomes* resistance.

TRENDLINES AND THEIR VARIATIONS

A *trendline* is one of the most basic and useful tools in assessing trends or trend reversals in stocks, stock averages, and other financial instruments. A trendline is, as the name implies, a line that attempts to measure and define a price trend in any market that involves prices set by the free actions of buyers and sellers. It is also by definition a line that either slopes up or down to some degree in keeping with the primary definition of a trend as having a predominant up or down price direction. On the other hand, lines that are drawn across the highs and lows of a sideways trend or *trading range* are usually referred to simply as horizontal lines rather than trendlines.

A *rising* up trendline is usually drawn by connecting two or more, generally three if available, of the lowest lows—the resulting line will then often be below the level of the later periodic price drops that occur in a rising market. Some of the other names for these kinds of minor countertrend movements are: price "dips," *pullbacks*, corrections, and *reaction* lows—for every action there is some re-action, for example, as caused by sellers who think a stock is overvalued, even if perhaps only temporarily. What really defines a rising up trendline is not the advancing price moves or price swings, but the low point of the downswings, dips, or pullbacks on the way up. You hear the saying "buy dips or buy weakness." This generally refers to buying the *corrections* in a rising trend, and buying pullbacks to the up trendline is a good method to employ for this. Downside reactions in an uptrend will usually stop above, at, or near the rising up trendline. Figure 5.18, which shows the same chart of the stock just examined in Figure 5.17 for another purpose, illustrates a simple up trendline connecting three and more intraday lows—and it demonstrates that you never have to search very far for examples of trendlines.

A down trendline slopes down as it measures a declining price trend and is typically drawn by connecting two or more, usually three if available, of the highest highs of the periodic upswings or rallies that occur in a downtrend. The points that establish the down trendline are the high points or peaks of the upswings, or minor rallies that run counter to the general downward direction. The advice to "sell rallies" is typically in reference to a declining trend, and a rebound to the down trendline would be a good way to do it. While there are always some countertrend movements in a decline, trendlines that slope down in a very steep manner are more common historically than those that have a radically steep upward slope. Rallies in a downtrend will often stop below, at, or near a down trendline. Trendline resistance is the expected selling that tends to develop on rallies up to a down trendline. Figure 5.19 is a line chart and connects three and more closing lows. Note that the rebound from the resistance trendline on the lower right of the chart illustrates the principle that support and resistance *trendlines* can also assume opposite roles at a later stage—here, the resistance trendline, once broken, later defines a support area.

This brings us an obvious question of which type of chart to use and does it make a difference. Generally, it does not make a difference whether

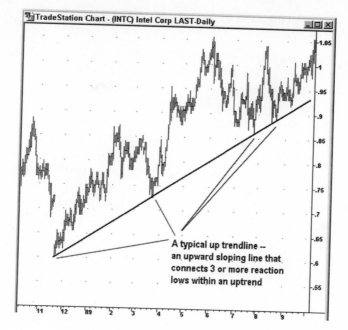

Figure 5.18

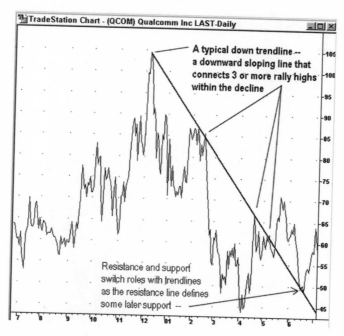

Figure 5.19

you use a bar (or candlestick) or line chart in terms of finding enough points to construct a trendline or in terms of whether one is better than the other. I use both and sometimes see slightly different things. A pullback in an uptrend may dip under the trendline that uses the lows, but not be apparent on a close-only line chart. I tend to prefer drawing trendlines on daily bar charts. For weekly and monthly charts, I generally draw a line first with a bar chart, then switch to a line chart for comparison. If the line chart gives me a clearer trendline definition, I save and use that one. You can also draw trendlines on point and figure charts, which makes a third choice as can be seen in Figure 5.20. The upside penetration of the down or resistance trendline at the extreme right suggests a reversal to the trend from down to up.

Using a ruler or straightedge and a pencil on a printed out chart or one in a chart book, will allow you to draw trendlines fairly adequately. There are also charting or technical analysis software applications that have drawing tools so you can construct trendlines on the screen. Online charting Internet sites like bigcharts.com have a *Java* chart choice that will allow you to construct a trendline on this chart type. You can start over

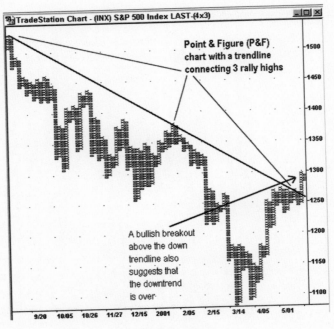

Figure 5.20

whenever you want to change the method of construction. A printout of what is on the screen will allow you to keep your work. Of course, you could always print out the chart and construct the trendlines on paper.

TRENDLINE RATIONALE AND CONSTRUCTION

As I demonstrate the methods and examples related to trendline construction, at the same time I will discuss more about what trendlines can and can't do to help you spot trends and trend reversals. Because the use of trendlines is something of an *art* rather than an exact science, people can get frustrated when the trendline *rules* do not seem to work. There is also the fact that it just takes some months and years to see how trendlines work in a variety of stocks and market conditions. What follows, I hope, is most everything you will need to know to start drawing and using trendlines and also a rationale for their use.

1. There is more than one way to draw a trendline but the guidelines for using them are the same as seen in Figures 5.21 through 5.24.

Conventional or traditional trendlines are straight lines drawn through at least two lows or highs, preferably three, and such a trendline never *bisects* or cuts through any bar (its price range) in a bar chart or any close on a line chart. However, if we remember always that trendlines are angular measures of price momentum and that momentum can sometimes only be loosely defined, we have made the case for trendlines that cut through some of the bars. I call these the "best fit" trendlines that go through the greatest number of highs and lows. And I always remember that I am trying to visually depict the *dominant* momentum of the trend. Trendlines that go through the most number of high and low points and/or involve subjective judgments as to best fit, have been called *internal* trendlines by Jack Schwager, who has frequently described this method of (trendline) construction.

The general guidelines for using trendlines regardless of how they are precisely constructed, is to buy on declines to or near a support up trendline and sell rallies that touch or approach a resistance down trendline. Conversely, a decline that goes through or *breaks* an up trendline is an indication that the trend has reversed and a sell is indicated; a rally that goes through or breaks out above a down trendline is an indication that the trend has reversed and a buy is indicated.

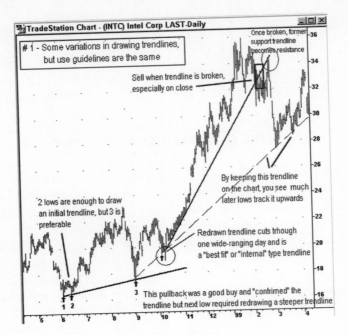

Figure 5.21

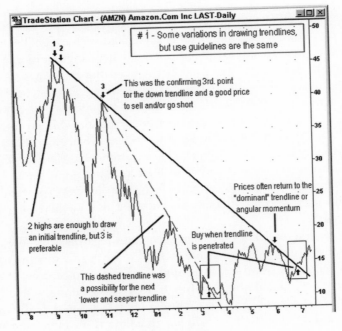

Figure 5.22

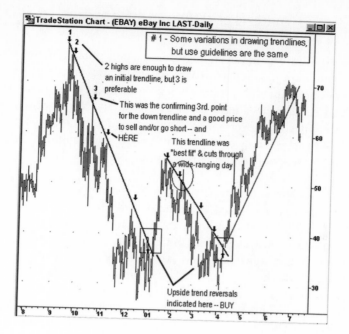

Figure 5.23

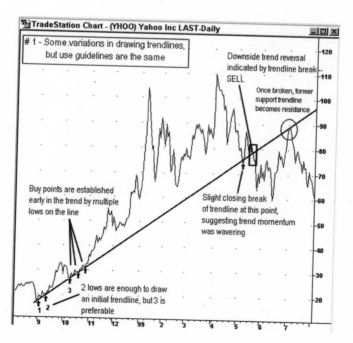

Figure 5.24

113

2. Trendlines are, in effect, angular measures of *momentum*, shown visually on a price chart. If you remember the nature of what trendlines are, you will remember that momentum is a quality of motion that is sometimes hard to measure exactly. Within this limitation, trendlines are nevertheless sometimes so accurate in depicting the trend that it's easy to forget this cautionary reminder. Figures 5.25 and 5.26 are examples of this point.

Trendlines show, in effect, the rate of change for prices in an up or down direction as expressed as an angle line. If prices are going up an average of three percent a month, this mathematical progression can be shown as a line. However, drawing trendlines must also take into account the extreme highs and lows (above or below the "mean" or average change), which are the most emotional points of excess in the market. Therefore, we can expect that there will be some false signals given by trendline breaks and breakouts—that is, downside or upside penetrations of the line that you are drawing—because points of excess go further than is normally predictable.

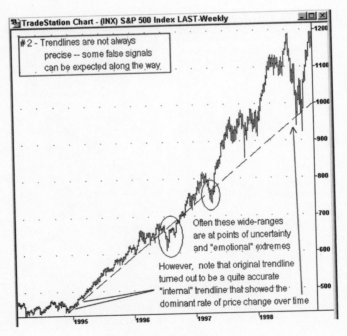

Figure 5.25

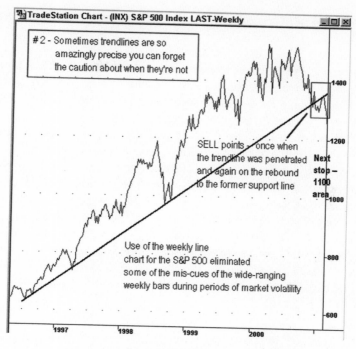

Figure 5.26

You can anticipate that you will need to periodically redraw trendlines to account for some new extremes if you want the most accurate visual depiction of the trend momentum. Remember the adage about putting in the time and work on technical analysis if you expect the rewards. The money management rules about always limiting losses will prevent the times that trendlines don't work—where they fail to identify the exact parameters of a trend or trend reversal—from causing a big dent in your investing and trading capital. Nothing works all the time in technical analysis. Getting in early on trends, for which trendlines will be of considerable help, provides the best opportunity for capturing the most profit from a trend. Accomplishing this more often than not will normally tend to make up for other losses along the way. The idea is to keep using trendlines and the other tools I will discuss—they'll work over time if you just keep using them and don't expect more than the tool can provide.

3. Trendlines look like they make identifying every trend and trend reversal easy after the fact. Once the price action has unfolded, it's

easy to see the dominant trendlines as is apparent in the series of charts shown in Figures 5.27 through 5.31.

Flying a plane looks easy when an expert is doing it. It will take some time for you to make as good use of trendlines going forward, as looking backward. When, for example, market action is unfolding and you are in a stock that you identified as having begun an uptrend due to its breakout above a down trendline, there can be points where it's hard to figure how to draw or redraw a trendline as they need to be adjusted. Some technicians will apply a rule that a trendline must be penetrated by a certain percentage or dollar amount to confirm the penetration. Then there is the question of whether to draw a trendline through an apparent extreme (cutting through a bar), and so on.

There is also the risk that placing a stop under a trendline will result in exiting a position because prices dipped under the line, then resumed an upward course. For this reason, exiting only on a close above or below the trendline, depending on whether you are long or short, could be a method

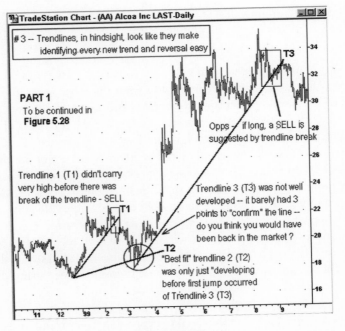

Figure 5.27

Figure 5.28

Figure 5.29

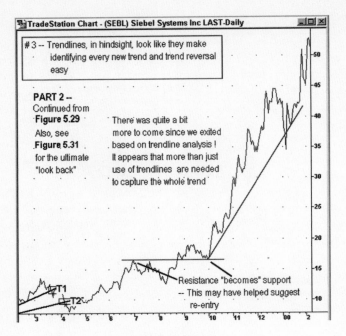

Figure 5.30

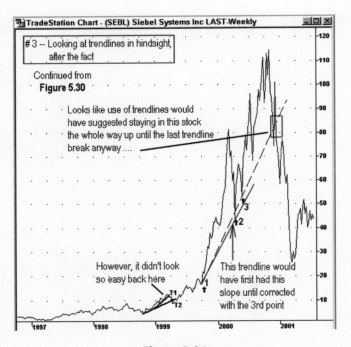

Figure 5.31

employed to try to confirm that a trend reversal has in fact occurred. However, this strategy is also a difficult trade-off in terms of a stop order entry strategy as "stop-close only" orders are accepted mostly in some of the futures markets. If you were unable to exit at the close, you have to have the discipline to do so the next morning and not backpedal in your risk control strategy. Also, exiting on a closing basis means you can't then adequately protect against the occasional severe price breaks, where the close, or next day's open, is far below the trendline in question.

One key to how to use trendlines relative to risk control is to know the nature of the market you are in. If you are in what Dow called the third phase of speculative excess, don't wait for the close and have stop orders in place. Of course, there is always the risk of a big earnings disappointment announced after the close in a stock or overnight news in futures or FX markets, but the markets are risk ventures. The key is to keep risk in balance with reward potential—and expect the unexpected, which is why you shouldn't trade with all of your capital.

4. Trendline breaks often lead to spotting some outstanding trading and investing opportunities later on if you continue to keep track of the previously broken trendline. See Figures 5.32 and 5.33 (also refer back to Figure 5.19).

This is the same concept as a support level, once broken, assuming the role of resistance later on and vice versa. An uptrendline that indicates support on the way up, if penetrated, often defines (becomes) resistance on a return to this line later. Market analyst Michael Jenkins used to call such broken lines "kiss of death" trendlines and it was often a very apt term. Once prices return to an up trendline like this, the line can act as a deflector to prices and they'll then start falling more often than not. This is one of the more useful patterns in chart analysis. A return to a trendline situation doesn't set up all the time, but when it does, it's a high-potential trade to take, by selling in the area where prices make the return. If short, (buy) stops can then be placed above the trendline because, if prices regain the line, it's a *pattern failure*. Moreover, risk can usually be tightly limited at that point as the stop-out point is just above the line. Downside potential, relative to risk, can be excellent.

The reverse situation is provided with a down resistance trendline during a declining trend, when the trendline is pierced by a rally—this trendline may come back into the picture later if prices drop back or return to this previously broken line. This return point can offer a second, more favorable, entry

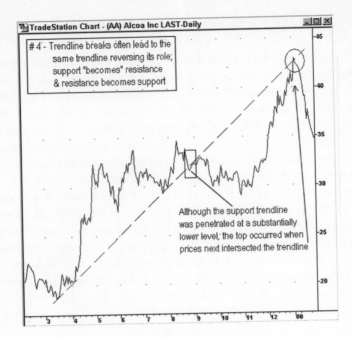

Figure 5.32

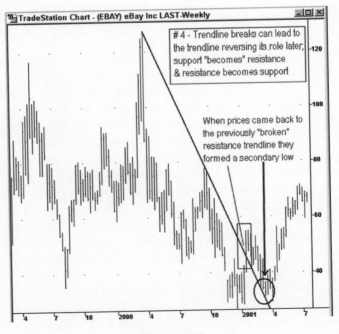

Figure 5.33

point. Expectations are that prices will rebound from this line, marking a final low before a secondary uptrend develops. Figures 5.32 and 5.33 are both examples of this principle and also demonstrate that the return to the prior trendline can be a more favorable entry than would be the case for anyone who bought or sold at the point where the trendline was first penetrated. Of course, since you don't know if this trendline return will happen, the strategy, by necessity, is to buy or sell when the trendline is *first* penetrated, with an appropriate stop. A return of prices to a previously broken down trendline but at a lower price point is seen fairly often, and when this pattern develops it offers a good *setup* or basis on which to take a trade, by those who favor trading. For investors, these return rebounds can offer a more favorable entry for a longer-term buy and hold. This strategy also offers a second entry point or place to add to a position. This is one of the few instances where I consider price averaging (down) with multiple positions.

5. Trendlines often have to be redrawn, especially in the beginning stages of a new trend as demonstrated in Figures 5.34 and 5.35.

Figure 5.34

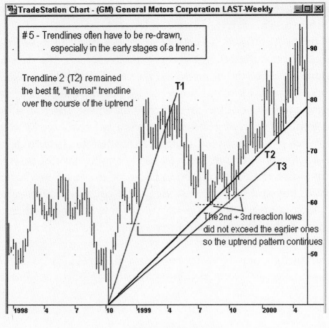

Figure 5.35

An upside or downside penetration of a trendline, especially in the early part of a trend, does not necessarily negate the emerging trend or confirm a trend reversal. As has been discussed previously, an upswing high that exceeds a prior high or a downswing low that exceeds a prior low can merely be an indication that the prior trend is continuing. Prices may also be undergoing a sideways consolidation or only a minor correction in the *initial* formation of a trend, so final definition for a trendline can take some time to form.

Within an emerging uptrend, one key to what is going on with a correction is whether a downswing stops above its prior low. If it has not, simply redraw the trendline from the lowest low through the bottom of this newest low. The reverse is true in an emerging downtrend—redraw the down trendline through a new higher high, as long as the top of this price swing does not exceed a prior significant high. It is more rare to have to as frequently redraw a down trendline, as declines that mark a new down trend often tend to fall more in a steep fashion. This goes back to the nature of bear markets and the fact that a lot of selling tends to come in all at once—a one-time decision is often the case for long liquidation, whereas buying is phased in typically by both individuals and institutions, especially in the stock market.

6. Different price *scales* can result in quite different trendlines and trendline patterns, as is apparent in Figures 5.36 and 5.37.

Use of the arithmetic scale versus the semi-log (*log*) price scales on longer-term weekly and monthly charts, especially where there has been a large price increase or decrease, can result in an indication that a long-term trendline has been penetrated that is not apparent using the other scale. There is no hard and fast rule on the question of which interpretation should be considered in your investing strategy. Generally, I lean to the semi-log scale as the most informative as to whether long-term trend momentum has shifted. However, I look at both scales and wait for other technical indications to confirm a trend change when price action relative to trendlines does not agree. And, of course, there is the ultimate validation for a trend change, which is when prices exceed a prior major low or high. If the two scaling types give different results on this point, I use the log scale.

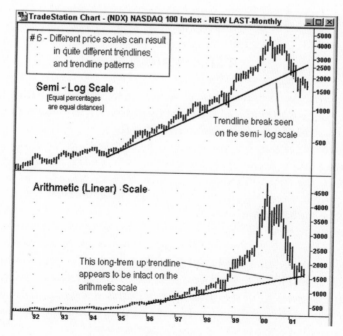

Figure 5.36

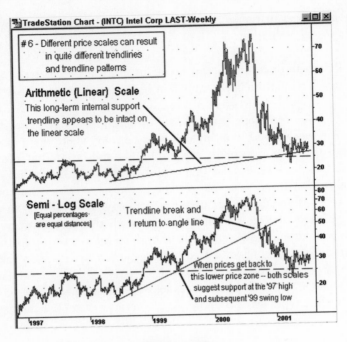

Figure 5.37

PRICE CHANNELS

A price *channel* is constructed by drawing a line parallel to either an up or down trendline that slopes in the same direction. A trendline is the first requirement, which can be constructed after two to three lows or highs form. The second parallel line can be drawn then with only one high or low point. In an uptrend there are minor price swings that go against the direction of the trend. These downswings are used to define an up trendline. The top of the first upswing can be used to define the upper boundary of a price channel within which a trend may be proceeding. Figure 5.38 shows how an uptrend channel is constructed. An upper channel line in an uptrend tends to offer minor resistance as prices move higher. Once reached, the upper line is where prices are often deflected and encounter resistance as in Figure 5.38. There tend to be three results if selling pressure at the upper end of the channel acts in this deflecting manner: Prices continue higher but stay just under or around the upper channel line, there is a pullback to about the middle of the channel, or prices drop back to the low end of the channel—back to the support trendline.

Figure 5.38

If a subsequent high forms that is above the first top that has been used to construct the upper channel line, the parallel line is typically redrawn with a parallel so that it goes through this higher high as is seen in Figure 5.39—the *widest* point is used, as we want to see the widest possible parameters for our channel in keeping with its intended use to define the potential extremes within the price boundaries traversed by a trend. An example of a downtrend channel is provided in Figure 5.40.

There is always a point or an area where prices get ahead of themselves in an uptrend or downtrend—by "being ahead of themselves," what is meant is that prices have overshot reasonable valuation levels for this time and place—markets and their prices go from undervalued to overvalued and back again. So prices will get ahead of themselves even within the dominant trend and they will adjust accordingly.

The usefulness of a channel line is that the upper boundary line of an uptrend channel and the lower boundary of a downtrend channel are potential areas for both profit taking and trading against the trend—for short-term traders. In addition, investors looking for an improved price

Figure 5.39

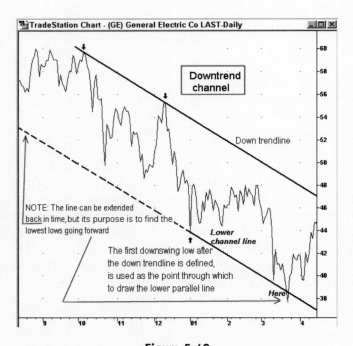

Figure 5.40

entry may want to look for a price channel if one can be defined. After the upper line is reached in an uptrend channel, there is an increased likelihood that prices will dip from there, at least to the midpoint of the channel. This would then suggest that a later and better (cheaper) price entry is a possibility.

The channel pattern does not always appear nor, once constructed, do the boundaries always deflect and contain the price swings that unfold during a trend. However, when you do see this pattern holding up over time, it often works quite well in defining the stopping places for repeated price swings. And if prices break out above or below a price channel that has been formed for some time already, it is a reason to look more closely at what is happening. An upside breakout above a well-defined uptrend channel is an indication that the trend momentum and strength are accelerating in the direction of the trend. If there is instead a decline to under the lower channel boundary, it is no different from any similar trendline break and is a possible reversal sell *signal*.

TRADING RANGES

When prices stop advancing or declining and start moving sideways, this pattern is called a "consolidation," as if prices had to mark time for a while and *digest* the new level that has been reached. A movement back and forth two or more times between two prices areas, one support, the other resistance, often develops into a *trading range*. Sometimes, a trading range can go on for weeks or months. A name applied by Charles Dow to such a sideways trend was a *line* or line formation. Such a pattern is also called a *rectangle* in current practice technical analysis terminology.

Continuation of a trading range for a lengthy period of time has implications for both traders and investors. Traders take note when the support and resistance areas for a market or individual security become well-defined and predictable—when prices get down to the low end of the trading range, a buying opportunity presents itself. Conversely, the high end of the *range* becomes the place to sell. It's sometimes said that a stock or commodity gets "bound" in a trading range or range bound. Stock investors will take note because their stock seems unable to *break out* of that trading range.

When prices do break out in one direction or another, above or below the trading range, it's common to see a sizable move develop in that direction. In a stock the trading range indicates that supply and demand, buyers and sellers, are in relative equilibrium. However, eventually something tips the balance. If it's on the downside, the buyers who have been accumulating near the lows, rush to exit. If it's on the upside, the sellers who have been selling, rush to cover shorts by buying and perhaps buy to go long as well—they are already interested in the stock. Two stocks in trading ranges, with both upside and downside resolutions, are presented in Figures 5.41 and 5.42.

A rule of thumb is that the longer prices go sideways on the horizontal time scale, the further will be the potential price move (up or down) when there is a breakout above or below such a long-standing price range. If the breakout is against you and you are long, you should probably exit, preferably by having a stop order that was already in place under the lower boundary of the trading range—otherwise, by the time you can act the potential loss can be larger than you wished to take. Conversely, if you are long and the breakout is in your favor above the high end of the trading range, this could be a time to add to your position.

Figure 5.41

Figure 5.42

RETRACEMENTS

We owe some debt to Charles Dow for his observations that an intermediate trend often will *retrace* (give back) anywhere from around one-third to two-thirds of the distance covered by the primary trend, before the major trend resumes. There were further refinements on retracements made by W.D. Gann, a well-known stock and commodities speculator in the first half of the 1900s.

But the origins of one of the most useful *retracement* theories for stocks and other markets came from someone who lived in the Middle Ages and was studying the population growth of rabbits. Leonardo Fibonacci was an Italian mathematician who was doing this aforementioned work in the early 1200s. The number sequence that is named after Fibonacci is where each successive number is the sum of the two previous numbers, that is: 1, 2, 3, 5, 8, 13, 21, 34, 55, 144, and so on. Any given number is 1.618 times the preceding number (approximately) and .618 times the following number. There are some technical *indicators* whose formulas rely on the *Fibonacci number* sequence, but a big application is to use the *Fibonacci retracements* of

.382 or 38 percent, .50 or 50 percent and .618 or 62 percent. The number 5 is in the Fibonacci sequence, and the others are *ratios*—.618 comes from the percent that each number is of the next higher number and .382 is the inverse of .618 (100 − 61.8 = 38.2). We'll stick to the shorthand and round off to 38 and 62 percent. Also, as I used to say in my CNBC.com columns, a "little bit" more or less than 50 percent—the little bit, being approximately an eighth of a point either way—someday I'll have to explain that they used to trade stocks in eighths of a point (dollar) increments but decimal trading is still fairly recent.

What you most need to know is that tracking what would constitute the 38, 50, and 62 percent retracement points, after a minor or intermediate price swing, is a common practice and a quite popular point of reference, especially among professional traders. There is a simple pragmatic reason for this popularity—buying or selling in these retracement areas often results in coming close to buying at the low and selling at the top. Maybe the saying "Buy low, sell high" owes something to the common retracements.

You can set most charting applications to calculate popular retracements ranging from .33 to .38, .50, .62 and .66 by pointing first at the low, then the high (pullback retracements) or first at the high, then the low (for retracement rallies in a downtrend). Or you can use a calculator and calculate the three percentage figures once it appears clearly that a high and a low are in place for the minor or secondary trend in question, and from which you can now calculate retracement possibilities. In an uptrend, once a minor downside correction begins, *subtract* the point figures that would represent a 38, 50, and 62 percent retracement (of the recent high minus the low) from the recent high. All you need is some degree of assurance or assumption that a price swing has run its course and that a countertrend move is developing. In a downtrend, the 38, 50, and 62 percentage figures are *added* to the most recent low. In a downtrend, once it's apparent that a minor countertrend rally is underway (prices and volume surge), the expectation is that in a normal market prices will rebound an amount that is equal to about half of the last decline—or "a little bit more" (62 percent) or "a bit less" (38 percent). Then, for example, if prices climbed to the 62 percent retracement level, in a downtrend, this would suggest a favorable exit if long, and trade entry to sell short.

Here are some guidelines relating to the use of *Fibonacci* retracements.

▌ A strong trend will usually see only a minimum price retracement— around one-third to 38 percent. If prices start to hold around this area, trade entry may be warranted.

▌ A *normal* trend, not powered by something extraordinary, will often see a retracement develop of about half or 50 percent of the prior move. A common area to buy or sell is at the 50 percent retracement level, with an exit if prices continue much beyond 62 percent, for example, 5 percent more.

▌ Within the range of normal, but not evidence of a particularly strong trend, will be a retracement of 62 percent or perhaps two-thirds (66 percent). If prices hold this area, it's also a good target for initiating a buy or sell with an exit if the retracement exceeds 66 percent.

▌ If a retracement exceeds one level, look for it to go to the next, for example, if a retracement goes beyond 38 percent, look for it to go on and approach 50 percent. If it exceeds 50 percent, look for 62 percent. If a retracement exceeds 62 percent, or a maximum of 66 percent, then I look for what I call a "round trip" or a return all the way back to the area of the prior low or high—this type of action suggests a *retest* of the low or high and is the ultimate retracement, of 100 percent.

▌ Retracements are most commonly done from the low to high, high to low and not based on the highest *close* to the lowest close, and so on. However, you can experiment with retracements based on closing levels as they also are worth exploring.

▌ The common retracement levels work on all time frames, for example, hourly (or less), daily, weekly, and monthly charts.

Examples of these points about the use of Fibonacci retracements abound, but a few are shown in Figures 5.43 through 5.46.

SUMMARY

We have explored the characteristics and behavior of trends and how to define their beginning, middle, and end with trendlines, price channels, retracements, and volume. These are some of the more important technical analysis tools. You will see instances where prices move against the primary trend without piercing the major trendline and where the price swing is merely a normal correction to the dominant trend. On the other hand, secondary trends can require frequent redrawing of trendlines and retracement levels—this is of major help in keeping track of accelerating moves,

Figure 5.43

Figure 5.44

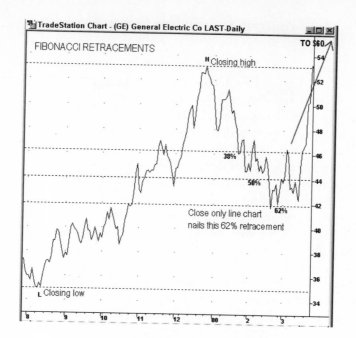

Figure 5.45

Figure 5.46

pauses, sideways consolidations, corrections to the main trend in a counterdirection and finally, reversals of the dominant trend. The more you practice drawing trendlines, the more you will derive from them, as there is also an art and *feel* to drawing trendlines.

Trendline construction should give more meaning to the old adage that "the trend is your friend" as trend and channel lines are ways to keep yourself on the profitable side of the trend. If you are positioned so as to profit from the direction of the dominant trend, you will have the force of others with you especially in an uptrend. In a downtrend, when a countertrend rally is ongoing, it's much easier to also go with the dominant trend and simply wait for a break of a secondary up trendline, especially after a 50 or 62 percent retracement and enter the market on the short side.

In an uptrend, when a decline has run its course, as suggested by a move back above a secondary down trendline, and by prior support, related volume activity, and a retracement percentage, buying is the "easier" side of the market to be on. During corrections, patience is required in waiting for the market to tell you that the trend is resuming as you're looking to get in the market. If you don't follow the technical clues and wait for the right time, you may wind up going against the current trend by trying to pick a top or bottom. If you want to go *against* the trend, I suggest lying down until the feeling passes.

Trendlines and channel lines are basic tools to define the "shape" and direction of price trends. Prices trace out other shapes and patterns that are not necessarily related to straight-edged trendlines, but that also have recognizable outlines. The study of these various chart patterns, which is another significant component of technical analysis, is the subject of our next chapter.

6

RECOGNITION AND ANALYSIS
OF CHART PATTERNS

INTRODUCTION

Technical analysis as a body of study and knowledge about the financial markets has made one of its most significant contributions in the area of identifying certain predictive patterns of price behavior that can be recognized visually on charts. Such patterns form because the market has reoccurring cycles of buying and selling activity. Because these patterns are the result of collective human behavior as it is manifested in the area of financial marketplaces, and such behavior patterns are not infinite, there are a select number of possibilities only. For example, at the bottom of a market cycle, the bulk of sellers have done their selling, and buyers are scarce. Prices have come to rest at an area where there appears to be some long-term value. This area might equal the low of two years prior. As business activity is cyclical, the prospects for the market will brighten at some point. Early buyers are more aware of this possibility and their buying alone will pull prices up as the sellers are not as active any longer. The more prices advance, the more this draws in other buyers who sense that something positive may be happening.

At this point we have the chart pattern called a *double bottom*, which is a low made in the same price area as at a prior bottom and is usually accompanied by an increase in average daily volume. This pattern alone has been found to have good predictive value because it is generally caused by a positive change in the outlook for the future prospects for the financial asset in question and enough knowledgeable people take action accordingly that prices start to rebound. Generally, a major prior low, the first part of the double bottom, marked the last time the prospects for the company or asset improved. The resulting upswings see follow-through often enough that we have the second dynamic of the double bottom—a trend, once underway, tends to continue. This is *pattern recognition* of the most basic kind and reflects natural, reoccurring, and fundamental forces of cyclical change. Because of this, patterns work in the sense of having predictive aspects. Did we need to know what caused the sea change in the outlook for the asset or company? Not necessarily. It is enough that knowledgeable people do know and that there is a proven past tendency for the pattern called a double bottom to suggest a change in trend.

We will examine the common technical patterns that have shown themselves to have forecasting value for either a *reversal* of the current trend or that have been shown to mark a *continuation* of the current trend—for example, after the double bottom, prices may advance for a time, then drift sideways for an equal period, perhaps retracing half of the first price rise, before rising beyond the peak of the first rally. The obvious value of the reversal pattern is that it allows me to profit from a *new* trend. A major value of the continuation pattern is that it suggests that I should *stay* invested. There are a variety of technical patterns and they are not always easy to recognize, especially early in their formation. This part of technical analysis, recognition of patterns, is the most potentially subjective as it is the most prone to different interpretations. Given time and some study of them however, the art of recognizing the different chart formations can greatly assist you in knowing what phase of a market trend is unfolding and where it's going next. This recognition, in turn, makes the ability to recognize chart patterns a prized tool for profitable investing and trading.

CONTINUATION VERSUS REVERSAL PATTERNS

Some patterns traced out by prices during a trend suggest that the trend direction that has been ongoing may be coming to an end. Seeing these patterns, for the most part, does not always depend on a trendline break. Any price or volume formation of this type is generally described as a *reversal* pattern. I have already described the *bull* and *bear trap* reversals which is a new low or high in a price swing, immediately followed by a strong countertrend move. However, these patterns can be seen only *after* they have formed. While bull and bear trap reversals do suggest a possibly strong initial move in the opposite direction from the prior trend, they otherwise have no predictive value as they are not patterns that set up before a trend reversal has already taken place.

Reversal Pattern Types

The price reversal patterns that tend to be seen *before*, or in the forefront of, a trend reversal include:

I *double* and *triple tops* or *bottoms*

I *W* bottoms or *M* tops

I *V* tops or bottoms

I *rounding tops* and *rounding bottoms*

I the *head and shoulders* pattern

I some rectangles

I *wedges*

I some triangles

I *broadening tops* or *bottoms*, which are traced out over an extended period

I *breakaway* and *exhaustion gaps*

The previously mentioned patterns are formed over a few or many sessions, but some reversal patterns are established after only one to two periods (e.g., hourly, daily, weekly) such as in a *key* upside or key downside *reversal*. Sometimes a price *spike*, where the high or low is noticeably above or below the close, warns of a trend reversal. As seen already in the discussion of candlestick charts, certain single candlesticks are anticipated to mark a trend reversal (e.g., the *hanging man* or *hammer*).

There are also situations where a volume pattern warns of a trend reversal as was described in the instance where prices surge and volume slackens or where the on balance volume (OBV) indicator line starts moving counter to the direction of prices. However, this type of pattern is better categorized as an instance of a price/indicator *divergence*, discussed already and which will be further covered in the next chapter.

Sometimes what is thought to be a continuation pattern will turn out to have an opposite aftermath, as a market reversal will occur instead—such an outcome for a continuation (or for a reversal formation also) is considered to be a pattern *failure*.

The categories of reversal or continuation patterns are useful general guidelines as to the most common types of pattern *resolution*, relative to the current trend. A resolution of a pattern is the next price move after a pattern has formed. We need also keep in mind the failure possibility. As with any risk control strategy, we should guard against the unexpected or the unusual. While chart patterns are very helpful as guidelines for trading strategies, the best rule always is to not get complacent and to recognize that any given pattern may fail to have any special significance on a particular occasion or will lead to an opposite outcome than expected. The patterns that we use in technical analysis mark some change in what is going on with an index, a stock, or other financial instrument—sometimes, the subsequent change is not a move in the direction anticipated.

REVERSAL PATTERNS

I put all top and bottom patterns such as *double tops* and *head and shoulders* into the category of *reversal* formations, even though they may form only after a lengthy period of sideways consolidation. The top and bottom formations themselves may take some time to complete and the actual trend reversal will not be seen until after this completion. This may be contrasted to a *V* top or bottom which is a sudden turnaround and quick reversal. Nevertheless, all such formations are part of patterns that tend to signal an upcoming conclusion to the trend that preceded them, the beginning of an actual reversal and a subsequent new trend.

Double and Triple Tops and Bottoms

There is a story used in the description of the process of doing Zen meditation where the practitioner says that after first learning to meditate, trees were no longer trees and mountains were no longer mountains but after many years of practice, trees and mountains were again simply trees and mountains. There is an analogy in this to my own practice of technical analysis. When I first learned about double tops and bottoms as possibly indicating an end of a trend, I saw many instances of the expected outcome for this reversal pattern and I was seeing markets in a different way. After more time spent observing market trends, I saw exceptions develop where for example, a second top was exceeded and I began to anticipate the exceptions to the rule and to pay less attention to the expected outcome for these patterns. I had become too *sophisticated* to believe necessarily in the probability that a second top was an indication for a future downside reversal. After still more time, I began to see the potency of double tops and bottoms and realize that while these patterns sometimes failed to bring the expected result, they were very good signals after all. For me, double tops and bottoms *became* double tops and bottoms again.

Double and triple tops are, as the term implies, situations where a high or low fails to exceed the price area of a prior significant top or bottom, on two or three occasions. It should also be noted that the second or third top or bottom does not have to occur at the exact level as the previous high or low as long as this subsequent high or low is in the same general price area as the earlier peak(s) or bottom(s) (e.g., within 5%). A significant prior high or low would be one that was the extreme point of an advance or decline to date. A stock or futures market that makes tops or bottoms in the same approximate area on more than three occasions is considered to be in lateral *consolidation* or *trading range*—a subsequent breakout above or below this range can also establish an upside or downside reversal of the trend but this is a different pattern.

We need only think about the concepts of support and resistance to understand what is happening in a double top or bottom, which is more common than the triple top or bottom. *Support* is a price area where buying interest is such that there are more willing buyers than sellers, and this buying will drive prices back up. *Resistance* is a price area where selling interest is strong, and sellers will overwhelm buyers and drive the price down.

Double bottoms form in a price area where in the initial bottom there was an abundance of willing buyers. If the potential buyers were strongly interested once in a particular area and there is no great change in the market outlook, they will be interested again in the same price zone and this buying will cause a rebound. Double tops form in a price area where the would-be sellers are in control because of their numbers and willingness to sell most or all of what they own of a stock or other financial instrument— this may also be an area where there is willingness to sell *short*.

It is when the outlook for a stock or other financial instrument changes, that a prior high will be exceeded, as enough buying interest develops to keep prices moving through the prior high. The reverse is true when prices sink through a prior bottom—there are too few buyers this time around. The significance for you, and a significant value in technical analysis, is that the price pattern alone will tip you off as to whether the most knowledgeable participants in the stock or other instrument find the value proposition to be different on the second or third time around for prices at the previous swing low or high. Generally the more time that separates the twin (or triple) tops or bottoms, the more significant is a subsequent trend reversal.

A confirmation is also required to determine whether a double or triple top or bottom is in place and the dominant trend has reversed. You'll recall that the definition of an uptrend is a series of higher highs and higher reaction lows. It is not the failure of prices to exceed a prior peak (this could always happen later), but a decline that exceeds a prior reaction low that initially confirms that a trend reversal has taken place. A double bottom is *confirmed* when a prior significant upswing top (in the decline just ended) is exceeded after the apparent double bottom. Another related confirming indicator, while secondary to exceeding a prior swing low or high, is having volume action in synch with price action. For example, on a break of any prior significant swing low or high, volume will normally expand significantly relative to before this break. We would also expect that the on balance volume or OBV line would move in the same direction as the breakout. Volume offers good secondary confirmation and should be looked at also. If there was no volume confirmation to price action and there is only a slight closing break of the prior low or high, it's usually a good idea to wait for a second consecutive close above or below the swing low or high in question.

It's useful to also remember the psychology involved in tops and bottoms that form in a repeat fashion over time. Market participants become convinced that a price floor or ceiling has been established. There is then more belief in the staying power of the trend after the double top or bottom has formed and more people get into the market, stock, or other instrument, which then helps keep the trend going.

The pattern of double or triple tops is a very useful one as a guide to getting into or out of the market for both traders and investors. I especially like entry at such points as I can then take a relatively small risk, as liquidating stops can be set just above or below the second or third top or bottom. Because of this, I will not necessarily wait for confirmation of the double top or bottom reversal pattern, which is achieved only when prices also go on to exceed a prior upswing high or low as described previously. This strategy assumes the risk of a pattern failure in exchange for a more favorable risk-to-reward ratio, which is especially relevant to traders. Investors looking to take a long-term position may wish to wait for the confirming price action. It is always important to pull together all aspects of trend analysis. If there is one to two years between the second low or top, this is more significant than a double top or bottom that formed over one to two months. Look also at what volume and the overall market are doing. It's quite relevent if the major market averages have bottomed or peaked. Remember Dow's adage that a rising tide lifts all boats. Conversely, swimming against the tide is only for the most powerful swimmers.

Further upside or downside potential can be guessed at when evaluating the possibility that a trend may be vulnerable to a reversal or is just consolidating. One way of setting at least an initial objective based on a double or triple top or bottom is to assume that the *minimum* objective is equal to the *height* of the trading range formed by the multiple tops and bottoms that form in the topping and bottoming process that occurs after a run in prices. For example, a stock trends higher until it hits $100. The stock drops back to $75, then goes back up to $100 and maybe back down to the $75 area again. The trading range at this point is $25. If the stock breaks out above $100, thereby confirming a double bottom (at $75), a minimum upside potential is probably to $125. Conversely, a break of $75, would suggest further downside potential to $50, where the stock would also complete a 50 percent retracement.

The risk-to-reward equation should be worked out, if those parameters are in your favor, at potential tops and bottoms. If long at a possible double top, your risk of giving back a substantial portion of any unrealized gain is generally higher than the reward potential of a further up leg. At such a juncture, it is not necessary to exit your position, as the old top may certainly be exceeded, but raising your exiting stop to just under the last prior significant downswing low is warranted. In the case of an investor with reason to anticipate the start of a primary trend reversal, waiting for confirmation of a double bottom is a good strategy. A more aggressive stance, especially if the prior downswing low is far under the possible double top, is an exit at the probable double top, especially if the prior top was a major one, while being prepared to assume a new long position if prices push through the most recent high by a significant amount (e.g., more than 5%) and on strong volume. Use of a buy stop above the prior high can put you into a new long position. An exiting sell stop can then be set not far under this new entry point, as the risk (exit) point ought to be just below the old high that was just exceeded. This prior top should now offer support on pullbacks—prior resistance, once exceeded, *becomes* support—if this is not the case, a bull trap reversal is a definite possibility (i.e., a push to a new high, followed by a downside reversal).

Figures 6.1 through 6.6 are examples of double and triple tops and bottoms, including a double top that was not *confirmed* (6.5) and a triple top (6.6) that was confirmed but was a *pattern failure* in terms of indicating a reversal in the time frame shown.

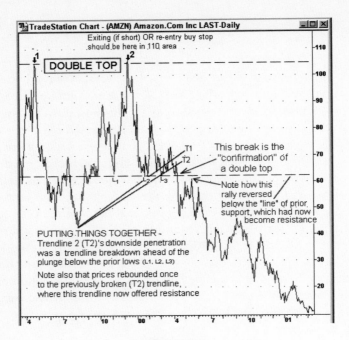

Figure 6.1

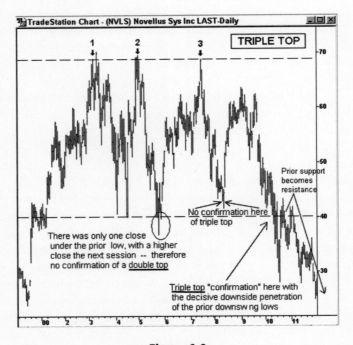

Figure 6.2

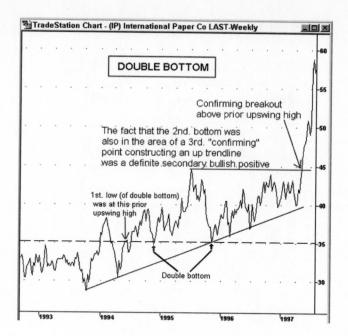

Figure 6.3

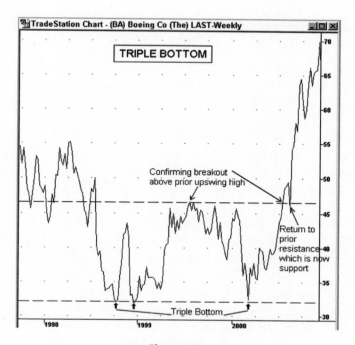

Figure 6.4

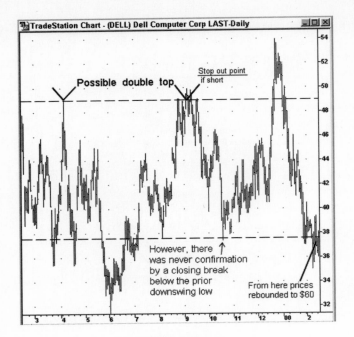

Figure 6.5

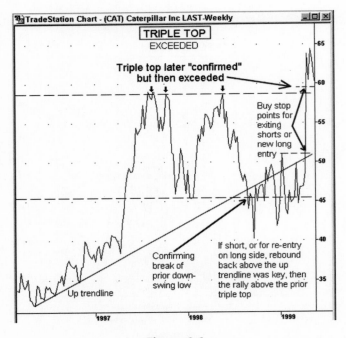

Figure 6.6

A slight variation and different name for double bottoms and tops is sometimes used when the double top traces out what looks like an obvious M, as in Figure 6.1—this pattern is called an M top. A double bottom is also sometimes called a W bottom. Not all double tops or bottoms have this obvious appearance, although when you look for it, as in the double bottom shown in Figure 6.3, you can usually see this type of outline. More obvious examples are shown in Figures 6.7 and 6.8. One reason that these names came about were that they clearly distinguished this type of bottom and top from the most common top and bottom pattern, that of the V top or bottom, which is discussed next.

V Top and Bottom Patterns

As implied by the shape of the letter V, an intraday or *intraweek* low formed at the end of a decline, when prices go into a final steep descent, followed by an equally sharp rebound, is a V bottom. The same letter

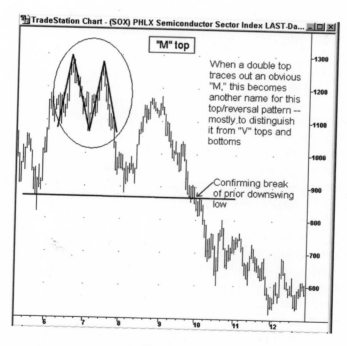

Figure 6.7

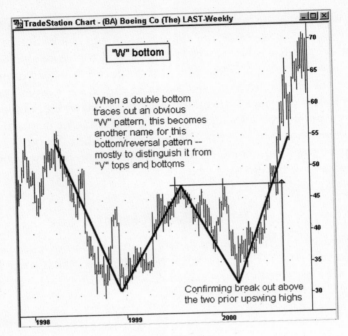

Figure 6.8

name is given to a top that is formed by a sharp advance, followed by an equally steep decline—a V top might be more accurately called an *inverted* V top, but it's generally not qualified in this manner.

As part of the discussion of V tops and bottoms, it will be useful and appropriate to more fully describe a *spike* and also what is sometimes called a *thrust* day. A spike is simply a sharp runup or decline whose *intra-bar* (e.g., hourly, daily, weekly) high or low substantially exceeds the respective high or low of the bar or bars (e.g., day or days) that immediately preceded the spike, as well as for some time after the spike has occurred. What we often see on daily charts at tops is a spike high well above the prior day or days, but a close that is well under that day's intraday peak. At bottoms we often see a spike low that is well under the prior day or days, but a close that is well up from the intraday bottom.

When a daily *close* is below the low of the prior day, it is sometimes also qualified as a *downthrust* day. When a *close* is above the high of the prior day, this occurrence is also sometimes called an *upthrust* day. Analogous to mechanical power, whenever thrust is used in technical analysis, it implies a strong force pushing the market in one direction or another.

An even stronger case for a trend reversal, after an uptrend has been underway for some time, is suggested by a day with a jump to a high well above the prior day or days (a spike), but a close that is under the low of the prior day—a downthrust day. Conversely, a stronger case for a trend reversal is made well into a downtrend, when there is a low well under what has gone before (a spike low), followed by an upthrust day whose close is above the prior day's high.

The concept of the thrust day, taking into account the close, relative to whether it is below or above the prior day's low or high, is something that is not necessarily significant as a single event. Thrust days are quite common—a series of them is what is significant. A strongly uptrending market typically will have a number of upthrust days and a market in a pronounced decline, a number of downthrust days. Figures 6.9 and 6.10 show charts with down and up spikes and thrust days, respectively.

The foregoing discussion on spikes, including spikes that have closes above or below the prior day's price range (up- or downthrust days) is relevant to V reversal tops or bottoms as they are often part of the "V" top or bottom pattern. Figure 6.11 is the same chart as 6.10 (Altera Corporation—ALTR) only not in the closeup view of a few individual days at the top and outlines the V top pattern of which the upthrust and spike highs of Figure 6.10 are part. It's very common to see even steeper V top patterns such as in evidence in Figure 6.12, in which there is a pronounced spike high at the very top and in the center of an inverted V top. Figure 6.13 is an example of a V bottom formation—V bottoms do not have as many instances of very steep angles making up the sides of the V as is the case with tops.

V bottom or top patterns are not easy to identify until after their formation. While they are developing, they are not much different in appearance from a pronounced further price spurt, followed by a correction. However, when there is also a definite spike high or low, accompanied by a confirming surge in volume, this provides further technical clues for a reversal pattern. Figure 6.14 is a chart that adds volume to the price picture alone of Figure 6.13. The jump in daily volume that mirrored the spike low (bottom of the V) offers an excellent confirmation of the likelihood of an upside reversal as suggested by a close in the middle of the

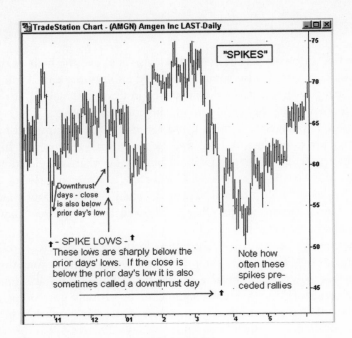

Figure 6.9

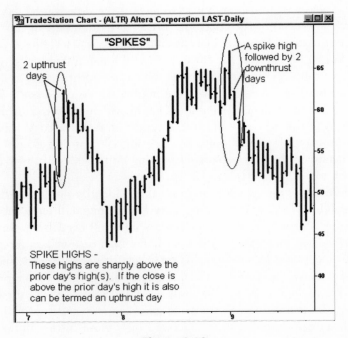

Figure 6.10

Figure 6.11

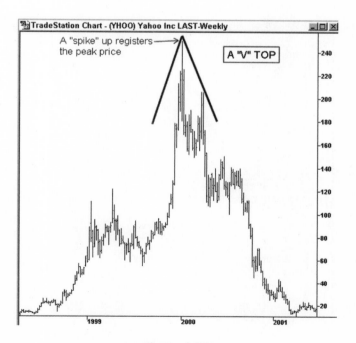

Figure 6.12

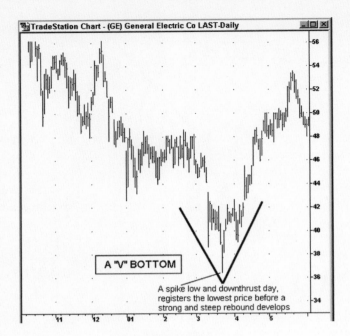

Figure 6.13

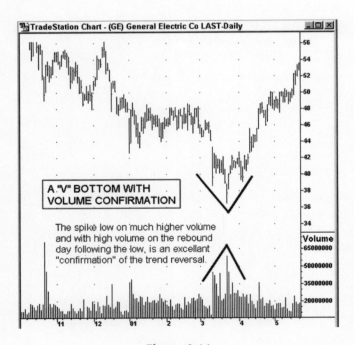

Figure 6.14

daily range, which was followed by a strong rebound in prices in the following day and days.

Key Reversals

What may be the strongest short-term reversal pattern, which is sometimes the start of a significant change or turnaround in the existing trend, is contained in the formation of what are called one- and two-day *key reversals*. Of necessity, we need first an explanation of some terms and agreements about what has to happen to fulfill the conditions that are part of short-term reversal patterns not always so well defined in technical analysis.

The following is the definition for what is called a *reversal* up day or *reversal* down day and also sometimes called a "key" *reversal up* or "key" *reversal down day*:

I Reversal up day—a day when there is a lower intraday low than the prior day, followed by a close above the prior day's *close*. Such days are fairly common, so I myself resist calling this set of conditions, a *key* reversal, as it is construed sometimes—actually there is no agreed upon textbook definition of what exactly makes a reversal a key reversal—by my fellow market technicians.

I Reversal down day—a day when there is a higher high than the prior day, followed by a close that is below the prior day's *close*. For myself, the same limitation applies to also adding the descriptive term key to this concept of a downside reversal.

What I believe is the more significant event, where the *reversal* conditions are more restrictive and which makes a reversal closer to a key reversal event, either up or down, is a different definition:

I *Upside key reversal* day (or week, if the weekly range is used)—a day when there is a lower intraday low than the prior day OR prior two days AND where the close is above the *high* of the prior day (a *one-day key reversal* up) or of the prior two days (a *2-day key reversal* down).

I *Downside key reversal* day (or week, if the weekly range is used)—a day when there is a higher intraday high than the prior day OR prior two days AND when the close is below the prior day's *low* (a *one-day key reversal* down) or of the prior two days (a *2-day key reversal* down).

The preceding descriptions would also apply to *intraday periods* when each bar was 15, 30, or 60 minutes.

My more restrictive definition for a *key reversal* involves a close that is above or below the prior one to two days' high or low for the simple reason that this is more definitive and more likely to signal a reversal pattern. The criteria relating to the prior high or low of the preceding bar is similar to the up/downthrust day definition—the thrust day definition implies nothing about first making a new high or low, but does mean that the close is above or below the prior day's high or low. A two-day key reversal is a stronger *signal* than a one-day key reversal. The same for a two-week versus a one-week key reversal. To eliminate a tendency to think only in terms of a daily or weekly time period or whatever specific time period is measured, I will also use the nonperiod-specific word "bar" rather than hour, day, or week (e.g., a *downside key reversal* is a move to a new high, followed by a close below the prior *bar's* (or *bars'*) low.

Short-Term Reversal Patterns

To rank reversal criteria, we need to bring in one other aspect relevant to potential reversals occurring over one to two "bars" (i.e., the time duration—day, week, etc.—being measured). Besides the concept of a spike high or low, it's useful to look at whether we are also seeing an *all-time* high or low—this would result in a type of ranking scheme useful for determining the likelihood that such reversals also mark final tops or bottoms of a secondary or primary trend, such as one taking the form of a V bottom or top. The characteristics making up the most pronounced reversal criteria occur infrequently. However, it takes only a few occurrences of these over time to create a relatively large payoff in terms of capturing far more of a market's gain—for example, by being quick to exit with profit intact when spotting a reversal unfolding. There are a large number of examples shown. What is important is not to memorize the exact characteristics of the different reversal criteria described. Rather, the repeated examples will begin to give you a feeling about what potential short-term reversal patterns look like. Trends tend to end in similar ways and the types of short-term reversal patterns demonstrated are useful alerts for that possibility.

Use of the term "bar" will represent the open, high, low, close (OHLC) for nonspecified time periods, as the same reversal criteria are valid for any time period that a *bar* could represent (e.g., five minutes, other intraday periods, hourly, daily, weekly, and monthly). It essentially doesn't matter whether an OHLC is for a bar that represents one hour or one week.

Within any given time period being measured, the technical analysis/charting patterns will tend to result in the same outcomes. You can substitute "hourly" or "weekly" (or "monthly") for any example where I use a *daily* bar—daily bars, followed by weekly bar charts, being the most common periods I use in my examples.

The following patterns represent a *continuum* or range of possibilities, from highest to lowest, in terms of the general potential they have to be associated with a trend reversal.

1. **High Probability of a Reversal.**

   ▮ A key downside reversal where prices go to a new high *substantially* above the prior bar's high (a *spike*) and this high is either an *all-time* new high or a new high for the secondary trend, followed by a close that is below the prior one or two bars' low. A similar jump in volume would be a good secondary confirmation.

   ▮ A key upside reversal where prices go to a new low substantially below the prior bar's low (a *spike*) and where this low is also an *all-time* new low or a new low for the secondary trend, but which is then followed by a close that was above the prior one or two bars' high. A jump in volume helps confirm the turning point. In stocks the chance of hitting an all-time low is slim, whereas it is more likely in a futures contract. Seek evidence of major reversal patterns by use of the longer-term weekly charts, especially to guard against a primary trend reversal after a major advance. Figures 6.15 and 6.16 indicate the pattern described (#1) here.

2. Same as the above conditions where the new high or low in question is both a spike and a new *all-time* high or low or a new high or low within a secondary trend, except that the close is below or above the *close* of the prior bar or prior two bars—not the previous low or high of the prior bar. Figures 6.17 and 6.18 illustrate this pattern (#2).

3. A spike to a new all-time high or a new high in the secondary trend, followed by a close that is nearer the low of the bar than to the high OR a spike to a new all-time low or new low in the secondary trend, followed by a close nearer the high of the bar than to the low. Figures 6.19 and 6.20 are examples of this pattern (#3).

4. A new high or low is made and this price is substantially above or below the bar that preceded it—a spike—but this new high or low is *not* an all-time new high or low (or new high or low within

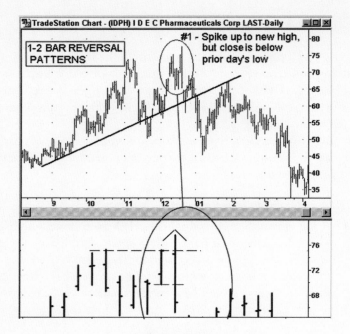

Figure 6.15

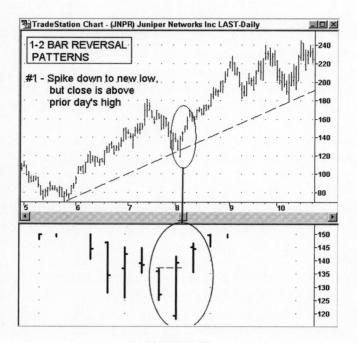

Figure 6.16

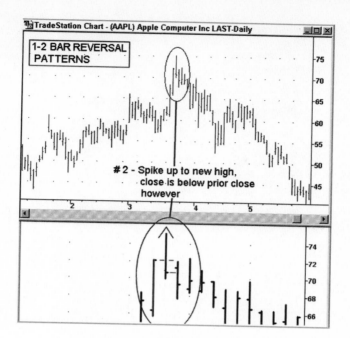

Figure 6.17

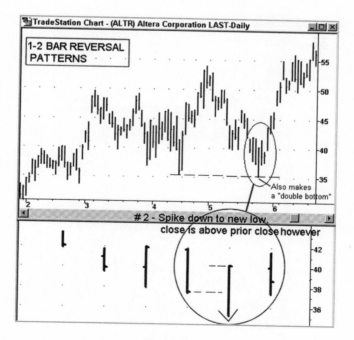

Figure 6.18

155

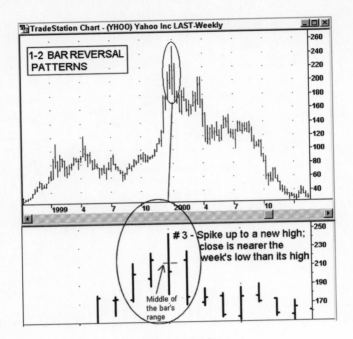

Figure 6.19

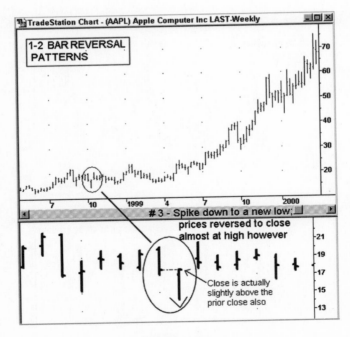

Figure 6.20

the secondary trend), but the close of the bar is below the prior close or prior two consecutive closes. More examples of market reversals are seen with this set of criteria, especially at bottoms. Tops are more likely to see both a spike up and a resulting new high that is an all-time peak—due to the emotional excesses of major price peaks made after a bull market is mature. Bottoms will see downward spikes, but a new low is less likely to be a new all-time low. Figures 6.21 and 6.22 are examples of this set of conditions (#4).

5. A *key* one- or two-bar *reversal*—this eliminates the *spike* high or low from our equation. Instead, we see prices go to *any* new high/low (for a day or week, etc., depending on what the bar represents). This action is then followed by a close below or above the prior one to two bars' high or low, depending on whether we are looking at a *key upside reversal* or *key downside reversal*. A "key" reversal, as I define it, would be a close above or below the prior (day's or week's) *high or low* rather than just its close. A key reversal

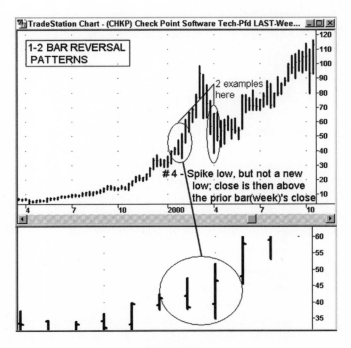

Figure 6.21

Figure 6.22

of this type is not rare but definitely occurs far less often than the simple up or down reversal patterns that use only the criteria of a close above or below the prior close. Figures 6.23 and 6.24 show charts with key one-day up and one-week down reversals (type #5). Figures 6.25 and 6.26 show charts with a number of two-bar reversals where the close exceeded either the high or low of the prior two days or weeks (#5). Some technical analysis software, such as the one used for this book, will allow you to define whatever set of conditions you can define and, once applied to a chart, will then show you all instances, if any, where those conditions were fulfilled (e.g., TradeStation's *ShowMe* feature does this).

6. Reversal patterns where a *spike* high is not a new high for a move, but the close of that day or week is below the prior bar's close OR there is a spike low substantially below the prior bar which is not a new low, but the close is then above the prior close, which suggests a possible reversal. This pattern can be an indication of a new minor price swing up or down. Figures 6.27 and 6.28 show

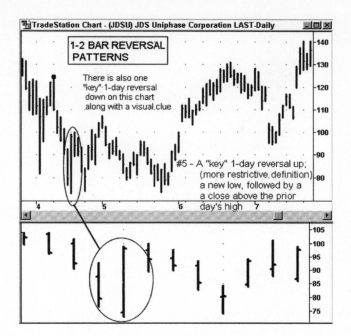

Figure 6.23

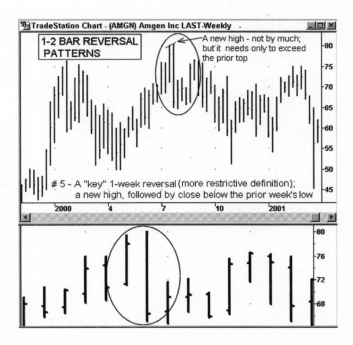

Figure 6.24

Figure 6.25

Figure 6.26

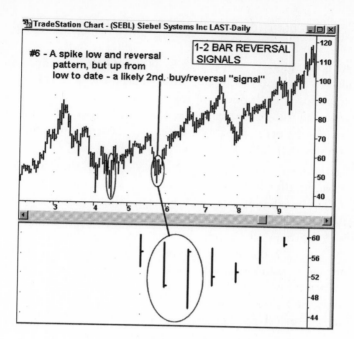

Figure 6.27

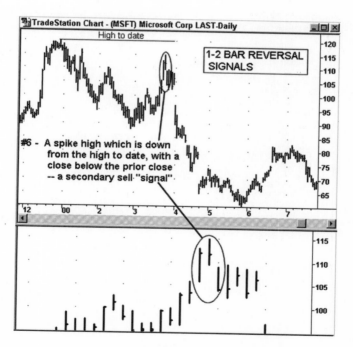

Figure 6.28

such secondary reversal signals as described here (#6). The chart shown in Figure 6.29 is a little different—there was a series of spike lows, each one marking a new low for the move, but only after the third occurrence was there an advance that began a new trend—the breakout above the most recent down trendline helped "confirm" this final reversal.

7. At the beginning, or well into a downtrend, there is a *spike* low substantially below the prior bar(s) but the close is nearer the high of that bar than it is to the low, suggesting a possible upside reversal OR at the beginning, or well into an uptrend, there is a *spike high* substantially above the prior bar, but whose close is nearer the low than the high of the period being charted (e.g., hour, day, or week), suggesting a possible downside reversal. These are not situations where the close exceeds the close of the prior day or week, and so on—however, they can be the start of a *trend reversal*, as such a pattern suggests a possible final buying or selling push (as seen in a price spike), but one suddenly lacking the neces-

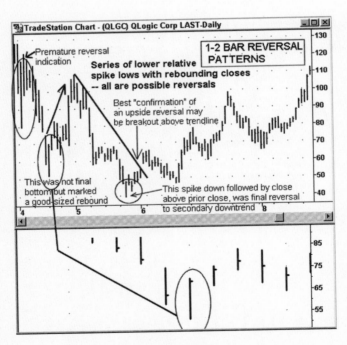

Figure 6.29

sary follow-through buying or selling to keep the trend going. Such times are points of bullish or bearish extremes, in terms of expectations and sentiment and often mark turning points in a market or financial instrument. Figures 6.30 and 6.31 have charts indicating one-day spike reversal patterns (#7). As always, having further confirmations of a trend reversal based on trendline breaks or volume considerations is a good idea. In the case of the chart shown in Figure 6.31, the third up spike reversal pattern was also in the area of a *double top*.

8. **Lower-probability short-term reversals.** A new high is followed by a close below the prior day's close or a new low is followed by a close above the prior day's close. This pattern is the simple *reversal up* or *reversal down* day or week but does not constitute key one- or two-bar reversals according to the criteria I have suggested. This pattern occurs fairly frequently as can be seen in Figures 6.32 and 6.33 (criteria #8) but is correlated with a significant top or bottom only infrequently as can be determined from the chart examples, which are typical.

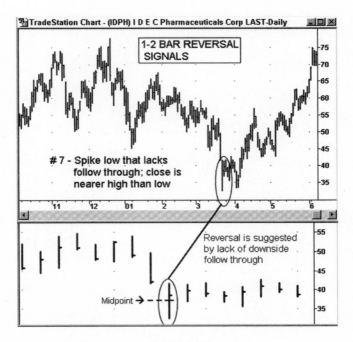

Figure 6.30

Figure 6.31

Figure 6.32

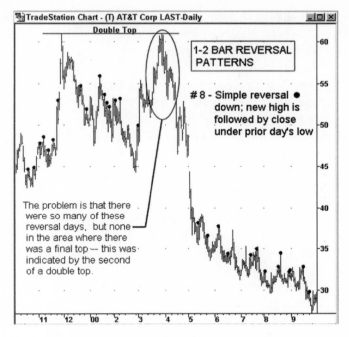

Figure 6.33

THE HEAD AND SHOULDERS PATTERN

The *head and shoulders (H&S) top* formation is similar to the triple top in that there are three peaks prior to a downside trend reversal—the difference is that the middle peak (the head) stands above the first and last top formations (the left and right "shoulders"), both of which form in approximately the same price area. The *head and shoulders bottom* formation or *inverse head and shoulders* is a mirror image of the head and shoulders top. It is also similar to the triple bottom in that there are three lows. However, the second or middle low (the head) is noticeably below the price level of the first and last lows—these lows form in approximately the same price area and are also described as the left and right "shoulders." The head and shoulders bottom pattern is reversed from the top formation—as if the outline of the head and shoulders was that of an upside down person. Drawing a line through the points formed opposite the rounding left and right "shoulders" is considered to be the "neckline" to the head and shoulders pattern as in the examples in the figures cited next.

Head and shoulders patterns, as is true of other top and bottom patterns such as double and triple tops or bottoms, are more likely to occur after a trend has been underway for some time. A head and shoulders top or bottom can be found visually by using either a bar (or candlestick) or line chart. Chart examples for the head and shoulders top are seen in Figures 6.34 and 6.35, with a further example in Figure 6.36 where prices, after piercing the *neckline*, rebounded back to it on two occasions before plunging to a price that fulfilled the *H&S* downside objective. Such a return to a neckline is not uncommon. Just as prior support, whether measured as a single price point, an area, or a trendline, once broken, can becomes resistance on a subsequent rebound, this, too, can occur in the case of the previously broken *neckline*.

In Figure 6.35 we see an instance where prices rallied back above the neckline and made a secondary top below the right shoulder—this does not invalidate the formation because a *complex head and shoulders* will sometimes have two left shoulders or peaks at about the same level and/or two right shoulders or peaks in the same area on the right side. The important thing to look for is symmetry—the left shoulders are formed from prices that peak in the same approximate area, as do the right shoulders. Relative to

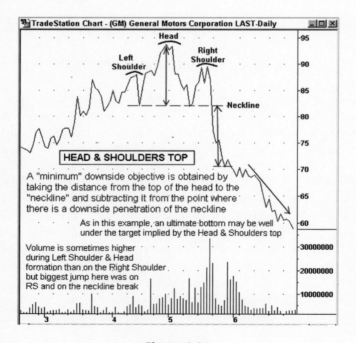

Figure 6.34

Figure 6.35

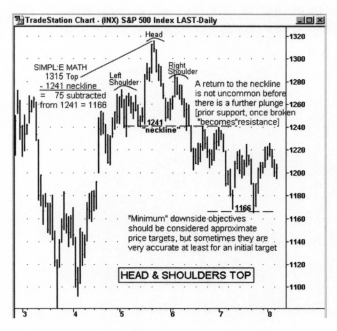

Figure 6.36

this, the head is a *single* top that is above the left and right outline of the shoulders—no formation with two heads is considered valid.

Examples of the head and shoulders bottom or "inverse" head and shoulders are found in Figures 6.37 and 6.38. As can be seen on all the chart examples there is a measuring technique that can be applied to the head and shoulders pattern. In the bottoming pattern, a trendline is drawn through the top of the rebound (initial point of a neckline) from the first cluster of lows (the left shoulder) that connects the top of the subsequent rally from the lowest cluster of lows (the head)—we then have at least two points to draw a line and that line has the relative position of the neckline of a human figure. The difference between the price that represents the top of the head (the lowest low) and the price on a vertical line where it intersects the neckline is our first needed value. Add this value to the point where prices achieve an upside penetration of the neckline after the formation of the third cluster of lows, representing the right shoulder. This then provides a minimum upside objective.

In the head and shoulders top formation the steps in calculating a downside are the same, only the final step involves subtraction rather than

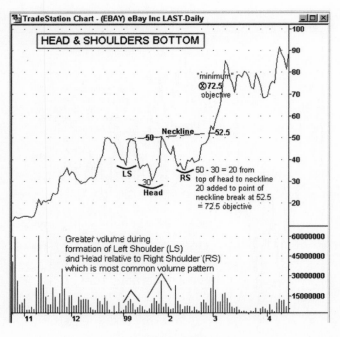

Figure 6.37

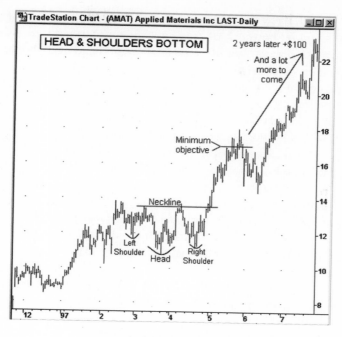

Figure 6.38

addition. In the H&S top, the highest high of the bar in the cluster of highs forming the head is used as the first value, and the price point on the neck-line intersected by a vertical line from that bar is the second—this value is then subtracted from the point on the neckline where there is a downside penetration on a decline after the right shoulder forms. The resulting value is a minimum price target only. This is similar to the rule of thumb for measuring a minimum objective for a double or triple top where the height of the trading range is added or subtracted to the breakout point.

The measuring convention for a head and shoulders objective should not be taken as an absolute. This measuring rule implies a minimum objec-tive only, and once a trend develops, the overriding principle is to stay with the trend as long as it continues. However, a significant value is provided by this measuring technique in that an initial price objective can be established. This helps determine where to set a protective stop so that the potential loss is a fraction of the *reward*, or minimum profit, potential (e.g., one-third).

The second point regarding price objectives is that the actual upside or downside potential of these top or bottom formations may be *less* than measured by use of the technique described. Thomas Bulkowski in his *Encyclopedia of Chart Patterns* found that the most likely rise after head and shoulder bottoms, once the neckline was penetrated, was a gain of between 20 percent and 30 percent. For the head and shoulders top, the most likely decline for the cases studied, was just over 20 percent. This information leads to a suggestion that when a head and shoulders pattern develops as expected and if the resulting gain as measured from the neckline exceeds 20 percent, it may be appropriate to protect any such gain with a liquidating stop that attempts to *lock in* three-fourths of the gain (a 15 percent profit), in the event of a reversal.

Another aspect to the head and shoulders pattern is that it has been found to have one of the more predictable outcomes of price patterns in technical analysis terms. For example, Bulkowski found that 93 percent of the head and shoulders top formations he studied broke out to the downside (penetrated the neckline) once they had formed. This suggests as a trading strategy, that when the formation of the right shoulder is apparent, going long in the case of the *H&S bottom* and short in an instance of the *H&S top* pattern—and to not necessarily wait for a penetration of the neckline. The liquidating exit (stop) point then is right where it is most opportune and where the liquidating price represents a small risk. The obvious and recommended place to set a stop is just beyond the top of the head, not far away from the entry point, assuming the buy or sell was initiated after the right shoulder formed. If the top of the head is exceeded once the right shoulder is formed, this constitutes a *pattern failure*. If the pattern *fails* it's not a good strategy to remain in an investment or trade that was entered into based on the expectations of a trend reversal implied by an initially valid head and shoulders formation.

Academic research also has been done in recent years undertaken to gauge the effectiveness of the predictability of price patterns like the head and shoulders. Dr. Andrew Lo and colleagues at the MIT Sloan School of Management did extensive statistical evaluation of a number of technical chart patterns and found five that yielded "statistically significant test statistics" (i.e., they had a level of predictive value that was greater than any random or chance occurrence). This study was reported in *The Journal of Finance* in August 2000. The five technical chart patterns that indicated to this research group as having predictive values based on what technical analysis said the outcome of those patterns should be included (1) the *head and shoulders* and (2) the *double top* patterns already discussed. (There will be explanations of (3) the rectangle top and (4) bottom, and (5) the broadening bottom formation, which are the other three.)

WHY REVERSAL PATTERNS WORK

A last discussion point concerns the question of why these price patterns or chart formations have predictable outcomes. It is always for the reason that the patterns describe a set of circumstances that relate to a cycle of attitudes and behavior on the part of market participants—such aspects of market behavior repeat again and again. In the case of a head and shoulders *top*, we can take a hypothetical example for XYZ stock. There is always a group of investors that comprise the most knowledgeable group that follows and invests in this company—we can call this group the *smart money* crowd. Let's assume our example stock has generally been in an uptrend but the value of the stock is getting a bit rich relative to earnings. However, fundamentals regarding the company still are positive overall and the smart money people decide to do some buying, perhaps after a period where the stock price has leveled off or declined a bit. This buying and perhaps some favorable news regarding XYZ Company, causes the stock to advance. Some other followers of the stock notice the increased activity and advancing prices and also become buyers. As the stock rises there is a point where the smart money people believe the stock to be overvalued and decide to take profits. This selling causes the stock to retreat some from the highs and makes the first peak comprising the left shoulder.

Other followers of XYZ stock are interested in buying price dips or in a period of weakness and the stock begins to rise again. The smart money group is a seller into any new high ground, as volume increases. The stock indeed gets higher than it did on the last rally but the aforementioned selling *caps* the price and a second higher peak forms. The continued selling eventually drives the stock down again. Believing that the price is again relatively cheap, less informed investors push the stock up a third time, forming the right shoulder. This time however, the stock has probably gone up on less volume with fewer willing buyers and some still determined sellers. A next downswing takes prices back to the prior support. If this level gives way, more holders of the stock decide to sell. There is a snowball effect as prices adjust downward by an amount equal to the prior rise—this happens to be equal to the distance from the low point after the first rally (the neckline) to the top of the biggest advance (the head). At this point it's very common that some facet of the company's business creating a drag on company profits—what caused the smart money to sell rallies—has become more widely known and the stock remains under pressure.

This same pattern and dynamic of the interplay of the most knowledgeable and less knowledgeable investors and traders, coupled with an asset that is getting rich relative to the *fundamentals* involved, plays out in other markets in a similar fashion such as in the commodities, futures, fixed income, and FX markets.

ROUNDING TOPS AND BOTTOMS

Rounding tops and rounding bottoms are patterns that I have found to offer one of the better buying or selling opportunities—they are not the most common patterns but gems when they occur, in terms of a tendency to precede substantial trends. Three examples of rounding formations are shown in Figures 6.39 through 6.41. A rule of thumb is to buy dips that carry prices down toward a circle that represents the line of a rounding bottom—if prices fall to below the line of this circular arc, especially on a closing basis and by a factor more than has already occurred, this is the exit point (i.e., the point where your sell stop should be in with your broker). This curved line or arc is like a trendline in this respect.

When *accumulation* (purchases made over some period) or *distribution* (the selling of one's holdings to others) occurs gradually in a market, creating

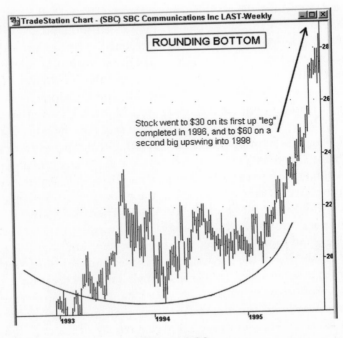

Figure 6.39

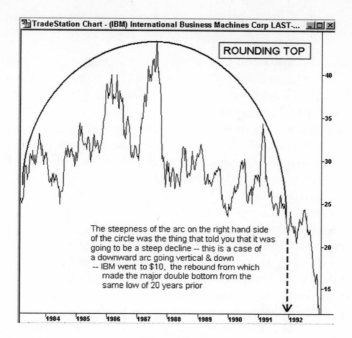

Figure 6.40

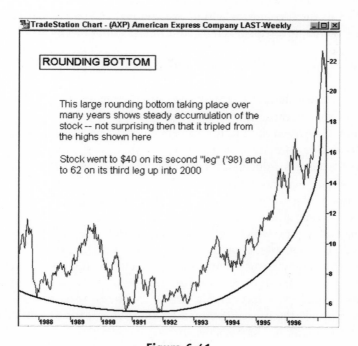

Figure 6.41

these types of rounding formations, it's usually because of the professional types of market participants—the ones whom Dow found to be the early buyers and sellers of stocks that they correctly perceive to be under- or overvalued, respectively. These smart money people will be very moderate in their buying or selling activity so as not to drive the price up or down overly much. Nevertheless, given this added volume—*volume precedes price*—the stock gradually moves either up from the bottom or down from the high. However, because this movement is so gradual and takes place over a lengthy period, the outline traced out on a chart is that of an arc or part of a circle.

A compass, the simple handheld drawing instrument that can construct a circle, when extended out, allows drawing an arc on a printed chart that has multiple touches of the lows of a bottom or highs of a top pattern. If the subsequent price action continues so that about a quarter of a full circle is completed, the stock or other item is then rather far along in terms of an accelerating trend, and there is increasing price momentum typically. Such momentum is created by the buying and selling activity of the widening circle of investors and traders who get involved in the stock because its price is moving. Usually at this stage, the increasingly positive or negative fundamentals become more widely known, written about, or discussed in such forums as within professional research departments, the business media, investments clubs, and Internet chat rooms.

BASE PATTERNS

Strong price trends and sizable moves often develop from rounding bottoms and tops because this pattern represents a broad and solid *base* that represents a firm *foundation* for a sizable move. This is similar to a rectangle (Dow's line formation) bottom or top that goes on a long time. The *width* of a base is important. The underlying idea is that the horizontal time axis and vertical price axis are interconnected. The wider the base (more time), the further the potential movement up or down the price scale. This concept is more refined in point and figure charts and in Gann charting techniques, which will be looked at later.

As an example of the factor of *time* or duration of a trend, an example can be provided by a stock that trades between $40 and $60 for two years. This duration can also be seen as forming a lengthy sideways support base that would suggest considerable upside potential, assuming there is a breakout above the aforementioned trading range—for example, a move up to $100 or more. Technicians sometimes talk about *big base patterns* and such sideways movements can extend to several years. The Dow Industrial average spent about 20 years trading just under 1,000, which represents 40 percent of the past 50 years—see Figure 6.42. You can see that the percentage increase since the ending of that enormous *base* in late 1982 was enormous. Of course, the other aspect of this situation was that the 20 years the Dow spent trading under 1,000 must have meant that many investors were consistently selling whenever stocks, in terms of the Dow Industrial average, approached the 1,000 area.

The big bases or tops that I am describing owe much to the activities of a professional circle of investors and traders who are, or represent, major buying and selling interests and are typically the ones first and consistently involved in the accumulation or distribution of the stock, stocks, or other market in question.

The initial accumulators of a single stock, for example, are the ones most likely willing to put the stock away and are not fickle traders in for the short haul—most are well aware that the big gains (Warren Buffett's accumulations for Berkshire Hathaway come to mind) are made when holding through the early formative stages and then the second main segment of a bull market. In the case of a *base* pattern, these individuals know

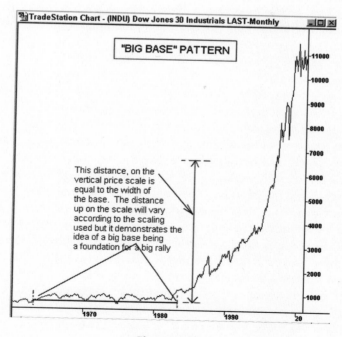

Figure 6.42

or foresee better business conditions for the overall economy, for the stock, or for a market *sector* like oil services or computer makers. Such a stock bought at lower levels by such accumulators, when the stock is said to be in *strong hands*, is not likely to be sold in times of further periods of price weakness—rather, it's more likely that there will be further steady accumulation. It takes some time for institutional investors to accumulate (or distribute) a large block of stock without moving the price substantially. The steady progression of prices that traces out a circular trend is best understood in terms of such steady purchases or sales—such professional activity is the best money to be following, so to speak. Visual evidence of this kind of accumulation or distribution is often the dynamic force driving the formation of the lower or upper arc of a circular or saucer shape traced out by the touches of the various lows of a rounding bottom or the highs of a rounding top. As the arc moves around to a steeper angle, up or down, this will tend to be the market phase where public investors are also participating in the buying or selling in a major way. Rounding bottoms and tops, especially the large ones, have a tendency to *support* very big advances or provide the push that gets major and steep declines going.

A broad base such as the mostly sideways movement of a lengthy trading range represents a long-term accumulation of a stock, stocks in general, or any other market. A long period of accumulation creates a big base pattern. A big base pattern can support a megamove such as may occur as infrequently as every few decades. When there is sufficient buying power unleashed, such as from inflation in the 1970s that drove gold prices to the stratosphere, leveraged buyout and junk bond money in the 1980s, or the boom in new technologies and the Internet in the 1990s, there is the possibility of seeing prices going up at geometric rates.

Conversely, the distributors or sellers of stock are often putting the stock out slowly and not all at once. Eventually, rallies will find more of this stock for sale. The smart money group on the bearish side is not going to be buying into the periodic rallies and will instead look to sell scaleup as any advances develop. It is the knowledgeable investors with the most buying power who are precisely the group missing to add the buying push necessary to take prices through the big resistance overhang of a major top, which amounts to a massive amount of shares for sale whenever the stock advances. This group of participants will be noticeably absent on the buy side and will concentrate on selling what they still own.

While there is not a particular name for it, the opposite of the big base pattern could be called the "big top" pattern when it occurs over a long period, as shown in Figure 6.43. A pattern of *distribution* that goes on over

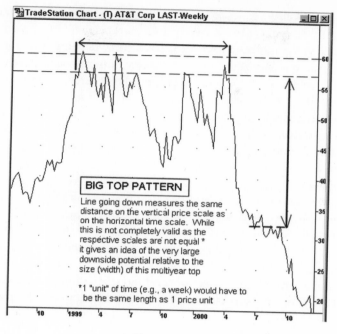

Figure 6.43

such a long time as in the preceding example, coupled with repeated attempts to break through the large amount of selling that must have been occurring, signifies that major holders of the stock were selling steadily—at least in an area that they no doubt considered to be overvalued. In Figure 6.43, the example of the large top in AT&T, the selling involved probably stemmed from a loss of confidence in the company or uncertainty as to the outcome of major U.S. deregulation and the metamorphosis undertaken in response to it by AT&T, the bluest of *blue chip* stocks. (Sorry, Grandpa, you weren't watching the charts!) The outlook for a stock or industry can be more and more subject to dramatic change in a shorter and shorter time span—such is the increased pace of technological and structural change. This fact makes technical analysis more important as it's vital to use all means available to identify major trend reversals as well as new emerging trends.

ARCS THAT GO VERTICAL

After a base that is sufficiently broad, the resulting megarise potential implied by a base big enough to support it can eventually lead to a huge advance—

that rise, if it takes the form of a circular arc, traces out a steeper and steeper arc or *parabolic arc* as can be seen in two markets where this pattern completed itself in Figures 6.44 and 6.45. It can also be seen in one individual stock that is in the aftermath of the vertical arc pattern—see Figure 6.46.

What these markets, whether gold, the Japanese real estate and stock markets of the 1980s, or the Internet bubble of the late 1990s, have in common is that what appears to be the inevitable result of this pattern—that it is unstable, with a rate of increase that cannot be sustained. What goes up must come down, as is said. When the parabolic rise of prices gets to that point—its arc going virtually straight up or vertical—we know one thing for certain, that the next major move or trend for the index, average, or individual issue will be straight down. It is only unknown as to what the final blow-off price peak will be, as such levels are quite unpredictable in the emotional final speculative stage. It is predictable that the final top will occur in a relatively short time duration, from the point where the price charts have a rise that is nearly vertical.

Moreover, speculative excess of this kind of extreme doesn't end with a moderate decline and soft landing. No, the foundation for the price levels

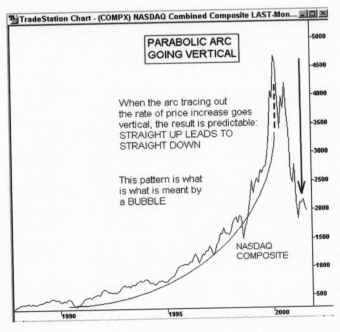

Figure 6.44

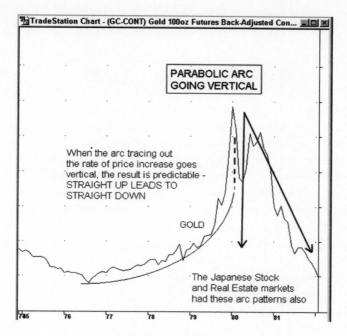

Figure 6.45

Figure 6.46

attained at this point is pencil thin—it's like the whole structure is based on a very long, slender pole rather than a solid foundation. When it comes down, it is going to come crashing down. This is still not qualitatively different from the panic selling phase that Dow talked about—of course, this is a BIG panic—and it is also similar, due to the collapse of the rationale that supported the huge valuations. At some point everyone realizes that only the willingness to pay higher and higher prices by more and more people is what can keep this market process going. Earnings could never grow at the exponential rate that was built into stock prices, especially tech stock prices, using the most recent and phenomenal examples leading to the 2000 market top. If one major source of money, that run by professional money managers, reduces their equity participation, the overall buying dries up significantly. The further evidence that a market is in for a severe decline, is that volume levels begin to fall steadily during the countertrend rallies that develop periodically.

In summary, this type of *reversal* pattern is the most extreme. It can be a once-in-a-lifetime event—if you understand the pattern, you will see it when it occurs again and you will know what the outcome is in advance. It's always the same, but never boring and not dangerous if you can withstand the crowd and the psychology that seems to keep most everyone participating as long as possible. Of course, this is not to say that you don't run the risk of stepping out of a market like this way too soon. I know professional advisors, early *bears*, who missed quite a bit of the last phase of the late 1990s *megabull* market when there were still huge gains being made—you will not want to get too bearish too soon, either. However, the tools you have learned so far are enough to provide all the confirming sell signals needed.

RECTANGLE TOPS AND BOTTOMS

A *rectangle* pattern is outlined by two horizontal lines that connect a series of highs and lows that occur in or around the same areas over time, creating a sideways *trading range* that most often interrupts an advancing or declining trend. The *rectangle* is usually a *continuation* pattern or sideways consolidation prior to the resumption of the dominant trend. In some instances, a rectangle acts *in lieu of* a secondary downtrend in a primary uptrend (or a secondary uptrend in a primary downtrend). On still fewer occasions, the rectangle can also form a top or bottom and becomes the prelude to a trend reversal. The key to a rectangle is to follow the direction of the price swing that breaks out above or below the top and bottom of the rectangle.

Dr. Lo's study done at MIT, mentioned earlier, found that *rectangle tops* and *rectangle bottoms* were two (of five) chart patterns they found significantly correlated to a predictable outcome. If a rectangle forms after an advance, but the breakout is downward and the reversal is to the downside, it could be considered to be a rectangle top. Conversely, if a rectangle formed after a decline, was preceded by a downtrend, and the direction of the breakout is up, it is a rectangle bottom. I should also note that most technicians simply call both patterns rectangles. When they do occur, rectangles followed by reversals are reliable patterns in terms of suggesting that there will be a follow through after the breakout. When there are one or two consecutive closes above the upper or lower horizontal line, or the line is exceeded by more than five to seven percent, any trade or investment made should be in the direction of the breakout, with a stop point just below/above the breakout point.

A rectangle top is preceded by an uptrend in Figure 6.47. The minimum objective for a low in the expected downtrend is equal to the height of the formation—that is the distance between the line of the highs and the line of the lows—added to the bottom of the rectangle at the downside breakout point. Sometimes, the line is not precisely defined, so an approximation must be used. Generally, the longer the sideways trend, the bigger will be the resulting move.

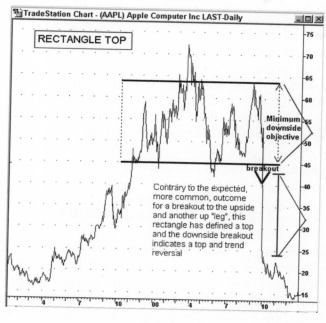

Figure 6.47

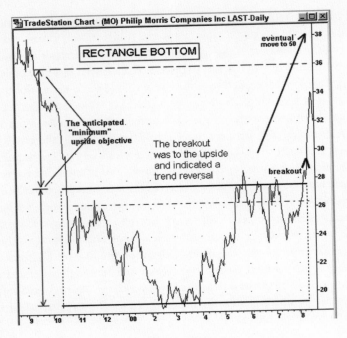

Figure 6.48

The rectangle bottom is preceded by a downtrend in Figure 6.48. The minimum objective for a high in the expected uptrend is equal to the height of the formation—that is, the distance between the line of the lows and the line of the highs—added to the top of the rectangle at the upside breakout point. As it is always true for any minimum price objective rule of thumb, they are useful for an initial objective at the time of the breakout. After the trend develops, you need to follow the trend developments and also use other technical analysis analytical tools (e.g., trendlines), in order to see just how the price trend will extend in terms of duration and price.

BROADENING TOPS AND BOTTOMS

The *broadening bottom* formation is the fifth pattern that the MIT study mentioned, found as having a prediction outcome that is significantly more than random chance would imply. The broadening *formation* is the same pattern in either instance. It can be labeled a broadening *bottom* when the trend preceding the broadening formation is down and a broadening *top* when the trend preceding the pattern formation is up. These are often reversal patterns because, unlike the *compression* of the triangle pattern we'll examine shortly, occurring when buyers and sellers get more and more finely matched, the broadening formation is decompression, so to speak. When price *volatility* increases as is the case when you have a rapid series of higher highs and lower lows, it is because participants in the market get less and less certain what the correct valuation (price) should be. This dynamic more often accompanies a reversal in the direction of the trend.

The *broadening bottom* is where the price trend is downward and a sideways series of price swings develop that form a series of higher (minor) upswing highs and lower downswing lows, which means there is one upward and one downward sloping trendline. There should be at least two to three price swings that result in the two to three lows and highs that allow drawing of the trendlines. The subsequent outline to this pattern is also triangular in shape but that shape takes the form of a megaphone. The breakout is upward as can be seen in Figure 6.49.

There is little to differentiate the actual broadening formation in the top or bottom varieties from one another *except* for the direction of the preceding trend. The preceding trend, before this series of higher highs and lows, is

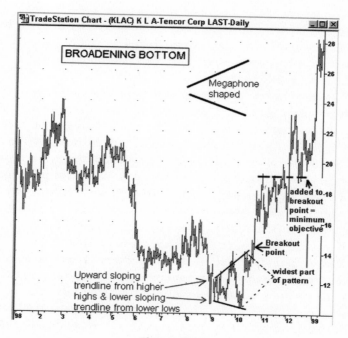

Figure 6.49

down in the case of the broadening bottom and *up* in the case of the broadening top. Even with this categorization, it's not always easy to determine whether the item being charted is in an uptrend or downtrend. For investment purposes, and if a trend direction is not readily apparent from the shape of the chart pattern or analysis of any relevant trendlines and other such visual markings, I suggest defining the trend direction by whether prices are trading below or above the average of the past 200 days' closing price (i.e., a 200-day "moving average" as it will be described later).

A breakout from the broadening bottom exists when prices advance above the highest high in the formation. The measuring implication for the height of the next leg is the same regardless of whether the breakout direction is up or down. The measuring implication for a broadening bottom is for a minimum objective equal to the height of the formation at its widest point added to the breakout price. The breakout price is the price point at which prices advance above through the upper trendline after it's formed by two to three points—three offering better definition. If this occurs at a much higher level after a further drift sideways, add the height to the highest upswing high within the megaphone shape, and that is the minimum objective.

The price objective rule of thumb for broadening formations in general is not as reliable as for the *head and shoulders* or regular *triangle* patterns. If the breakout is to the upside, and any subsequent gain after the breakout is equal to 20–30 percent, a liquidating stop order can be placed just below the closest prior downswing low to lock in as much of the gain as possible, while still staying with the trend.

The *broadening top* is made up of the same upward sloping trendline composed of higher upswing highs, coupled with a down sloping trendline connecting lower downswing lows. The result is the same *megaphone* shape outline. When the trend that precedes this formation is up, assume that the resolution of the pattern will be a breakout through the lower line as in Figure 6.50. However, the breakout direction is the most important thing. We need to be prepared for a *pattern failure* when the broadening top does not precede a downside reversal, and the breakout is to the upside instead. A sideways drift is another possible outcome, in which case the risk of loss is not great, but neither is the profit potential.

A *pattern failure* is when the outcome reverses from the usual. In this case (Figure 6.50) it would have been if the pattern turned out to have led to the same result as a *continuation* formation, and the breakout was to the upside in the direction of the prior trend. There is significant price *volatility* being shown in a *broadening formation*—higher highs and lower lows—and the direction of a next leg preceded by increased volatil-

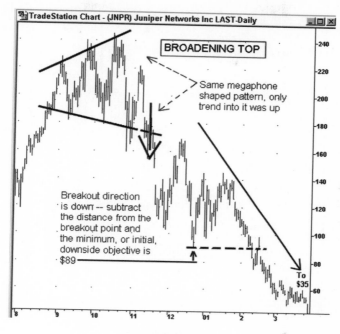

Figure 6.50

ity is never going to be completely predictable. Even if we see no reason to anticipate a reversal to a trend, we should nevertheless watch carefully for a breakout at either trendline. The price objective on a breakout either way is the same and is as suggested by a measurement of the height of the formation added to or subtracted from the breakout, depending on the direction. The broadening formation is not as common as other types of reversal patterns, such as double tops.

BULLISH FALLING WEDGES AND BEARISH RISING WEDGES

Wedge patterns are not seen so commonly either, but when they do develop and I see them—you do have to *notice* them—the wedge pattern has proven to be a reliable *setup* to an eventual trend reversal. In a *rising wedge*, prices move gradually higher but in converging trendlines or a "narrowing in" pattern of higher highs and lower lows, such as seen in the rising wedge pattern in the chart in Figure 6.51—this pattern occurred over a five-month period. There should be at least two to three upswing highs and downswing lows that comprise the points through which the trendlines are drawn—there typically

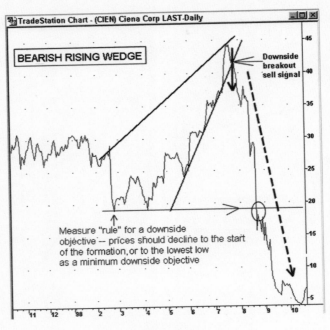

Figure 6.51

are more points than this minimum number for drawing the two converging lines. A wedge pattern can form over a lengthy period. Figure 6.52 shows one such pattern occurring over a nearly two-year time frame.

What is being suggested in the rising bearish wedge is that buying is being met with stronger and stronger selling as prices edge higher. When prices fall below the lower up trendline in a rising wedge pattern, a trend reversal is suggested. Prices may rebound to the trendline again, but will not likely get back above it. Place a liquidating buy stop just above the broken trendline when a short position is established on the downside break.

A declining or *falling wedge* is typically a bullish pattern as it suggests that selling is being met with increasing buying. Eventually, this sets the stage for an upside reversal—see Figure 6.53. There is an expectation that prices will at least rebound back to the high point seen in the downward sloping wedge (i.e., the highest high). According to Thomas Bulkowski, an even higher percent of bullish *falling wedges* result in upside breakouts, versus downside breakouts after formation of bearish rising wedges. This finding suggests being ready to buy an upside breakout to the declining wedge as soon as it occurs. One tactic is that of making ongoing downward adjustments of a buy stop order so that it remains just above the upper down

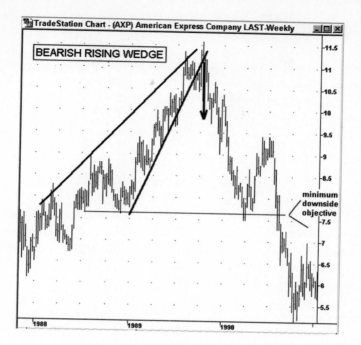

Figure 6.52

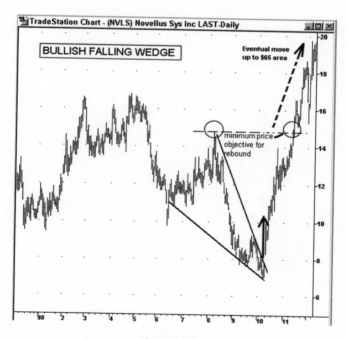

Figure 6.53

trendline. This way a position can be taken in the market or particular item as soon as prices achieve a decisive upside penetration above the falling wedge. Liquidating stops are then placed just below the trendline that was penetrated to the upside, as there should be no further return to below this line, especially on a closing basis without suggesting a pattern failure.

TRIANGLE TOPS AND BOTTOMS

A triangle is where the outline of a sideways movement, after an up- or downswing, traces out a three-sided pattern based on a pattern of higher highs and lower lows, and the resulting trendline angles converge or narrow. Each trendline, to be valid, should be *touched* two to three times. At a point that nears the end point of the triangle, there is a breakout above or below the upper or lower trendline. The triangle can be viewed as the result of *compression* of the price range. This happens when buyers and sellers get into a closer and closer balance with each other. A physical analogy is that of compressing a spring and letting go, with the result of a strong snap back movement. *Compression* is a price tug-of-war—the springboard action carries prices most often in the *same* direction as the prior trend. For example, if the trend has been up, buyers have been in control. When prices break out (expand from) above a price range that has become more and more narrow, the buyers suddenly see the trend affirmed and step up their buying. Sellers step aside as they still are mindful of the trend. Because of this dynamic the triangle is actually one of the most common *continuation* patterns.

Occasionally however, triangles become top or bottom formations that precede trend *reversals*. The key event is to follow the *direction* of the *breakout*—if this is in a countertrend direction, it's a reversal signal.

If the triangle line is *flat* on the *bottom* and the topmost line is sloping down, this is a *descending triangle*. The downward slope to the trendline formed from the progressively lower minor rally highs, indicates that sellers are doing scale-down selling and are taking what they can get, price-wise. The descending triangle is considered to be a bearish pattern, with breakouts to the downside as a common outcome after the triangle forms. Therefore, if seen at the top of an uptrend, such as in Figure 6.54, this can suggest that this pattern is a *triangle top*. In a breakout of the triangle in either direction, there will commonly be a jump in trading activity, which will be apparent in the volume figures.

Another type of triangle consists of a *flat* horizontal line on *top*, as highs hit the same level repeatedly, while the line drawn along the bottom consists

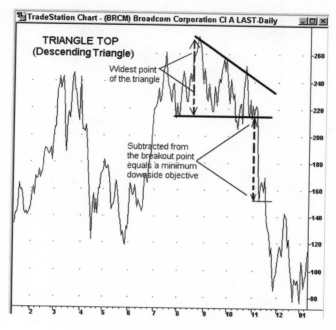

Figure 6.54

of higher downswing lows, so is a rising line. This pattern is called an *ascending triangle*. The lower rising trendline, formed from progressively higher downswing lows, indicates that buyers are willing to purchase at gradually higher levels—whereas sellers are selling only on advances back to where rallies have been ending, as suggested by the topmost level line of rally peaks. The ascending triangle is assumed to be a bullish pattern. If this formation is seen after prices have been trending lower, it suggests a triangle bottom formation, such as the one shown in Figure 6.55 and would also fall into the category of a reversal pattern. Triangles as reversal formations are not common.

The measurement for a minimum price objective is the same in either the case where the outcome of a triangle leads to a trend reversal or where the outcome is the *continuation* of the trend that existed before the triangle formed. The minimum price target after a breakout is equal to the height of a vertical line that connects the widest point between the upper and lower trendlines where there is a price *touch* to the line. The difference between these two intersecting points is added to, or subtracted from, the breakout point at the upper or lower trendline.

In the case of the triangle top or triangle bottom, I normally anticipate

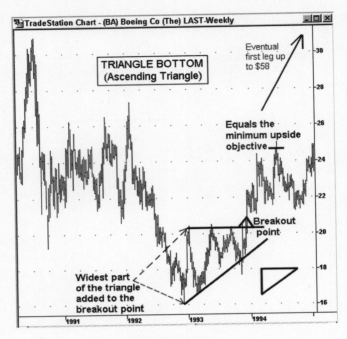

Figure 6.55

the total move following a price reversal may exceed the minimum price objective implied by the triangle formation. If a stock or other financial instrument has reversed its trend after forming a triangle top or bottom and has entered a new secondary trend, the first move may be only the first segment of a trend that will typically have several segments or *legs* to it (e.g., a rally, correction, second advance, another downswing, and a final rally in an uptrend).

GAPS

Price "gaps" can occur at the beginning ("breakaway" gaps) or ends ("exhaustion" gaps) of trends, and therefore be part of *reversal* patterns. When price gaps occur in the middle of trends ("measuring" and "runaway" gaps), which is more common, they are part of *continuation* patterns.

Price Gaps in General

A price *gap* is formed when any traded item has a low that is above the prior day's high—an *upside gap*—or when the item's high is below the previous day's low creating a *downside gap*. Gaps are price areas where no trading took place from one session to the next. This space between two consecutive days' price ranges, as seen on a bar or candlestick chart, has various degrees of significance in terms of predicting possible trend reversals that may be underway.

Generally, gaps below the market tend to act as a support area; gaps above the market suggest resistance and an area where there will be selling interest. Most price gaps occur after news has come after the close of trading (e.g., company earnings announcements or commodity reports that are more bullish or bearish than expectations). Since a consensus expectation is "built into" the last traded price or close of every stock or commodity, significant new influences affecting the market's perceptions for the current price level tends to cause an immediate adjustment in the opening price. Either buyers will be willing to pay more and potential sellers will want higher levels to induce them to sell, or sellers will be aggressive in offering the item at lower levels and buyers will not be interested in purchasing unless prices drop.

Upside gaps are price areas where buyers were unable to make any purchases, as selling occurred only above the gap area. Downside gaps are price areas where sellers were unable to make any sales as they could only affect a transaction at levels below the gap. This is behind the notion that gaps below the market will tend to act as support and gaps above the market act as resistance. A move back down to a gap will tend to bring in additional buying interest unfulfilled at this lower level from earlier, and a rebound back up to an overhead gap can attract interested sellers that had unfulfilled offers before in an area where prices had previously "gapped up." There is a saying that "gaps get filled in." This occurs when perceptions change and a market settles down in subsequent days and weeks after the gap event. But to see what is what with gaps, we need to differentiate among different types of gaps and see which ones are part of a reversal pattern. Gaps that are typically part of ongoing trends will be mentioned again in the section on *continuation patterns*. However, the primary explanation of gaps is given here.

❙ **Common gaps.** So-called "common" gaps occur frequently and are merely part of normal price activity and are not especially significant. These gaps tend to get filled in regularly. In the stock market, because of the tendency to halt trading in a particular issue if news comes out that affects the stock, resumption of trading can easily result in a price gap. Overnight news affecting stock and commodity price is common, as various economic and business reports often are released after regular trading hours. Earnings reports and to some extent other company announcements that might materially affect a stock's price are released after the close of regular trading. Given the extent of after-hours, or 24-hour, trading, there is some ability for participants to react to news in marking prices up or down, but the official price record occurs only during regular trading hours, and gaps are the result. Price gaps are uncommon in the interbank currency markets as these markets are trading in at least one major regional center for about 22 hours out of 24. If charted globally, which is common, few if any gaps will appear. Price gaps are seen frequently on chart types that display the session low and high. Gaps will, of course, *not* be seen on close-only *line charts*. Point and figure charts will account for the up or down jump that causes the appearance of a chart gap *as if* there were actual trades that occurred in the gap area.

I **Breakaway gaps.** A *breakaway gap*, as the name implies, is a gap that bursts out of the pack, so to speak—it is a gap that develops when prices jump well above or below what has been the normal trading range up until this gap event. This type of gap can mark an upside acceleration of a trend that is already underway, or it may act as the first signal of a trend reversal (e.g., the trend was up, but then a downside breakaway gap occurred that was the beginning of a trend reversal from up to down), as can be seen in Figure 6.56— some common gaps are noted on this chart also. Another example is found in Figure 6.57 for the same stock when its trend reversed to up. Some stocks and many futures markets have more of a tendency for gaps than others. The general rule of thumb for stocks is that the very widely traded stocks will tend to have fewer breakaway and exhaustion gaps. The breakaway gap will tend to either just get filled in or not be filled in at all, at least during the price move that follows. Either buyers are eager to buy dips back *into* the upside breakaway gap area or sellers are active in selling rallies that approach an overhead breakaway gap. Breakaway gaps tend to be *milestones* on a chart and are widely followed. Once the move is over and during a later trend, prices may return to the area of a prior breakaway gap, and this occurrence now lacks the special significance it would have had immediately after the gap formed.

I **Runaway or measuring gaps.** A *runaway gap* describes a gap occurring when a trend *accelerates* in either direction. This tends to occur in the second phases of bull and bear markets when there is more interest and participation in the traded item. A series of these gaps can occur,

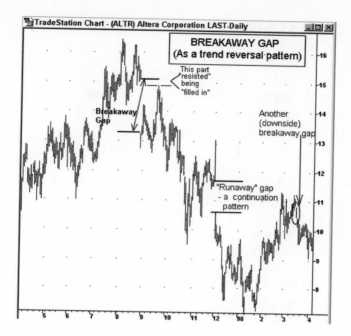

Figure 6.56

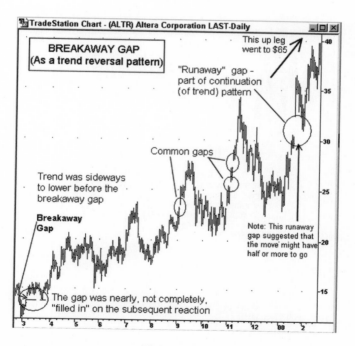

Figure 6.57

but this tends to be more common in the futures markets. A runaway gap will also have a measuring implication for the possible upside or downside potential of the move underway, as it often appears about midway in a price swing. In this role it is also called a *measuring gap*.

▌ **Exhaustion gap.** The *exhaustion gap*, which tends to be more common in the futures markets, occurs after a trend has been underway for some time. It typically stems from a final burst of buying or selling activity that "exhausts" the participants or depletes their trading capital. It's also common after such a gap, that another gap forms in the opposite direction that leaves one or more isolated bars. The resulting open spaces left after these price gaps create the pattern known as an *island* formation or *island reversal*. Without subsequent price action that suggests a top or bottom is forming, an exhaustion gap would initially be hard to distinguish from a common or runaway gap. Exhaustion gaps are the most likely to signal a trend reversal, especially in conjunction with a subsequent gap that also forms an island pattern—see Figure 6.58.

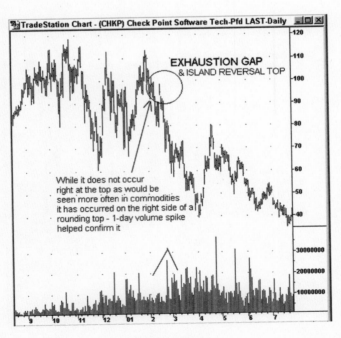

Figure 6.58

Island Reversals

As island formations involve gaps, this pattern is listed in this section on gaps. An *island bottom* is a formation where prices gap lower after an extended downtrend (an exhaustion gap), then trade for one or more days below the low end of the gap, leaving the chart space of the gap open. This activity is followed by a gap higher that again leaves open space above the single bar or cluster of bars and results in the appearance of an *island* that is underneath the subsequent uptrend. For examples see the charts in Figures 6.59–6.61. The more "pure type" island bottoms and tops tend to be a feature in the futures markets, but there are some island/gap type patterns that are seen in stocks, especially the more volatile ones—in stocks, a looser interpretation is required for these formations.

You can add this to your recognition list of quick forming reversals to accompany *spikes* and one- to two-day *key reversals*. One key to a true island top or bottom is that they need appear near the top of an uptrend or the bottom of a downtrend, as proven by subsequent market action. The best strategy before concluding that an island top or bottom reversal pattern has formed is to wait a few days to see if the gap or gaps

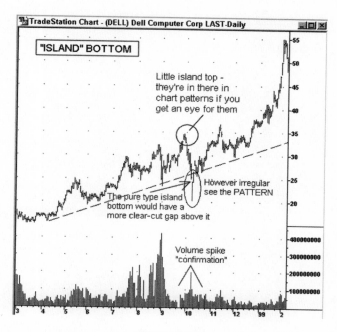

Figure 6.59

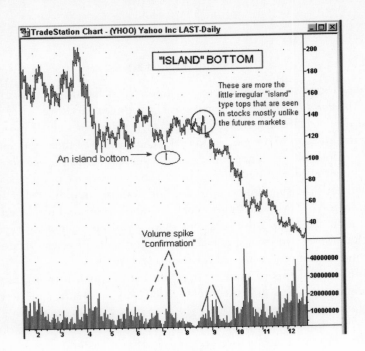

Figure 6.60

Figure 6.61

created during the island reversal formation get "filled in." If a gap or gaps remain after this period, the probability of there being a final top or bottom in place increases substantially. In stocks, you also see these reversals occurring on the way down, rather than at highs or lows, more often than other markets.

An *island top* is the opposite of the island bottom and occurs when prices gap higher (an *exhaustion gap*) after an uptrend has been underway for some time, then trade for one day or for several days where the lows remain above the gap, leaving this space completely *open*, ideally. This price action is then followed by a gap down that results in open space below the single bar or bars, or there will be gaps on either side of the cluster of bars making the formation resemble an "island"—see Figure 6.62. A new trend then begins from this point, the island top is typically left intact, and prices do not fill in the gap(s) that has created the isolated bar(s), at least during the duration of the following price move.

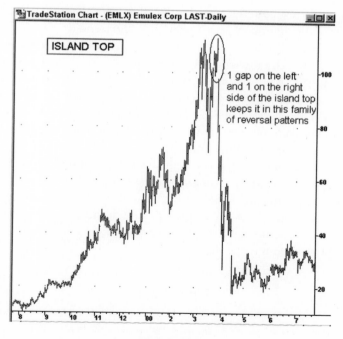

Figure 6.62

CONTINUATION PATTERN TYPES

The other broad category of significant technical price patterns is made up of ones that suggest a pause only in the movement of the stock or other financial instrument in the direction of the trend, and that the dominant trend can be expected to continue at some point—these chart formations are therefore aptly described as *continuation* patterns. Continuation patterns include

- *Flags*
- Most *triangles*
- Most *rectangles*—virtually the same as a line formation
- *Runaway* and *measuring gaps*

CONTINUATION PATTERNS— PAUSES OR CONSOLIDATIONS IN TRENDS

The word "continuation" comes from the verb "to continue." In technical analysis, these are patterns that develop that *consolidate* the prior movement within the dominant price trend. In a new trend or price swing, there is an initial strong move in one direction. After the initial buying and selling activity, prices reach temporary equilibrium. The participants on the winning side will take some profits and sell what they own, or cover some of their short positions. Hence the idea of *profit-taking* that the financial press likes to describe as being so frequent—we wish there were as many profits taken as they say there are! This activity will tend to cause prices to retrace some of the initial surge.

The investors and traders on the losing side, who bought high and sold low, are trying to also help themselves—but in their case it's to reduce their losses. They may not be desperate but have decided to get out if they can exit at a better price. If on the losing side of a decline, they'll sell on rallies. Those short, or looking to get in because they think the stock is now cheap, will want to buy the dips.

RECTANGLES

The aforementioned process creates the rectangle formation—a pause in the trend, when two to three (or more) upswing highs form around the same level and two to three (or more) downswing lows are created as buyers and sellers transact within a limited (price) *range*. The tops and bottoms are each at a similar price level—enough so that we are able to draw horizontal lines through the upper and lower ends of the *trading range* that has developed. As time goes on and the formation *broadens* out, the overall shape of it takes on a definite rectangular form. Charles Dow called the same type of pattern a "line" formation. No doubt he was looking at it from the point of view of the major trend, and usually a sideways trading range that is part of a secondary trend is not much more than a narrow line across the chart. We have the fortune to be able to zero in on this pattern online or with charting applications, and we can change the time duration so as to see the rectangular nature of this pattern I'm describing.

Eventually one side or the other is ready to do another round of buying or selling—the market typically only *trends* about 30 percent of the time—and there is a breakout above or below the rectangular trading range. A next price leg carries on in the same direction as the prior trend. If the trend was up, the most common next leg is up, after the rectangle completes. If the trend was down, the most common next leg is down when there is an eventual downside breakout. Sometimes, the rectangle goes on for weeks, sometimes for months and sometimes even for years, as can be seen in Figure 6.63. Another good example is in Figure 6.64. You can see why some technicians are tempted to use a rough rule of thumb regarding the width of the pattern equaling the *potential* distance up the vertical price scale (especially if the price and time scales get closer to a 1:1 relationship in *scaling*) after such a broad and solid *base* provided by the long sideways trend. The time spent in the lateral sideways movement or *trading range* suggests good balance in buying and selling. When this changes it often swings to another extreme. As Dow noted, the market goes from one extreme to the other—the movement of a *pendulum* is the perfect metaphor. Anyway, buyers were in control of the next two years as evident in Figure 6.64, as they pushed the first leg of the primary trend up to $70. Figure 6.65 provides an example of a rectangle that is a pause or consolidation in a downtrend.

The implication of a *breakout* from the rectangle is twofold. Look for follow-through when prices pierce either the top or bottom of the rectangle. The extent of the next price swing that follows should at least be equal to the height of the formation added or subtracted to the breakout point. This brings into play the concept of the *measured move*, where a next price swing should travel *at least as* far as the first. This is a minimum objective and sets up an initial target only. A subsequent up or

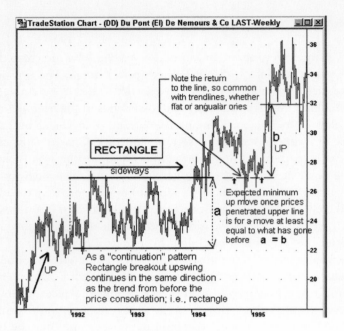

Figure 6.63

Figure 6.64

Figure 6.65

down *leg* (trend segment) will often carry further than the prior one, as we'll see later in a brief foray into Elliott wave theory.

GAPS AS CONTINUATION PATTERNS

Gaps have already been well defined in the previous segment on *reversal* patterns, which is the case with breakaway and exhaustion type gaps. "Common gaps" occur frequently and are part of continuation patterns. Common gaps occur so frequently that you may stop noticing them after a while. Figure 6.66 is of a daily stock chart that has a circle drawn around most of the common gaps—they are numerous and typical for this market. The sometimes numerous nature of common gaps should not obscure the important pattern information provided by the noticable gaps that occur with definite price *acceleration*. Gaps that tell us that the current trend is accelerating, and constitute a definite sign that the trend is continuing, are *runaway* or *measuring* gaps.

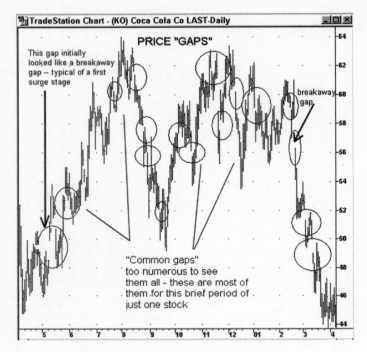

Figure 6.66

I **Runaway gaps.** Sometimes after a trend is already established, a stronger, more accelerated move begins and a bigger gap occurs that qualifies as a *runaway gap* as in Figure 6.67—showing that either buyers or sellers are now more firmly in control. There may be more gaps seen around the part of a trend phase of accelerating momentum, a situation where prices go up or down at a faster and faster rate—for example, a stock or the overall market was going up at a rate that would equal a 15 percent annual increase, but this rate of increase jumps to a rise that would translate to 30 percent, then to 50 percent—the rate of price increase is moving up dramatically. Accelerating upside or downside momentum has traditionally been more common in the commodities markets, as are breakaway and runaway gaps.

I **Measuring the move.** A *measuring gap* is another term applied to a runaway gap, as it involves the possible measuring implications for an upside objective for the total move underway. As such, these

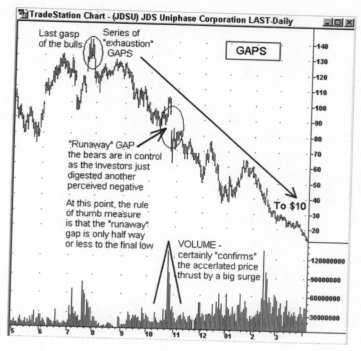

Figure 6.67

gaps are also indications that the bullish or bearish conviction about, for example, a stock or the market as a whole, has broadened to include many more market participants. If this is a bullish attitude, the gap higher suggests that a next wave of buyers have joined in and are willing to pay up for the item in question. When an expanded group of sellers becomes convinced that the value of their holdings is vulnerable to a more severe drop, they become more active sellers and are willing to sell even at a sharply lower opening. This second wave of buyers or sellers, as they represent a second stage of bullish or bearish news or conviction about the market or item, is a phenomenon that often occurs about *midway* in a move. The upside or downside *gaps* could as easily be called midpoint gaps. For example, a new up leg, perhaps marked with a breakaway gap, began at $50 and there was further substantial price gap or gaps in the $75 area—further upside potential suggested by such a measuring gap is for an objective to around $100.

TRIANGLES

The *triangle* is the most frequent continuation pattern, so triangle formations are generally considered bullish in an uptrend and bearish in a downtrend. Because of this, it is assumed—unless or until contrary price action develops—that a *breakout* from a triangle will take prices in the *same* direction as the prior trend. The triangle forms generally after a pause in an up or down move, when prices start going sideways. A series of minor upswings and minor downswings trace out two angles that form a triangle pattern, and these lines converge over time. Each of the two sides of the triangle consists of at least two to three points made by highs and lows, which make it a valid trendline. The shape of the trendline can vary, but common to all types is that after prices get close (within 20–30 percent) of where the lines would touch, prices typically break out above or below the topmost or bottom-most line.

Variations in these shapes have already been discussed. The *symmetrical triangle* is the most common form of triangle—see Figure 6.68—when the two angles have approximately the same slope. Sometimes, there is more of a sideways movement after a breakout of the triangle in the expected direction of the prior trend, but the eventual outcome is still the same, as seen in Figure 6.69. Usually prices are unable to even return to the trendline that was pierced—see Figure 6.70. The triangle is often a first pause after the initial segment of a trend—often, what follows is an even stronger move in that same direction. In an uptrend, potential buyers become more confident that the emerging trend will not be aborted. Sellers are already a little nervous as prices have risen—another wave of buying coming in will push them out of the way pretty quickly as the trend intensifies. The reverse situation occurs in a decline. Potential buyers are not at their most confident, due to the trend turning against them. As sellers see that buyers are not able to take prices back up much, they gain more conviction that prices will go down more.

If the series of two to three or more tops occur in the same area and the downswing lows are rising, this is called an *ascending triangle*—see Figure 6.71. What are *ascending* are the reaction lows. An ascending triangle is generally considered to be bullish as each upswing is starting from a progressively higher point, suggesting upward momentum and that buyers are willing to pay up for the item. If the trend preceding the ascending triangle was sideways, look for a bullish move after its completion. Of course, the ultimate determinant is the direction of a price breakout or the direction of any thrust out of the triangle. If an up direction would be in

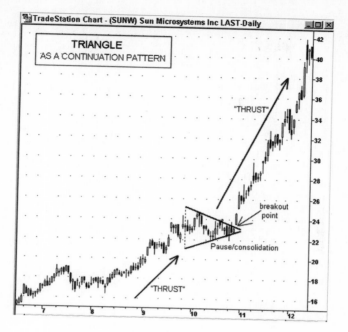

Figure 6.68

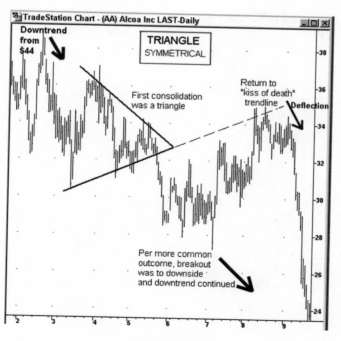

Figure 6.69

Figure 6.70

Figure 6.71

the direction of the trend and the move is down instead, this is a rarer instance of the triangle acting as a reversal pattern.

If two to three or more minor upswing highs have tops that are declining, and the downswing lows are occurring in the same area making a flat line on the bottom, this is generally called a *descending triangle*—see Figure 6.72. What are *descending* are the minor rally peaks, as each succeeding upswing tops out a bit lower, suggesting declining momentum within that movement. The descending triangle is sometimes thought to be bearish because waning buying is taking each rally to a lesser top. If the trend prior to the formation of the descending triangle was down, seeing the ascending triangle type developing as a (trend) consolidation is also consistent with the idea that the breakout move will be in that direction also. Assume, until the market shows otherwise, that the resolution of a triangle will be in the *same* direction as the secondary trend. Note that the descending triangle shown in Figure 6.72 achieved the expected *upside* breakout, demonstrating that the prior trend will assert a general dominant influence. The

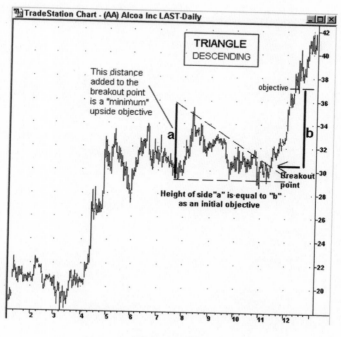

Figure 6.72

actual breakout was the defining event, and any contrary expectations are then unimportant.

Regardless of the specific shape of the triangle, all have the same *measuring* implication related to a minimum upside or downside objective after a triangle breakout. A minimum or initial objective is for a move equal to the height of the triangle at its widest point added to the upper breakout point, or subtracted from the lower breakout point—see Figure 6.73.

FLAG PATTERNS

Flag patterns are also very common continuation patterns and are considered bullish in an uptrend and bearish in a downtrend. *Flags*, and a variety of flag called a *pennant*—although I find it easier to just label them all flags—are relatively short-term sideways consolidations of or after a prior sharp move in prices. A flag pattern's outline is formed by a series of relatively narrow price

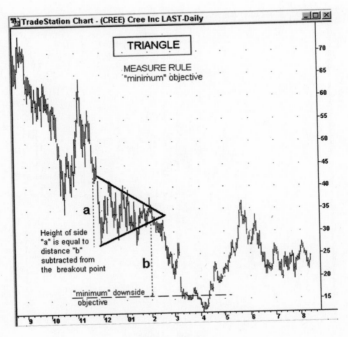

Figure 6.73

range sessions following a sharp, but relatively short, price spurt. The more or less straight up nature of this spurt causes a rise that looks like a *flagpole*, long and narrow. The narrow range days that form the flag have tops and bottoms that trace out short trendlines. The two resulting trendlines will usually slope in the *opposite* direction from the trend. Some examples, including the rare one (for stocks, not as much with futures) with a pennant shape, can be seen visually in Figures 6.74–6.76.

What is going on in the battle for investment survival represented by the flag formation is that either the bulls or bears had recent sizable profits that were made quickly. There is an old trader's saying to "take quick profits." It's natural for some of these winners to want to take profits on all or some of their holdings. The losing side may have held on during the recent strong move against them, especially because it happened so quickly. Some participants, on reflection, decide to get out. The resulting buying or selling occurs in dribs and drabs (on less volume) and this is what makes the pattern what it is. After this back and forth action, the emboldened bullish or bearish factions go back on a buying or selling spree, and there is a further breakout in the direction of the dominant trend.

Figure 6.74

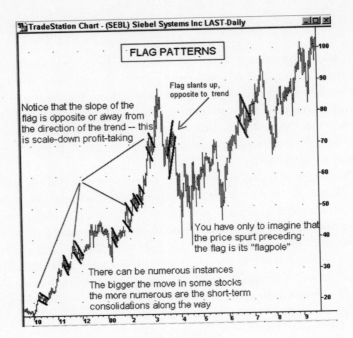

Figure 6.75

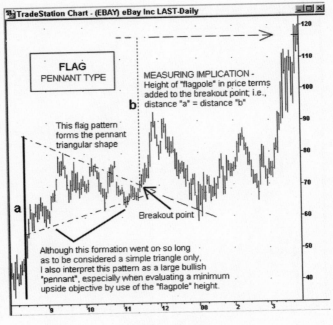

Figure 6.76

There is a measurement implication for the height of a further move after the breakout from a flag pattern. This minimum upside or downside objective is equal to the height of the flagpole added or subtracted to the breakout point—see Figure 6.77. I find this a reliable measure, and flag patterns are among my favorite trades when I run across them in time to buy/sell the breakout. The stop-out point, if the pattern fails, is near the breakout point. The stop will be near the entry point if you take a position only if prices exceed the top or bottom of the *flag*. A highly favored trade can be the result when the risk to reward ratio is 3–4 : 1; that is, for every dollar risked you project a minimum upside profit of three to four times this. For a series of reliable sell signals generated by a series of flag formations, see Figure 6.78.

All the measuring implications studied so far with rectangles, triangles, and flags are variations of the *measured move* concept. This is the rule of thumb that says that a next price swing will at least equal the extent of the prior move. By taking measurements at the widest points in the triangle, for example, and adding it to the breakout point, it does approximate a minimum objective that, if achieved, would make it equal to the

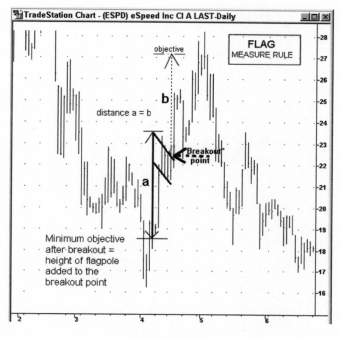

Figure 6.77

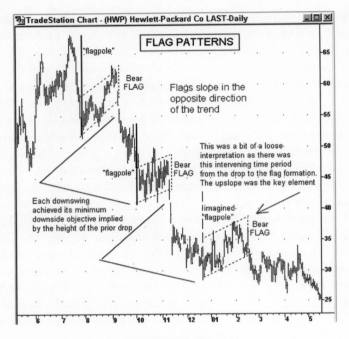

Figure 6.78

prior price swing. This subsequent price swing may be far greater than this minimum objective, but having such a target is valuable in order to establish some parameters as to trade potential. If a minimum move that can be projected is $30, a maximum objective could be $90.

The flag composed of two sloping trendlines set rather close together, will generally slope against or opposite to the dominant trend. Slope is not relevant to the pennant variation as it makes a triangular shape, and it is usually of a shorter duration than a *triangle*. In an uptrend the slope of a flag will be down typically and in a downtrend, the slope of the flag will be up. I find this rule less true in the commodities markets but quite true in stocks. Generally we could say that when the thrust creating the *flagpole* is up and a subsequent flag slopes down, this pattern is a *bull flag*. When the initial thrust is downward and a subsequent flag formation slopes up, this pattern is a *bear flag*.

A flag that forms near either extreme in a trading range will usually be significant. If a bull flag forms at the top end of a recent trading range, it suggests there may be enough new buying coming in to kick off a second leg. The reverse would be true at the low end of a trading range—a bear flag there would suggest that another secondary downswing was coming.

SUMMARY

There is a lot in this chapter, because there are a sizable number of significant technical patterns and to learn them takes some explanation and thought and especially a number of examples to understand them. It is suggested that you come back to the explanations and examples frequently, when you look at your own charts, especially when you see a chart formation that appears to be like the ones described and shown in the examples. Ability to quickly and easily see these things takes time as it involves both looking at some number of charts, past and present, and also having the experience of going through different cycles in the markets, which can take some years even. If you are seeing a bear market in stocks, you may not see a bull market firsthand for awhile. Of course, you can go back and look at past charts of during the last bull market, although, in U.S. stocks, don't expect them to all have the power and duration of the last one. Study of prior market cycles and looking at chart patterns from them, is an excellent way to learn, but there is also nothing like seeing the events real-time, so to speak, as you get the feel of it, too, which is also quite important.

Pattern recognition is the most visual aspect of technical analysis and one that perhaps benefits the most from repeated looking at charts and follow up, over time, to see if, for example, what you thought was a flag led to the anticipated later advance or decline. The twin pillars of technical analysis are (1) *patterns*, which broadly also includes trendlines and channels and (2), *indicators*. Some people will tend to rely more on one aspect than the other. *Classical* chart analysis is a term used sometimes that implies more of a reliance on pattern recognition than on indicators. Indicators, the other pillar of technical analysis that we examine next, may appear more straightforward—for example, prices are either above a moving average or below it. However, indicators are also open to quite varied interpretations and uses also, as we will see.

7

TECHNICAL INDICATORS

INTRODUCTION

Technical analysis makes extensive use of various mathematical models or *studies* to show various aspects of price activity, such as ones measuring *momentum*, or the rate of price increase or change. These models are generally called "technical indicators" or simply *indicators*. This chapter will describe the most common technical indicators and provide examples of how they can be used effectively in measuring aspects of market trends. The goals in using indicators are the same as for pattern recognition—to better identify current and emerging trends and the points subject to trend reversals, in order to increase profitable investing and trading decisions and decrease unprofitable ones.

Some choices had to be made as to which indicators to include, as there are so many and this is an introductory book. However, the technical indicators in most common use are described in this chapter. Some indicators have marginal or specialized uses or are similar to others that are in common use. If you use one or two of the class of indicators called "oscillators," which show market momentum, only marginal benefit will be gained by using minor variations of them.

Indicators and their use have a tendency to be misunderstood. Because they are mathematical and precise, there is a tendency to also use them *mechanically*, which often does not work out. For example, oscillators typically have levels at the upper and lower range of possible readings that are considered to show the point at which a market or financial instrument is "overbought" or "oversold." The rationale for such an indicator interpretation as *overbought* is as an attempt to identify where price momentum may be at an extreme and the market susceptible to a reversal. However, this notion runs contrary to what happens in a strong and prolonged trend and where a mechanical formula like this will have limited likelihood of identifying a top near its point of occurence or even a predictable likelihood of a minor setback. However, when the same market is in a *trading range* and nearing the top end of that range and also registers as "overbought," according to an overbought/oversold indicator, it can be a valuable tool in identifying a trading opportunity. As you go through this chapter it's useful to keep in mind that indicators will most likely be of the most value when used:

I In the *appropriate situation* for their use

I *Along with other tools* of technical analysis, including the study of chart patterns

I With a goal to achieving a skill or an *art in interpretation* of them rather than using them mechanically

TECHNICAL INDICATORS IN GENERAL

Indicators involve or consist of mathematical formulas usually based on *price* activity. For example, an average is calculated of the last 10 hourly, daily, or weekly closes. Along with analyzing chart *patterns*, indicators in technical analysis provide a second major method of evaluating market activity. They also can help us forecast the continuation or possible interruption of price trends. We've already discussed an indicator, or mathematical formula, based on daily trading *volume*, the on balance volume (OBV) indicator. The other technical indicators we will study are based on *price* as the primary input and usually the particular price is the *close*. The open, high, and low are used far less often. An example using a value other than close is computing an average of the high for the past 20 days, in order to see how today's high compares to this average. Again, the term "indicator" is the most common name applied to such technical formula, although the term technical "study" is sometimes also used.

The indicators that we examine mostly use the closing price level to compute its values and this is the *default* setting on most indicators. The closing level, as discussed in relation to the rationale and methods for candlestick charting, is the most important price of the day, relative to either the high or the low. The emphasis on the close in terms of indicators relates to the nature of a formula, which must take one value or another, and not visual *charting* techniques that rely on our brain to take in a variety of information. Indicators are useful in different ways, at different times. Five important uses of indicators are to help in identifying

1. *Direction* of a trend, ranging from short- to long-term
2. *Strength* of a trend
3. *Support and resistance levels* in a trend or in a trading range
4. *Divergences* that occur between indicators and price, suggesting a possible future *trend reversal*
5. Trend reversal *confirmations*, also ranging from short- to long-term

For an introductory treatment of technical indictors we can say that there are basically two types: *moving averages* and *oscillators*. Of the two, moving averages are the more important indicators for longer-term investors and for *trend-following* purposes. Trend-following techniques are, as the name implies, concerned with identifying the dominant trend, particularly the major trend, in order to participate, by investments, in that trend for as long as it continues. Moving averages are used to *follow* the trend, an apt term, as moving averages are "lagging" indicators or formulas that identify a new trend only after price momentum has developed fully for some period of time or after a time "lag."

Common oscillators include the *relative strength index* (*RSI*), *stochastics*, and *MACD* (*moving average convergence–divergence*) and are of significant use for shorter-term trading, but are also of some benefit for longer-term investors, just less frequently. When prices are confined to a *trading range*, which is most often the result of the consolidation or correction to a prior up or down trend, oscillators can be quite effective for identifying buy and sell entry points. They become more accurate in trading range situations in providing an indication of likely support or resistance, or the condition known as *oversold* or *overbought*. "Overbought" and "oversold" will be discussed next, ahead of the section on oscillators, to which this concept is normally linked. However, I'll first demonstrate the linkage of the concept of overbought and oversold to moving averages.

OVERBOUGHT AND OVERSOLD

In general, a market is said to be *overbought* when prices have a rate of price increase that is strongly in one direction and beyond its recent tendency to rise, and *oversold* when there is a relatively steep decline that is greater than its recent history. For example, a stock for weeks or months has never traded at a price that took it above its closing average price for the prior 50 days by more than 10 percent. Then comes a period, when there is a steeper advance and the stock soars to a level that is 20 percent above this same average and this item may then be seen as being overbought. *Overbought* here implies simply that any surge in buying well in excess of what is usual on a historical basis, also creates a likelihood that the stock price is vulnerable to a correction. Another example is offered by a stock that falls for 10 days straight. Assuming that this price behavior is *over* or beyond what is usual for this item, it will be considered to be *oversold* and susceptible to a rebound—an analogy to a rubber band is a good one—market *valuations* get stretched, so to speak, but then eventually tend to snap back toward the *mean* or an *average* price that is typical for the item in question.

The concept of overbought and oversold refers to rallies or declines that are steeper than usual, but the degree of this can vary a good deal. There are not always precise, objective, or agreed upon measurements of what this means. The first example mentioned is a more objective measure in that it examines how far the current close is above the *average* close of the prior 50 days. The example given of *oversold* based on 10 days of consecutive down closes is a more subjective criteria, as all down closes together may total only a minor overall decline.

A central important aspect of overbought or oversold is that the concepts relate to a situation where there is a preponderance of hours, days, or weeks, or some specified period of time, where prices are moving *strongly* in one direction. The concept of a specific price area that represents a level that is overbought or oversold does not normally come into play. Only that price *momentum*, or the rate (speed) at which prices change, is stronger than usual and predominantly in one direction. Experience suggests that at some point, after a market gets into these kind overbought or oversold ranges, there is an increased likelihood that there will be a price *correction* or countertrend move.

MOVING AVERAGES

A price *average* in its simplest form, consists of taking some number of prices, such as the close, adding them up and dividing by that number (e.g., 5, 10, 20, 50, or 200 days). A *moving average* is said to "move," as after the close of each bar, the close of *x* number of bars ago is dropped off and replaced by the latest close. The resulting average changes or *moves* relative to the preceding period. For example, in a 50-day moving average, at the end of the day's session a new calculation is made by dropping the close of 51 days ago and adding the last 50 days that now include the most recent close. The most common visual representation of a moving average is by creating a line that is plotted on the same graph as prices on bar, candlestick, or line charts. Point and figure charting does not involve the concept of a closing price for some specific period, so moving averages will not be seen on this chart type.

Moving averages are not unlike trendlines in that they also help measure the direction and momentum (the relative angle) of a trend, and prices that move above or below a trendline can alert us to a possible trend reversal. However, whereas a trendline has some validity being projected into the future or beyond the current period, as an angular measurement of price momentum, a moving average is a *lagging* indicator based on past prices only. We can't make an assumption for example, that a moving average that is climbing will turn down based on trading that hasn't happened yet. We see only at the end of the period being measured, whether the latest close is above or below a moving average, whereas when prices pierce a trendline, this is seen immediately, at least on an intraday basis.

Simple Moving Averages

The most common moving average is the "simple" moving average, where equal weight is given to all the prices in the period being examined. This is usually the closing price. Simple moving averages of varying *lengths* are shown in Figures 7.1 to 7.4 for stocks that are both trending higher and lower. Each period's close that is being calculated, whether intraday, daily, or weekly, is equal to all the other closes. In a simple 200-day moving average, any close, such as from 150 days ago, is equal to today's close, and

Figure 7.1

Figure 7.2

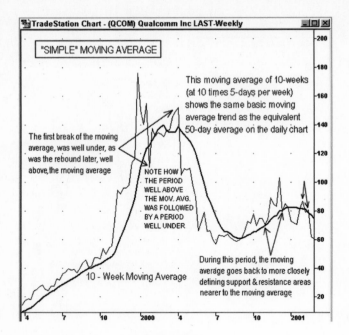

Figure 7.3

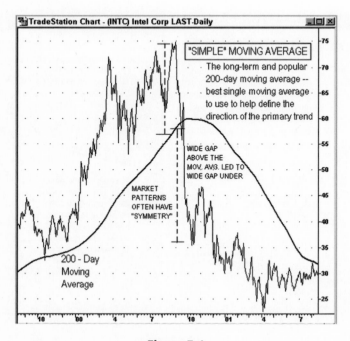

Figure 7.4

one close is simply one two-hundredth of the average. If there is a sharp upturn or downturn, the current close may quickly be well above or below a simple moving average, as the average itself will change relatively slowly unless of a short duration (e.g., 3, 5, or 9 days).

In the charts in Figures 7.1–7.4, you'll see that frequently the moving averages coincided with areas of price support, or resistance, on both daily and weekly charts. In an uptrend, as with an *up trendline*, the moving average line shows more instances where the average coincided with or *acted as*, support and in a downtrend, similar to what happens using a *down trendline*, there are many instances where the moving average coincided with *resistance*. The 200-day moving average is one often used, such as by professional money managers, to help define whether the primary stock market trend is up or down. If prices are trading above this average, the stock's major trend is more likely to be considered up, with the reverse situation being seen as characteristic of a stock that is trading under its 200-day simple moving average. In the futures markets, the 200-day moving average is too long to be useful. One of 30 to 50 days' duration is more helpful to identify the longer-range trend.

A moving average is, in a way, like a "curved trendline." However, a sharp price move will not cause anything but a very short simple moving average to shift rapidly, as the latest price change doesn't count for more than any other day of the average. This situation may be contrasted to a trendline where, after a steep move, a break of the dominant up trendline may be seen. The trendline in question may then no longer be valid and we need to redraw the line. Here the most recent price action is what determines a break of the trendline and in effect, a recent close takes on a greater importance. Of course, a sharp decline may quickly put prices under a long-term moving average, but the longer-term simple moving average itself changes rather slowly. However, there are other methods of calculating moving averages that have the *most recent price action* count for more than price activity that is further removed from the present, which we see next.

Weighted or Smoothed Moving Averages

The simple moving average is the most common type of moving average. I tend to use it in most instances and it is what most investors will look at exclusively, perhaps as much due to the fact that this type of moving average calculation is often the only type of moving average indicator on chart producing web sites. For the person who becomes interested beyond the basics and acquires a charting application, there are other moving average options that give more weight to the most recent price activity. A *weighted* moving average assigns a greater percentage value to the closes for *x* number of recent periods, thereby giving a reduced weighting to closing prices further back in time. The practical effect is to make the weighted moving average line follow current prices more closely, with less of a lag than a regular simple moving average.

Such *front-loading* is the most popular method of calculating a weighted moving average, but it is not the only possibility. A common variation called linear *step-weighting*, assigns a fixed increment weighting to each day that is dependent on the duration of the average. For example, in such a 5-day weighted average the most recent day's close is 5 times the weight of the first day of the 5-day period, the prior day is 4 times the weight of the first day, the third day back is 3 times the weight of the first day of the period, and so on.

The *exponentially smoothed* average is a type of weighted moving average that is a popular variation and method of allowing recent price activity to generate a more rapid change in an average. Such a *smoothed* moving average assigns a percent value—for example, .15—to the last bar and this value will be added to a percentage of the previous day's close. The percentage of the previous day's close is the *inverse* of the weighted percentage: 100 − .15 or 85 percent in this example. Because of this method of calculation, all daily moving average values are modified once the first exponential weighting occurs. The higher the percentage weighting given to the most recent close, the more sensitive will be the resulting moving average to the most recent price change. All data previously used are always part of the new result, although with diminished significance over time.

As a trend continues, the exponentially smoothed moving average will lag the trend somewhat more than the weighted moving average, due to the inclusion of all prior closes because of the *smoothing* factor. Days don't begin dropping out of the calculation of the average, past a certain number. A longer moving average of the *simple*, equal-weighted type, will lag even more as the most recent close will be averaged equally with many prior closes. For example, all prior 49 closing prices, in the case of a 50-day simple moving average.

In Figure 7.5, a 50-day *simple*, *weighted*, and *exponentially smoothed* average are all applied to the same price chart. For this period of time, the lag is greatest with the simple moving average and least with the weighted moving average. Both types of moving averages giving more weight to the most recent price react more quickly to a change in the trend. For shorter

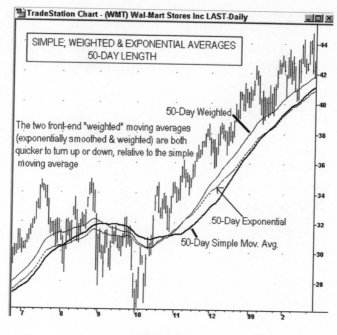

Figure 7.5

time durations, as in Figure 7.6, which uses a 10-day moving average *length*, there is little apparent difference between the three moving average variations. Taking a closeup view of a 30-day period when there was a minor trend change, as shown in Figure 7.7, it becomes apparent in this example that the first moving average to turn up was the exponential. This, of course, along with the weighted average can be made more, or less, sensitive to the most recent price changes by what "weighting" factors are used. They will turn up or down significantly quicker than a simple moving average unless all are of a very short duration, such as three days. At 10 days or longer, the gain in quickness of response in *front-weighted* averages, will appeal to traders who can deal with the periods of getting premature up or down turns in the weighted moving averages. Such changes may be premature as far as signaling a significant trend change is concerned.

As should be apparent, front-weighted moving averages are more appropriate for shorter-term trading purposes. Simple moving averages, especially in the 50–200 length range, are appropriate for an *investment* oriented time frame of many months or as long as a major trend continues. If there is concern that a trend is vulnerable to a reversal, there may be a

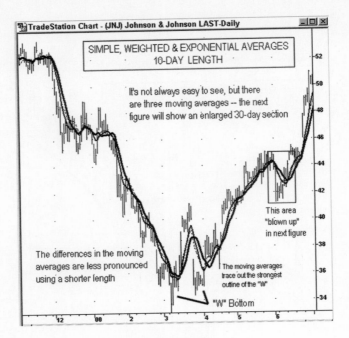

Figure 7.6

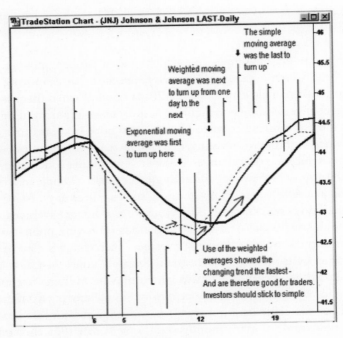

Figure 7.7

desire for the shorter *trigger* of the weighted moving average. It will provide the fastest alert of slowing momentum as far as a moving average, with a trade-off of perhaps being too quick. The exponentially smoothed average will principally be encountered by most users of basic technical indicators, of the popular *moving average convergence–divergence* indicator or *MACD*, which uses the smoothing technique as is discussed in the section on oscillators.

Moving Average Time Periods (Length)

There were always many questions that I received from readers of my CNBC.com columns as to what *length* of moving average is *better* or best. The answer is that it depends on your trading or investing horizon. A 5 to 21 bar length will track the short-term or minor trends—9, 14, and 20 are fairly standard lengths. You will often see the "default" number in moving average studies as 9. I prefer a 21-day moving average as a means of tracking the week-to-week trends. The result of using 21, versus the more common 20, is virtually indistinguishable. Use of 21 would be explained by a fondness for using 8, 13, or 21, as they are *Fibonacci* numbers. I tend to use 8 as my length for weekly and monthly moving averages and a 21-day daily moving average, along with 50- and 200-day averages to track the intermediate to long-term trends.

For the intermediate or *secondary* stock trends, the 50-day moving average, or 10 weeks on a weekly chart (5 trading days in a week: $10 \times 5 = 50$), is one of the most commonly used moving averages. The reason for this length, versus some other, is partly a matter of convention. I also think that it is because it is half of 100, in terms of days, and one-tenth of 100, in terms of weeks—100, its fractions and multiples, is a significant number in stocks as it is in the decimal system. I suspect also that 10 weeks has also proven to be the *right* length to capture trends in the market of secondary duration.

Examples of 21-, 50-, and 200-day moving averages can be seen in Figures 7.8–7.10 and examples of the 10-week and 40-week moving averages on the longer-term weekly charts in Figures 7.11 and 7.12. When changing time periods from daily to weekly, you need to remember to change moving average *lengths* to view the equivalent trends on the longer-term charts. Leaving the values and just switching time frames may be of interest also, but then you are comparing "apples and oranges," so to speak. A 50-week moving average encompasses almost a full year rather than the 10 trading weeks measured by the 50-day moving average.

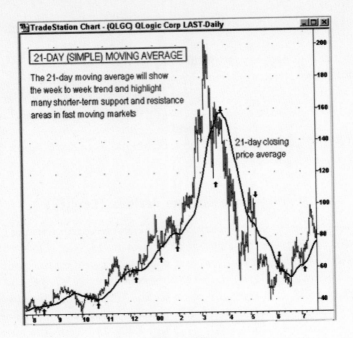

Figure 7.8

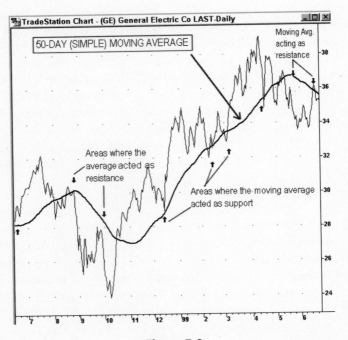

Figure 7.9

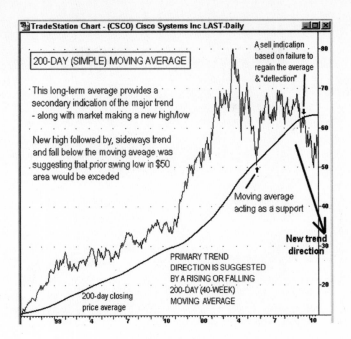

Figure 7.10

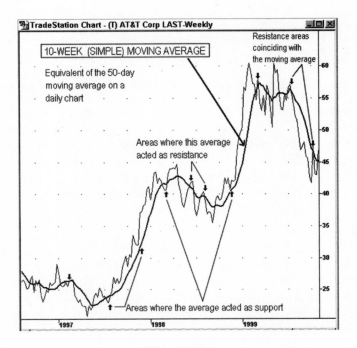

Figure 7.11

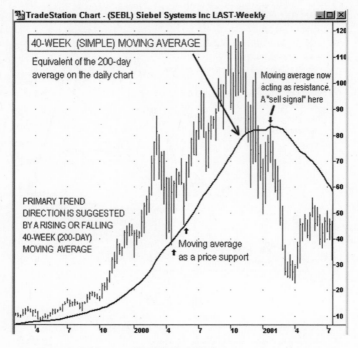

Figure 7.12

The Long-Term Trend and the 200-Day Moving Average

For defining the long-term (major) trend, the 200-day moving average is the moving average most often used in the U.S. stock market. The level of this average is followed by many investment-oriented stock market participants. Some chart books and commentators refer to the equivalent average in weekly terms, the 40-week moving average. One commonly accepted definition for the major overall stock market trend is that it is *up* as long as the 200-day moving average of the S&P 500 Index is trending higher and defined as being *down* as long as it is trending lower.

Some would view the major trend as shifting once the Index starts trading above or below the 200-day moving average, but the rule of thumb I employ is that this is a precursor of a long-term trend reversal, but that the definitive *signal* is given when the average itself turns up or down. Sometimes, its direction will be sideways for some time, in which case the price level of the Index as above or below the 200-day average would have to define the trend.

Support and Resistance Roles for Moving Averages

As discussed with trendlines, there is a *support/resistance* role reversal that also develops with moving averages. Take the example of where the level of the 200-day moving average of the S&P 500 stock index has been coinciding with a series of lows in the Index as stock prices retreat. If the Index has been holding above this moving average, the moving average is defining an area of ongoing price support. Suppose then that the S&P Index falls below its 200-day average, and, on the next rebound, rallies generally start reversing in the area of 200-day average and it *deflects* the rally. Price action relative to the moving average should be assumed, until otherwise resolved, to be a bearish sign of a significant trend reversal and that the average will now define an area of likely price resistance. What was support, the moving average, has *become* resistance—a similar dynamic to what is often seen with major trendlines. Stock investors may then want to consider reducing their participation in the market if prices continue falling, signaling a major trend reversal. In other markets, such as futures and FX markets, the 21-day and 50-day moving averages can play a similar role of defining support or resistance and sometimes, one then the other, in the same kind of role reversal.

An equivalent example in a bear market in stocks is an upside breakout above the 200-day moving average, perhaps after the 200-day average has been acting as resistance. When the S&P or Nasdaq indexes advance above this average, then fall back to it, only to rebound again, this is an alert for a possible bullish upside trend reversal. If other technical considerations also support this view, such as a major trendline penetration, and so on, it can provide a good reason to enter the market. If so, the *stop* or exit point at this juncture could be any daily or weekly *close* back below the moving average, or on a two to three percent intraday penetration of the moving average.

For futures markets, the 50-day moving average is going to be about as long as will be used due to the time duration of individual contracts, although a 200-day length might be used on a *continuous futures* price series. Common for individual commodities markets is the use of the 9- and 18-day moving average. You will find the moving average lengths that *work* best for the markets you are following by observation and experimentation.

When a market or individual stock begins a sideways consolidation or is contained within a trading range, the 50- and 200-day moving averages will, over time, flatten out. At this juncture the moving averages will act as a support area at times, then offer resistance at other times as can be seen in Figure 7.13. Difficulties can be presented in knowing whether to stay in a shifting trend like this. If prices are moving above or below a key moving average during these sideways trends or *nontrending* periods (per the more restrictive definition of *trend*), use of exit points based on moving averages can result in being *whipsawed*. Being whipsawed is a way of saying that soon after entry, there develops an opposite trend direction signal as closing prices *whip* back and forth or above and below the moving average(s) in question. To help avoid this frustrating situation, it's suggested to use whatever technical analysis tools are providing a clear direction, such as provided by the formation of any top or bottom patterns, *trendline* analysis, and Dow theory signals, or the secondary use of the key moving averages as *confirming* indicators only, as in Figure 7.14.

Moving Average Crossovers

Two moving averages are commonly used for "crossover" buy or sell indications. Two of the most popular moving average lengths employed in the

Figure 7.13

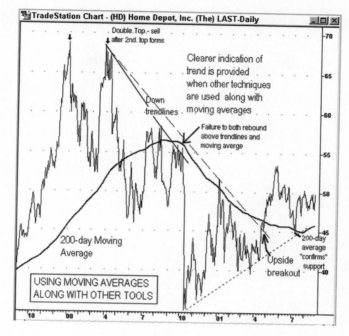

Figure 7.14

U.S. stock market, 50- and 200-days, have been already discussed as separate items. Used together, the shorter 50-day moving average is considered to suggest the initial stages of an uptrend by crossing above the longer-term 200-day simple moving average or a downtrend by a downside penetration—see Figure 7.15. The arrows show where the shorter-term moving average has crossed above or below the longer moving average. As long as the short moving average is above the long, it is an indication of upward momentum and suggests being in the market on the long side, especially if the other technical aspects to the market are bullish.

If a market was approaching a prior *top* that represented a major previous reversal point, this consideration would suggest a watchful attitude regardless of the moving average picture. The averages are, after all, lagging indicators whereas a prior top presents a *forewarning* of possible heavy resistance or selling interest. When, due to a price decline, there is a downside bearish *crossover* and the shorter average begins a period of being below the longer average, this is a suggestion to look at all the technical aspects of the trend and take action appropriate to your investment or trading plan (e.g., tightening stops, exiting long positions, selling short, etc.).

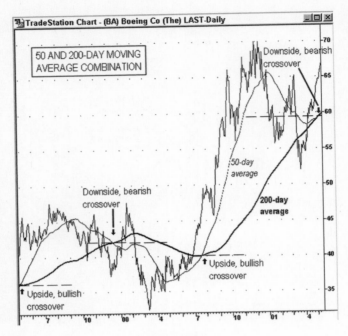

Figure 7.15

Popular moving average number combinations for the short-term are 5 and 9; a common default setting is also 9- and 18-period settings. Fifteen- and thirty-period (or forty) combinations are also used for a medium-term view. In stocks, the 50- and 200-day averages are most common. Figure 7.16 is a chart with a 9- and an 18-day combination applied. There are many crossovers shown in this figure, with a number of those leading to being "whipsawed." The trade was short-lived and incurred a loss as an opposite crossover developed relatively soon, as the shorter averages whipped back and forth, along with prices, before settling into any sustained trend.

Figure 7.17 shows the same stock as in Figure 7.16, for the same period, with better results, as a 13- and 30-day combination resulted in fewer, more profitable, trades. Some charting software packages allow *optimization* of the moving average lengths, as well as lengths for other indicators, for *profitability*. That is, for any time frame selected, the computer will go through all possible combinations of two moving averages from a selected *range* (e.g., from 9 to 50 or 30 to 200) to determine which crossover combination led to the most profitable results. There is a further discussion of optimization in a later introductory chapter on *trading systems*.

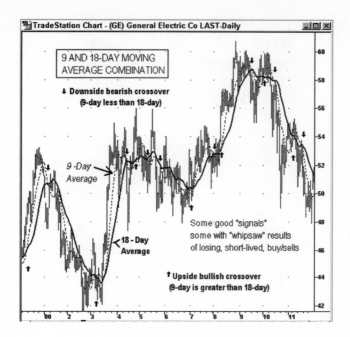

Figure 7.16

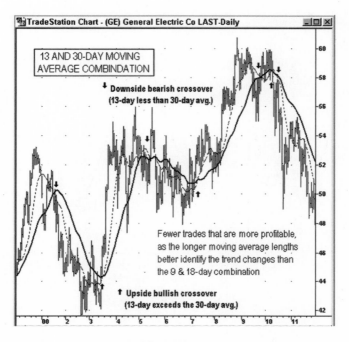

Figure 7.17

There are also moving average combinations that employ three moving averages, such as lengths of 4, 9, and 18 bars. The principle is similar, just that the shorter-term moving average must cross above the next one, which should in turn cross above the longest to generate a bullish crossover buy signal—or, cross below them in the case of a bearish downside crossover. The use of three moving averages would not appear to have an obvious additional benefit, but some shorter-term traders like the concept of an initial *alert* when the shortest crosses the next longer, or like to *scale* into multiple share or contract positions as multiple signals get generated as per the example in Figure 7.18.

Moving average *types* can be used in combinations, even when the averages are of the same time duration. A (front-end) *weighted* average will move faster than a *simple* (equally weighted) average. An initial alert or trade strategy is signaled when the weighted average changes direction and then *crosses* the simple average, with confirmation coming when the simple average also changes its up/down direction. Going back to Figure 7.7 provides an example of instances where 10-day weighted averages turned up or down first, then crossed above or below the slower moving simple aver-

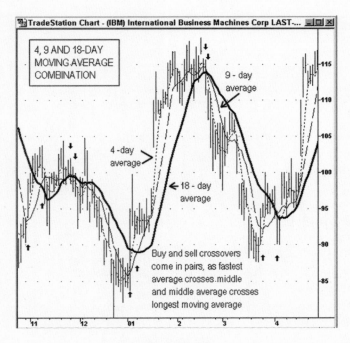

Figure 7.18

age of the same length. A more common strategy would be to weight the shortest of a system of two to three moving averages, to provide more of a hair-trigger alert that momentum or rate of price change is increasing or decreasing. The crossovers of the short weighted average with the other two provide a "get ready" and the middle average crossover with the longer average, a "get set, go" signal.

Moving Averages as Overbought/Oversold Indicators

The widening of the *spread* or point difference, between a shorter-term moving average and a longer-term one, is an indication that upside or downside momentum is strong. An example can be seen in Figure 7.15 when the 50-day moving average went far above the 200-day average. As can also be seen in Figure 7.15, the widening of this *spread* between the two averages did precede an eventual trend reversal. Market momentum can carry prices to highs not dreamed of when investments are taken—this was certainly the case in the megabull market of the late 1990s. Stay with the trend, but as it gets extreme do not get complacent and start planning how you are going to spend the profits. The market gives you what it gives you, not what you want it to. I have known investors who didn't get out of situations where they had huge profits because the amount wasn't quite enough to buy that vacation house, second car, or dream vacation just yet.

When prices of the major averages or stock sectors reach an historical extreme relative to long-term moving averages—for example, as seen in Figure 7.19—when the Nasdaq Composite, at its highest daily closing level, was well over 50 percent above its 200-day moving average. Such an extreme percentage *spread* also functions as an alert or warning that the market is at an overbought extreme, as I alluded to earlier in discussing how moving averages can function to alert us to extremes in momentum. Of course, the other possibility, besides the sharp reversal that occurred, was that a (sideways) consolidation would allow the 200-day average to *catch up* with the market. However, often one market extreme is followed by another. Certainly, the extreme situation described in Figure 7.19 could have put more market participants into a high alert of watchfulness for a trend reversal. The only uncertainty seemed to me to be *when* this would occur at the time, based on a knowledge of past market cycles and psychology.

When a market moves far above or below a long-term moving average, suggesting a very stretched or extreme market situation, such as

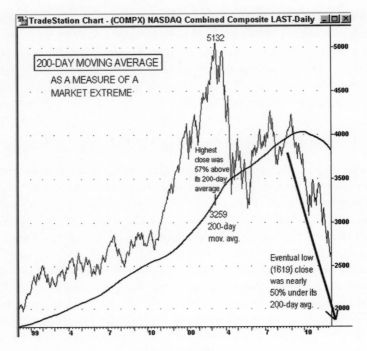

Figure 7.19

was the case with the Nasdaq at 5,000 in early 2000, it is time to go on high alert for signs of a trend reversal. Such extremes are relatively uncommon and not likely to persist. Moreover, it is not a situation to use the more conservative techniques related to prices falling below longer-term moving averages to trigger an exit, as a collapse from an extreme can be very sharp and steep. For example, waiting for the moving average to turn down or the use of a two moving average *crossover* to exit long positions, can risk a substantial portion of unrealized profits before these events occur. Strategies might include taking partial profits if prices cross below the 50-day moving average and again if prices cross below the 200-day moving average, but even that could be a long wait. I prefer especially to not wait for such a crossover to occur when there is a break of a significant *trendline* after the market is so *extended* above its long-term averages.

For any stock or other market, provided there is sufficient price history, it's wise to go back and look at prior major tops or bottoms to develop a feel for what is a usual or unusual price pattern relative to indicators like long-term moving averages. A sharp narrowing of the spread or *difference* between the shorter-term and longer-term moving averages can be an alert of *momentum* changes. Volume is another indicator to look at. If the market or particular stocks, sectors, or other items no longer have the same participation that put prices up so strongly, the average daily and weekly volume will taper off, especially on rallies.

In Figure 7.20, one of the first indications of the major top and subsequent trend reversal of one of the most prominent and important Nasdaq stocks, was provided by the narrowing *spread* or difference between the 21- and 40-week moving averages. The 21-week average had acted like a type of trendline, a "curved" trendline, as this average tracked the lows of a steep rise. As this average turned lower, prices fell below it, and the average itself crossed below the 40-week average, these events provided an early warning of the major reversal that followed. Also note that the weekly volume numbers fell off significantly during the sideways consolidation, but then begin to rise as the stock dropped under the averages shown.

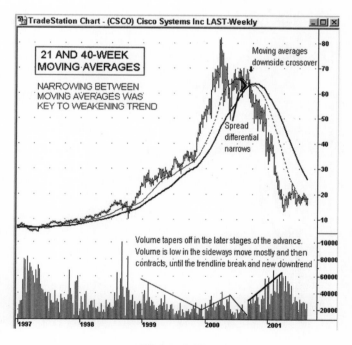

Figure 7.20

Moving Average Envelopes

Another significant means to see support and resistance levels and one that will help define specific price levels where a market may be overbought or oversold, is by the use of *moving average envelopes*. Moving average envelopes are formed from upper and lower lines that "float" at a set percentage above or below a particular moving average. My favorite moving average length to use to gauge the near-term trend is 21 days. The stock market, especially as represented by the S&P 500 Index, in an *average* market cycle and trend, will tend to see prices fluctuate in a range that is approximately three percent above or below this moving average. As we are interested in also seeing the high and low extremes relative to the envelope lines, *bar charts* are used. In a strong uptrend, this band or envelope can expand to four or five percent or more to contain within the envelope lines most of the highs and lows. Figure 7.21 shows a bar chart with a moving average envelope.

More volatile markets, stock averages, or individual stocks may regularly trade at 5 to 7 percent or more above or below the 21-day moving av-

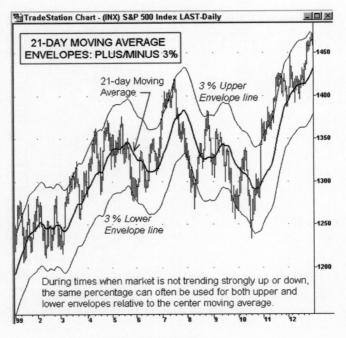

Figure 7.21

erage. The percentages best used as the envelope values, will vary from period to period. In a bull market, the upside rallies will usually extend to a greater percentage and the downside will be contained by a lesser percentage (e.g., 5% on the upside, 3% on the downside). Charting software will typically allow different numbers to be used on the upper envelope or band versus the lower envelope. It is important that the moving average, which is in effect the center line, should also be displayed as a key support and resistance area. Someone looking for trading opportunities, either just on the side of the trend, or on both sides of the market, can benefit from the use of the moving average envelope indicator. An investor looking for initial or additional entry buy points can often improve their entry point, if they wait for prices to dip to the lower envelope line. A seller should do the reverse and watch rallies for an approach to or above the upper envelope.

The following seven characteristics categorize the tendencies of market action and behavior that are commonplace relative to moving averages and upper and lower *envelopes*.

1. Determination of what moving average to use is somewhat arbitrary but is found by what *works* best in the most number of markets, which is a trial and error process and also develops through *experience*. The biggest variation is with the percentages above and below the moving average selected. I suggest starting with a 21-day moving average for most daily charts in stocks, most commodities, and for other markets. For a longer-term view and analysis, try a 50-day or 10-week average, with envelope sizes on weekly charts ranging from 10 percent to 20 percent. The direction of the trend determines whether the upper or lower envelope percentage should be larger.

2. A common starting point for the envelope size is three to five percent. The envelope size varies from trend to trend and market to market. For an envelope size that *works* best—for example, the percent figure that contains within it 90 percent of the price swings above and below the moving average—use three to five percent and expand or contract the envelope size as is appropriate for the chart.

3. If the last high was five percent above the moving average, keep the upper envelope line set at five percent—the next high will often reflect the same extreme. Conversely, if the last significant downswing low was three percent below the moving average, keep this figure as the lower envelope setting until market action otherwise dictates.

4. If prices cross above the moving average, assume that this line will act as *support* on pullbacks and the next rally will have the potential to advance to the upper envelope line. If the stock or other item is in an *uptrend*, the envelope line may act as a rising line of resistance for multiple rallies. The rally tops will *hug* the upper envelope line, but prices will tend to keep going up.

5. If prices cross below the center moving average, assume that this line will act as *resistance* on any rebounds and that downside potential is to the lower envelope line. If the trend is *down*, the envelope line may act as a falling support line and there may be multiple downswings that touch or hug the lower envelope line.

6. In an uptrend, buy declines to the lower envelope line. This area will both define where the stock or other item is both oversold and the specific price area that offers a potential buying opportunity. In a downtrend, sell advances to the upper envelope line. This area will help define where the market is both overbought and the specific price area that may be most opportune as a selling point.

7. Even if there is an extension of a price swing to above or below the envelope lines, the probability for a significant further move in that direction is limited, especially if the price swing is a countertrend move. At a minimum, there should be a reaction once prices are above or below the envelope line in question.

Figure 7.22 provides a further illustration of these points.

Bollinger Bands

Fellow market technician John Bollinger invented the Bollinger band envelope variation. Any reservation I have about their use focuses on it being hard to pinpoint a specific buying or selling area, as these bands expand or contract according to market *volatility*. This is, I suppose, both the technique's strength and its weakness.

Bollinger bands combine the envelope technique with a measurement of current or recent price *volatility* to determine the optimal placement of the upper and lower lines. Just as with envelopes, two *bands*—the convention is to call these lines "bands" to distinguish them from fixed percentage envelopes—are placed above and below a centered moving average, which is most often set, or *defaults* to 20 days. Unlike lines that are a fixed percent above or below the moving average, Bollinger bands are plotted two

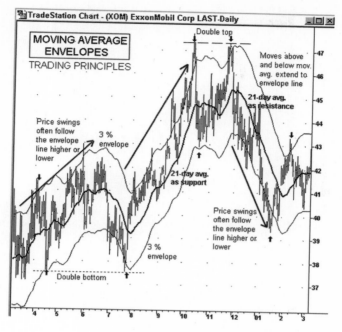

Figure 7.22

standard deviations above and below the average. See Figures 7.23 and
7.24 for examples of an item that was in a stable trend and another in a
more volatile period of wide-ranging price swings. In the former, the bands
are of a relatively narrow width and in the latter, significantly wider apart.

Standard deviation describes how prices are arrayed around an *average* value. One standard deviation is a set of values that contains approximately 70 percent of the price fluctuations that occur above and below the
moving average used in the Bollinger band calculation. Ninety-five percent
of the fluctuations will occur within two standard deviations of the moving
average in question. Since each Bollinger band is placed at a fluctuating
line that is equal to two standard deviations, 95 percent of all price action
will theoretically occur within the upper and lower lines. Each band represents, therefore, implied support or resistance. Price swings are unlikely to
be sustained above or below these lines for long.

Because of how they are constructed, Bollinger bands expand or contract in order to adjust to market *volatility* or the degree of price fluctuations at any given time. If prices are moving within a relatively narrow
price range, this is a situation of low (price) volatility. If prices are experi-

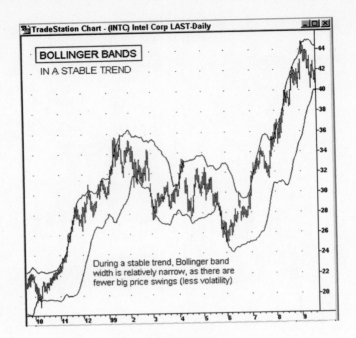

Figure 7.23

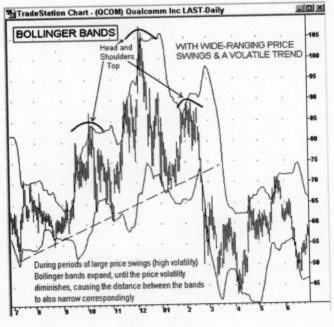

Figure 7.24

encing wide-ranging price movement, the bands expand to reflect the higher volatility that exists. If the bands are wide—and you can usually quickly see this visually in the pattern of price activity—the market is experiencing higher volatility. The lines then suggest where an extreme may be reached based on a more volatile and stronger recent price trend. If the bands are relatively narrow, the market is experiencing lower price volatility (narrower price swings) and the lines will intersect at upper and lower points that should mark the extremes for these quieter market conditions. As with envelope lines, they can be used on everything from intraday to daily to weekly charts, although the most common use is with daily charts.

SUMMARY—MOVING AVERAGES

Moving averages offer another powerful tool to supplement other technical analysis techniques that also help define the trend direction and pinpoint support and resistance areas. Moreover, moving averages highlight situations where a powerful trend puts prices at extremes well above or below what has come before. As markets experience a *pendulum* effect that often takes values from an *undervalued* to *overvalued* extreme, we also know that prices will tend to come back to an *average* rate of price increase or decrease sooner or later. This can be seen by the absolute distance of prices above or below longer-term averages and by the use of moving average envelopes, including Bollinger bands, which especially can help define short- to intermediate-term trading parameters. Moving averages are very useful in trending markets but do *lag* rather than *lead* price action. Moving averages will also visually demonstrate a nontrending or trading range market by a line that flattens out and moves in a sideways direction. For technical indicators that can work more effectively in a *trading range* market and can also predict the likelihood of a price reversal after a strong *trend*, we next examine indicators called *oscillators*.

OSCILLATORS—INTRODUCTION

A dictionary meaning of "oscillate" is "to swing backward and forward like a pendulum or to move back and forth between two points such as from a minimum to a maximum." This is exactly what the technical analysis indicator formula comprising an *oscillator* does—often, but not always, the minimum and maximum values are between 0 and 100. While the formulas may seem complex, what an oscillator measures is relatively simple. An oscillator measures market *momentum* or the rate of price change (e.g., a sharp run up or steep decline equals strong momentum). Oscillators help us seek out the strongest trends as they have the strongest momentum, just as weaker trends have a lesser rate of price change. The concept of momentum also leads to an analysis of the points where upside or downside momentum can no longer be sustained. As originally interpreted by Charles Dow, markets tend to have regular "oscillations" between cycles or periods of extremes—expressing the idea of a pendulum, where the two extreme points of the swing are, on the one hand, a condition where a market is considered to be oversold and the opposite condition, where a market is considered to be overbought. These are also points where a market is vulnerable to a trend *correction* or *reversal*, either on a short-, intermediate-, or long-term basis.

Oscillator Limitations

Overbought and *oversold* should always be thought of in relation to what time frame is being considered. Traders are interested in short- to intermediate-term reversal points, and investors are primarily concerned about a situation where a market is at a possible overbought or oversold extreme on a long-term basis. Overbought or oversold relate to a *potential* vulnerability to a reversal. However, a market can stay oversold or overbought for a relatively long period. It is also true that rapid and steep advances or declines are not sustainable for an unlimited period. A market *will* correct at some point after a steep rise or fall, but *when* is an open question in a strong trend. This is important because there may be a tendency to think that the first time or two an oscillator reaches an extreme reading, whether we are using a daily chart or a longer-term weekly or monthly chart, it is time to trade out of that stock or other item. However, we see many instances where the trend takes prices significantly higher or lower before there is a correction. Moreover, a correction may just turn out to be a sideways *consolidation* period, before there is yet another push in the same direction as before. Oscillators work well in terms of timing trend trades contrary to the most recent trend, by buying dips in a downswing and selling rallies in an upswing, especially in markets that are experiencing two-sided price swings rather than trending strongly in one direction.

The twofold nature of corrections is something to keep in mind always, as markets will tend to have either *price* or *time* corrections. A *price* correction is what is usually thought of as a "correction"—there is a countertrend move down in an uptrend or a countertrend move up in a down-trend. Markets can also correct by standing still. A *time correction* is where a strong trend in a market is followed by a sideways consolidation and will cause oscillators to reverse direction to a greater or lesser extent, depending on how long the sideways movement goes on. A *sideways* price move will *throw off* an overbought or oversold condition. Such a sideways consolidation in fact is a common occurrence in very strong trends and is often overlooked as a second possibility by analysts, traders, and investors as the alternative possibility to a *trend reversal*.

TYPES OF OSCILLATORS

Momentum Oscillators and Rate of Change

The *momentum* oscillator is a type of technical indicator that calculates and plots the net change, expressed in points, between the close of two periods. I should note that open, high, or low values could also be used for these and any other indicators like moving averages. It is necessary to set some number for the period being measured—10-day *momentum* would be today's close minus the close of 10 days ago—see Figure 7.25. A 10-hour or 10-week momentum could also be established provided the data is available. Measuring current prices versus earlier prices sheds light on the pace of a trend relative to whether it's slow or fast—if fast and steep, there is always also the possibility of a trend reversal. Examination of past reversals in that market is useful in identifying levels that represent overbought and oversold conditions, which is when momentum is very strong, either in an up or down direction.

The *rate of change (ROC)* oscillator shows virtually the same kind of change as the momentum model, only the scaling is different, as it's a fraction. The *ROC* indicator takes a current bar's price and divides by the price of x number of days ago (e.g., 10). The rate of change calculation creates a *ratio* rather than a price differential. An example of the ROC indicator is shown, along with the same length momentum oscillator for comparison, in Figure 7.26. The same item and time frame are used for both figures. You'll note on both types of oscillators, a middle line called the "zero" or *equilibrium* line. The concept of a zero or midpoint line indicates that readings above the line are a positive number, suggesting a bullish advancing rate of change, whereas readings below the midpoint line imply a bearish or declining momentum. In an uptrend, the current close

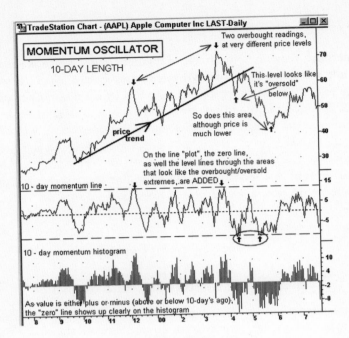

Figure 7.25

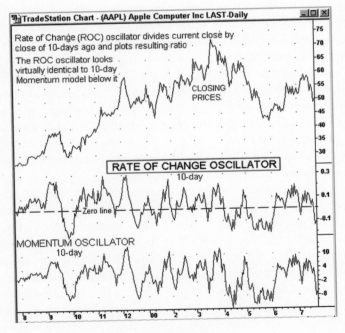

Figure 7.26

will generate a reading above or below the zero line, which is easily seen; this is not always the case on the price chart—especially in a sideways trend or in an area of *congestion* (i.e., where there is a cluster of closes around the same price).

Using Momentum and Rate of Change Oscillators

When either indicator is above the midpoint line and the line is rising at a steep rate, it provides a visual indication of strong upward momentum. When the rise of the line above the horizontal midpoint (zero) line shows a more moderate slope, the momentum indicated for that item is a more moderate one. When either of these oscillator type indicators have lines that are below the center line, the momentum indicated is more or less strong depending on the slope of the line. Some of the extremes noted on the chart examples in Figures 7.25 and 7.26 corresponded to tops and bottoms and some did not. The strongest trends will usually have the greatest extremes. As always, combining the analysis of a pullback in an oscillator line from an up or down extreme, with what is going on with *volume*, prior tops and bottoms, *moving averages*, and *trendlines* will provide ancillary or related clues about true reversals in the trend versus where the item is just registering an extreme reading.

Strictly speaking, a momentum or ROC crossover above the line (whether referred to as the midpoint, zero, or equilibrium line) is a bullish, or buy, indication. If a price drop pulls the indicator line below the midpoint line, this is a bearish, or sell, indication. Traders will use these signals in various ways. It may simply be to look for selling opportunities only when the line is at a high point relative to past weeks and to look for buying opportunities when the line is below the midpoint, indicating downward momentum and probably also at a low point extreme relative to the item's past history.

A shorter length selected for an oscillator, will result in a more sensitive indicator. Shorter time frames on daily charts, like 5- or 9-day periods, will generate both more fluctuations and more indications of overbought or oversold extremes. However, these shorter lengths are only potentially useful to short-term traders. Even traders who are geared to profit from smaller price swings will find that they can easily get *whipsawed* in their trading efforts. An example of being whipsawed is buying at what appears to be an oversold reading on the oscillator, only to witness a further drop. Generally, I suggest that investors use either a 20- (4-week) or 50-day (10-week) length at a minimum, to best gauge the secondary and primary trend momentum.

Historical Data Considerations for Oscillators

The specific levels that mark an overbought or oversold condition can only be judged in an "unbounded" oscillator by examining past extremes. Unbounded means there is not a preset scale with maximum limits such as from 1 to 100. This by necessity means examining a chart with some amount of price history, in order to see its past patterns and previous high and low points with that oscillator. There are *preset* levels that suggest overbought or oversold areas with other oscillators like the *relative strength index* or *RSI*. Even with the RSI, there is some degree of interpretation as to what constitutes the extremes at any given market phase. This interpretation is more wide open in the momentum and rate of change (ROC) indicators, and an overbought or oversold level is always relative to the period being examined. There are some who will attempt to set an objective measure for overbought and oversold areas, by specifying that only the readings that make up the highest and lowest 10 percent of all readings for the period examined will be used. I prefer the eyeball method and drawing a level line at the point where there are the most extreme peaks and troughs (similar to constructing trendlines), but this is also partly a reflection of years of experience, which facilitates a certain amount of intuitive feel for these parameters.

The longer the period of price history that is studied, the more that can be learned about the overbought/oversold parameters for a particular item in different types of markets. Technical analysis in general becomes more refined and useful when you have a greater amount of history to study. I sometimes used to be asked by readers of my weekly commentaries to look at a stock that was a recent initial public offering (IPO). I answered that even a year's history is rather short to do any meaningful analysis of that item. Better would be several years, within different degrees of up- and downtrends. Of significant importance is if the stock or other item has already had both major up and down market trends and whether this was also in the context of a major bull or bear market in stocks. However, a chart of between one and two years' duration will provide some useful information about what constitutes an area that appears to be overbought or oversold for this item.

Price Oscillators

Another unbounded oscillator is a *moving average–price oscillator* variation that subtracts a moving average from a prior price, rather than a current price from a past price, as in the momentum oscillator. Here the midpoint line will represent a level where the price is above or below the moving average and can be useful to quickly see any instance where current price levels are above or below some particular moving average.

Similar to this is what is usually called a *price oscillator*, which calculates and displays a line that represents the difference between a fast or short moving average and a longer or slower moving average. The moving averages themselves are not plotted. One approach to analyzing moving averages is to note the relative position of the two averages: If the shorter moving average is above the longer average, this makes for a *positive* price oscillator value and is generally bullish. If the shorter moving average is below the longer average, the value is a negative one and is generally considered to be bearish. This is another way of displaying the same information as is provided by two moving averages as lines on a price chart and seeing where the shorter crosses above or below the longer moving average—see Figures 7.27 and 7.28. As you will see in these chart figures, when the shorter moving average is above the longer, the differential line is above a midpoint or zero level line. When the shorter moving average is below the longer, the price oscillator line is below the midpoint line. You'll also note that this allows a faster and easier directional read, which is not always the case with trying to see the crossover of two lines when they are close together.

Moving Average Convergence–Divergence (MACD)

The well known *moving average convergence–divergence* indicator, most commonly referred to by its initials *MACD* (pronounced "macdee"), is a variation of the *price oscillator*. The MACD indicator is calculated by taking the difference between two exponentially smoothed moving averages of 12- and 26-days. Usually these are the only values ever used, although I would just note that Gerald Appel, the market technician who formulated the MACD indicator, suggested that a slightly different set of values should be used as a crossover *sell* signal. In my opinion, only a purist who relies heavily on this indicator need be concerned about using a variation for this purpose. I have not heard or seen anecdotal or empirical evidence that constructing the slight variation and applying it only in declining trends adds enough value to make it worth this complexity.

The MACD line is the difference between the two averages described, as the longer average (26) is subtracted from the shorter (12). A moving average of 9 periods then is calculated of this differential (the result of the subtraction), which is called the "signal line." A buy or sell signal is generated when

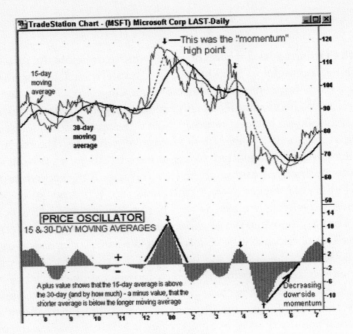

Figure 7.27

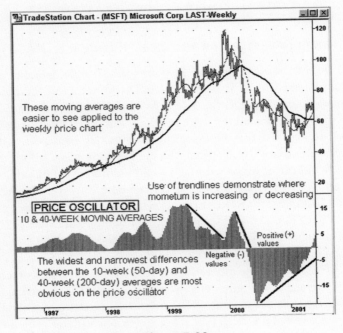

Figure 7.28

the MACD line crosses above or below the signal line. The exponential smoothing technique of the MACD line weights the most recent price changes more heavily and is therefore quicker to track the latest price changes. The signal line will be slower because it is a simple moving average of the last nine values of the MACD differential and is not weighted. There is usually a third line plotted, which is a *histogram* (vertical bars) used to show the difference above and below a midpoint line, of the difference between the MACD line and the signal line. This line is included in the standard MACD study to better see the points where there is an upside (the bars go above the midpoint) or downside (the bars move below the center or zero line) crossover. I sometimes dispense with the histogram part, as the zero line can be seen anyway. Use of the MACD indicator is shown in Figures 7.29 and 7.30.

A reason to include the *histogram* is that those bars will sometimes present a clearer picture of when the difference of the two moving averages is at the widest and narrowest points. It is often difficult to see these details, though, given how much is shown on the MACD indicator, which often occupies a small section below a price chart. It's common as you gain

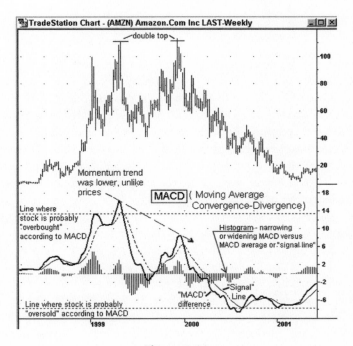

Figure 7.29

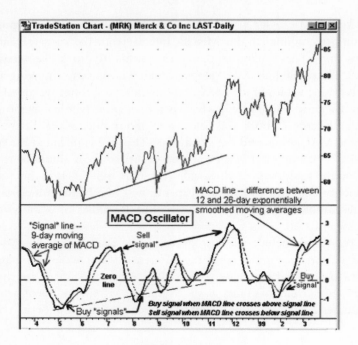

Figure 7.30

experience, to use indicators with minor modifications such as I describe, and relates to how much experience you have gained with it or the way in which you use the indicator. For example, if you use the MACD in order to generate a crossover buy or sell signal only, then the narrowing or widening of the histogram component of the indicator is less important.

The common use made of the MACD is similar to the *crossover* technique of other moving averages. A buy indication or signal is generated when the MACD line crosses *above* the slower signal line, and a sell indication is suggested when the MACD line crosses *below* the signal line. Use in this manner is like the trend following benefit that is gained from moving averages, where one, or a set of two moving averages define and track the dominant up or down trend. I suggest using MACD on either daily or weekly charts. Its usefulness on longer-term charts being a good measure of the momentum of the primary trend. Once there is a weekly chart buy or sell signal, I may take market action after the next MACD crossover signal on the daily chart that is in the same direction as the weekly signal.

The foregoing describes using MACD as a trend following indicator, but we are also focused here on its use as an *oscillator* and, as such, we can also employ it for buying when the market we are following is oversold and for a possible long exit or shorting, when the MACD suggests an overbought condition. "Overbought" and "oversold" zones are defined as being *above* or *below* the zero line, respectively. There are times when the two MACD lines are somewhat above the zero line and have crossover signals. Conversely, there are times when the MACD lines have crossover sell signals below the zero line. In general these are not seen as the best or strongest signals as shown in Figure 7.31. Some technicians also suggest that when *both* lines cross above or below the zero line, this is *confirmation* of the oversold buy or overbought sell signals described.

When the two MACD lines get unusually far above or below the zero lines, this relative position and distance from the midpoint or *zero* line can in itself be a strong added indication of an overbought or oversold extreme. However, as with the other *unbounded* oscillators, there is no *preset* area or position on the right-hand (MACD line) scale that suggests that a market is in a greater or lesser degree of *overbought* or *oversold*. The RSI, as we'll see, has a scale that goes only to 100, with an overbought zone by convention set that begins at 70. So a reading of 90, for example, is very extreme.

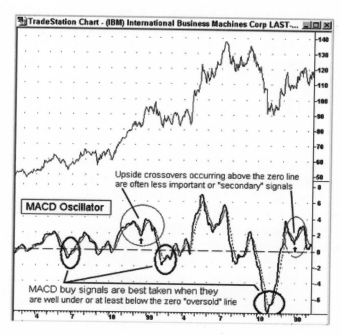

Figure 7.31

With unbounded indicators like the MACD oscillator where its values range up or down limited only by how far one average moves in relation to the other, it's necessary to look at and rely on past high and low readings of the MACD at prior market tops and bottoms as guides to the current situation.

The Relative Strength Index (RSI)

The *RSI*, as well as the *stochastics* indicator, are oscillators that are constructed in such a way that they are statistical models with *normalized* values, which relate to the indicators having a set *scale* that goes from a fixed point on the low end (0) to a fixed point on the upper (100). Mr. Welles Wilder developed the relative strength index—usually called the "RSI." A simple way to understand the RSI is that it is a *ratio* (one number divided by another) that compares an average of the up closes to the down closes for a specified period. There is only one variable, which is the *length* or number of periods (e.g., hours, days, or weeks). The common RSI default or preset value for length is usually either 9 or 14. The relative strength index calculations will be based only on the number of closes specified as the length setting. The reason for the widespread use of either 9 or 14 is mostly a matter of convention. A setting of 9- or 14-days does not represent an even number of 5-day trading weeks. Nevertheless, 9 and 14 are the most common default settings for *length* and there is a repository of experience among users of the RSI with these settings. The most commonly used setting to represent an oversold reading is 30 and below and 70 and above to suggest an overbought condition.

Optimum length settings are also a function of your time horizons relative to trading or investing. Five to nine for the RSI length is more appropriate for the minor trend and short-term trading. A length setting of 14 or 21 for daily charts is generally appropriate for evaluation of the *relative strength* of the secondary trend. My preference is to use an 8-week period for an RSI indicator applied to a weekly chart. Eight represents a two-month period or one-sixth of a year, which will usually provide a relevant picture of the secondary trend. While it may be necessary to go to a 12-to-16-week setting on the weekly chart in some very strong and prolonged trends, to best gauge overbought or oversold conditions on an intermediate-term basis, an RSI setting of 8–10 on a monthly chart usually provides useful information on the major trend.

RSI is derived by calculating the average number of points gained on up closes, during the period selected (e.g., 14), then dividing this result by the average point decline for the same number of bars. This ratio is "RS" in a 14-period formula for RSI or 100 – 100/1 + RS. RS = the average of 14-days' up closes divided by an average of 14-days' down closes. Every up close during the period is added, with this sum divided by the number of bars that had up closes, to arrive at a simple average. Every down close during the same period is added, with this sum divided by the number of bars that had down closes. If 10 of 14 days had up closes, the result of this division is a ratio that rises rapidly. Subtraction from 100 of the result of the division is what makes for the normalized scale of 1 to 100. Figures 7.32 through 7.35 demonstrate different facets of using the RSI oscillator.

In a period of a rapid and steady advance the RSI will reach levels over 70 rather quickly, and RSI can then remain above 70 for some period of time. The reverse is true in a decline, as readings under 30 are seen. In such situations, such as the late 1990s strong bull market, there was little value in selling stocks whenever the RSI suggested that they were at overbought extremes. Once the RSI retreats from such high levels, this can offer an alert that the trend may be reversing. It is also true that relatively brief sideways consolidations or even a minor countertrend movement will

Figure 7.32

Figure 7.33

Figure 7.34

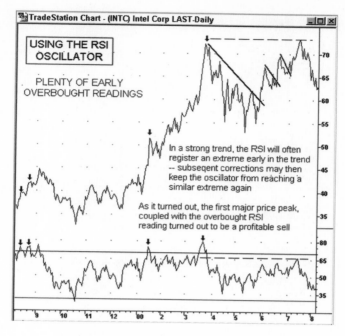

Figure 7.35

cause the RSI reading to move out of the preset 70:30 extreme zones and fall below 70 or rebound back above 30. Once a strong trend continues, the RSI can quickly get back into oversold or overbought territory again, but often, intermittent and minor corrections keep the RSI readings out of the extreme ranges.

In a strong up trend, it is often advisable to use longer length settings of the RSI—for example, 14 to 21 on daily charts and 10 to 16 on weekly charts. Defining "overbought" as a level above 70 such as in the 80 to 85 zone and in a strong down trend changing to a lesser oversold setting is also appropriate such as at or below 20. Changing the default setting for length varies the number of overbought/oversold *signals*, as does changing your setting for what constitutes an overbought and oversold extreme to an area that has been reached in the past as a high and low RSI reading— see Figure 7.36.

In market situations where there are very steep rises or declines, RSI serves a useful function in alerting you to a potentially volatile or high-risk situation. At a minimum, RSI readings under 30 and over 70 warn you of the potential high risk or unfavorable risk-to-reward balance in initiating

Figure 7.36

new long or short positions. If you already have a position, such extremes may be an occasion to tighten stops or take partial profits. While it is high risk, traders often do short-term trades that probe the short side in an over-bought situation or the long side in an oversold condition. Here, making additional use of *channel* lines, if available, is valuable for finding specific price areas in which to put on such countertrend trades.

A common situation is where there is a strong initial price swing, then a period of consolidation, such that the RSI stays within the 30 to 70 bound-aries. While RSI levels are in this *normal* zone, the RSI is of less practical use for trading. More value is gained in using the RSI in a market that develops a well-defined trading range. If prices falter in an area of prior highs, accompa-nied by even one day when the 14-day RSI is over 70, this indicator gives an added indication to sell in a prior resistance area. In an area of prior relative lows, accompanied by even 1 day with an oversold 14-day RSI reading at or under 30, the indicator provides some technical reinforcement for buying while prices are in a likely price support zone. The use of indicators to *con-firm* other technical developments relating to prior highs and lows or such things as price reversals at trendlines, is one of their most useful aspects. A *rounding* or *rectangle* bottom coupled with an oversold RSI reading would be a good technical validation for purchasing, especially if prices also broke out above a trendline. Trendlines may also be applied to a series of lower RSI highs or higher RSI lows, with the same implications for a breakout above or below the line. This may lead or confirm similar price action. Of course, the RSI is based on price changes, so the RSI will at times trace out patterns that are similar to what is being seen on the price chart. However, sometimes there is a good definition of a predictive pattern only on the RSI, as in Figure 7.37.

For investment purposes, when the RSI or other oscillators suggest that a market is overbought on a long-term basis, this may not imply doing anything to significantly alter your long-term investments just because of these extremes. However, this situation should suggest taking a more watchful approach and doing your homework diligently as regarding any other collaborative technical signs of a top. Taking strategic precautions like raising exiting stop points to just below relevant long-term trendlines and/or moving averages in case they signal a reversal, can help protect some, or the bulk of, unrealized long-term profits. This strategy should, at a minimum, keep you from being swept up in the euphoric final stages of

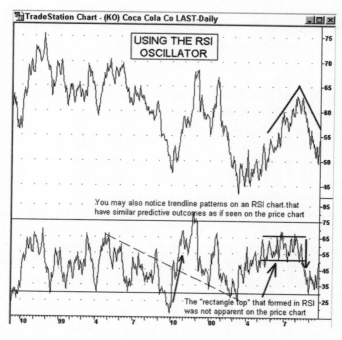

Figure 7.37

major bull markets and adding to your investments in the final bull market phase. If nothing else, looking at the overbought extremes reached in prior bull markets and the resulting decline that followed will serve as a visual reminder that the market works in predictable reoccurring cycles in terms of moving from *undervalued* to *overvalued* extremes and back again.

The Stochastics Oscillator

Stochastics works in a complementary fashion to the RSI oscillator and shows much the same in the way of momentum strength, as well as areas where a market will tend to reach a high or low *extreme*. However, sometimes one indicator shows something that the other similar but different indicator does not. If I could only use one or another oscillator, I would favor the RSI, but I like using them both for slightly different reasons. The stochastics indicator, sometimes called the *stochastics process*, was popularized by George Lane. The most common lengths used are the same as the RSI, either 9- or 14-periods (number of trading sessions), and the stochastics scale also ranges from 0 to 100. The common stochastics *default* oversold and overbought levels are pegged at 20 and 80, due to its having more wide-ranging fluctuations. The stochastics indicator is composed of two lines, rather than one. A slower line called the "percent D" (%D) line is a simple moving average of the faster "percent K" (%K) line. As with the MACD, the two lines of varying speeds lead to *crossovers* that generate buy and sell *signals*—see Figures 7.38–7.40.

Unlike the RSI, which is composed of a ratio of an average of up closes and down closes—which makes this indicator slower in moving up and down—the stochastics model looks at the current price in relation to the highest high or lowest low in the period being measured. Stochastics plots the current close in relation to the price range over the length set for this indicator and gives this a percentage value. The initial calculations for a stochastic of 14 days are twofold, establishing a *fast* and *slow* line. The fast line or %K formula is 100 − (the close minus the 14-day low) divided by (the 14-day high − the 14-day low or the *price range*). The "slow stochastics" variation of the basic stochastics formula applies a *smoothing* calculation to slow down the speed of the movement of the line, hence the name. The important thing to remember is not this alphabet soup, but the fact that the slow version of the stochastics oscillator (*slow stochastics*) is the version that is in the most common use and is most likely what you will be using, if you choose the *stochastics indicator* to apply to a price chart. If a choice is given, select slow stochastics.

The key concept relative to the stochastics oscillator is that in any trend

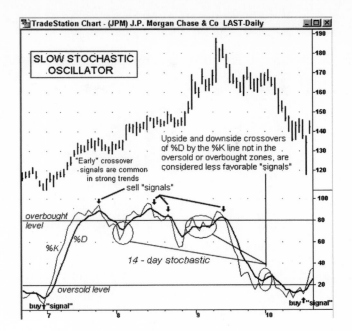

Figure 7.38

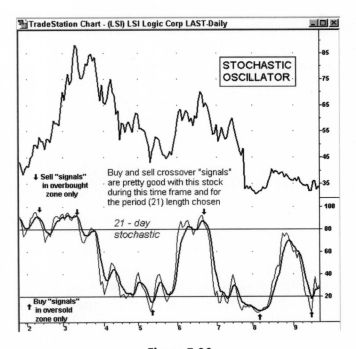

Figure 7.39

261

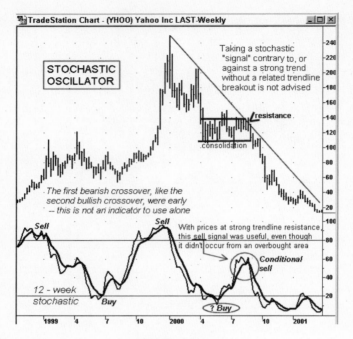

Figure 7.40

of x periods, especially one that is accelerating, prices will move away from the lowest low or highest high, at an increasing rate and this is what the stochastics oscillator is showing visually. If the upside or downside acceleration is especially strong, the two stochastics lines will reach an extreme, usually defined as a reading of 20 or below, or 80 and above, on its percentage scale. At a (slow) stochastics reading of 80 and above, the rate of price increase is thought to be too steep to be sustainable at the same rate of upside momentum and suggests some likelihood that the market in question will undergo a correction. At or below a reading of 20, the rate of decline is relatively steep and is considered to be unsustainable or unlikely, without a corrective rebound or sideways move.

Buy and sell crossover signals are considered to be optimal if they occur in the overbought (above 80) and oversold (below 20) zones, respectively. There will be instances of crossovers that occur in the middle of these ranges and these instances should not be utilized unless there are compelling other technical considerations that are guiding you—for example, deflection at an important trendline—see Figure 7.40.

The most frequent use made of the stochastics indicator is to serve as a model to show price momentum visually and as an overbought/oversold indicator. Stochastics, as well as the RSI and MACD—think of these as the *Big Three* of technical indicators, certainly of the *oscillator* type—are also worth their weight in gold for the occasional divergent buy or sell signal given when the indicator does not confirm a new high or low, in line with price action. There will be more on bullish and bearish *divergences* in the next chapter. Due to the importance and great usefulness of divergences in occasionally signaling a major trend reversal ahead of their occurrence, such nonconfirmations are worth treating as a separate topic and being a chapter in themselves.

OSCILLATOR USE ON LONG-TERM CHARTS

I tend to use stochastics somewhat less on weekly charts. I do suggest monitoring stocks or other financial items of interest such as bonds, futures, and FX markets, with at least one of the three major oscillators on a weekly and monthly basis. I tend to use RSI and MACD with longer-term charts by habit and keep such a selection *open* in my charting application so that I am reminded regularly of the longer-range momentum trend, and if the oscillator in question is at an extreme and possibly suggesting a buy or sell *signal*. The RSI tends to do this by climbing above or below the overbought or oversold levels, then *reversing* direction.

Whether seen by use of stochastics, RSI, or MACD, once price action registers at an overbought or oversold extreme, there is simply a greater *probability* of a correction or trend reversal at some point. With the ease of switching from charting one time frame to another—for example, going from daily to weekly—it's easy to retain the indicator and see what the overbought/oversold or momentum picture looks like when you are viewing the bigger picture weekly or monthly charts. I know *day traders* who also want to be regularly reminded of the longer-term overbought/oversold picture for the markets they trade. A picture is really worth 1,000 words, which is why looking at many chart examples is so useful. You tend to learn or progress in technical analysis by looking at charts, a lot of them and over time. Time is what brings the reoccurring cycles in the market and the valuable observation of the different types and phases of bull and bear markets.

Money Flow: A Hybrid Indicator Using Price and Volume

Blending price and volume analysis is the *money flow* oscillator, involving a formula for gauging momentum not unlike the RSI. This indicator incorporates volume information so this data has to be available—which, of course, will not usually be the case with intraday charts.

The money flow indicator calculates an indexed value based on price and volume for the number of bars specified in the input length. Calculations are made for each bar with an average price greater than the previous bar and for each bar with an average price less than the previous bar. These values are then indexed to calculate and plot the *money flow*. The use of both price and volume provides a different perspective from price or volume alone and this oscillator is of potential interest from that perspective and for identifying periodic overbought and oversold conditions, although this occurs less frequently than momentum models that use price only—see Figure 7.41.

INCREASING VELOCITY IN MARKETS

One fortunate thing for technical analysis in the new millennium may be that financial markets cycles (at least in the late 1990s) are occurring at a faster pace. Stock market movements during this period were more like the com-

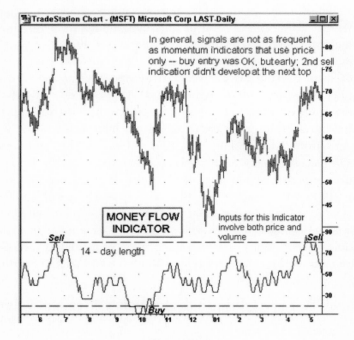

Figure 7.41

modities markets of earlier decades. If this continues it will mean that diverse chart patterns set up more frequently as the cycles, as in the futures markets, become more *compressed*—as is the case with an asset class that includes perishable items or ones requiring storage and "carrying" costs—where it was more likely you didn't have to wait decades to see what a major bull or bear market looked like. Of course, a major bull market in one asset class, whether in commodities, real estate, or bonds, is not unlike a major bull market in another, as all such market cycles are driven by similar human and *supply and demand* processes.

SPECIALTY INDICATORS—U.S. EQUITIES

The Advance/Decline (A/D) Line

This indicator, in widespread use in the U.S. stock market, can be calculated on both a daily and weekly basis and is the most basic and widely used indication of *breadth* in the major three U.S. stock exchanges (i.e., the New York Stock Exchange, the Nasdaq exchange, which is electronic, and the American Stock Exchange). Breadth is the calculation of how many stocks are advancing on any given day or week versus how many are declining and therefore concentrates solely on the *breadth* of participation in all stocks trading on an exchange.

Construction of the advance/decline line is calculated by subtracting the number of stocks declining on any given day, from the number advancing relative to the prior close. When more stocks are moving up than are moving down, this line is advancing (i.e., it has a positive slope and its direction is higher) and vice versa in a declining trend. These figures do not take into account stocks that were *unchanged* on the day or week, but only those up or down from the prior close.

The value of the A/D line always begins from some fixed starting point, and this means that the initial value begins at 0. What is most relevant in the advance/decline figure is the *slope* of the line, not the absolute cumulative value. Studying the direction of the A/D line is a means to determine whether there is *broad* participation in a rally or decline. Fewer and fewer stocks may in fact be carrying prices higher, as (1) the minority that are going up, are going up more in price than the stocks that are not in an arithmetic average like the Dow Jones or (2) are stocks that are weighted heavily in capitalization-weighted indexes such as the S&P 500 and Nasdaq Composite indexes.

When fewer and fewer stocks are participating in an advance, this fact will show up in a lagging *advance–decline line*, especially on a weekly basis. A/D charts are seen on some of the business media channels, but not often on web sites or via charting software. Ability to calculate and display the A/D figure may require that you have both the data and the ability to create a *customized* indicator, that is, one that is not standard.

The McClellan Oscillator

This oscillator will be applicable to equities markets that have a substantial number of individual stocks that trade actively. The McClellan oscillator also provides an indication of the trend in market *breadth* and is presented in a familiar way, as a (smoothed) difference between the number of advancing and declining stocks on the NYSE. It was developed by Sherman and Marian McClellan, as mentioned in their *Patterns for Profit*. Because of the nature of momentum, a strong bullish trend is accompanied by a large number of stocks going up. A weakening bull market is signaled by a smaller number of stocks making large advances in price, as discussed already with the A/D line. The McClellan indicator is another way to measure whether the broadest number of stocks are participating in the rallies. By participation, I mean a good majority of all the stocks in that average or index are also going up consistent with the trend of higher prices.

Buy indications are given when the McClellan oscillator falls into an oversold area, which is defined as –70 to –100, and then turns up. Sell signals are generated when the McClellan oscillator rises into the overbought zone of +70 and +100, and then turns down—turning down being the actual signal. When the oscillator is above +100 or falls below –100, it is a sign of an extremely overbought/oversold market—such readings can be associated with powerful bull or bear market trends. The rule of thumb with such extreme readings is to assume that the existing trend has staying power for only another couple of weeks or somewhat longer. Like the MACD and stochastics models, the McClellan oscillator is best employed looking for upside and downside crossovers, from within an overbought/oversold area. There are often crossovers, for example, in the slow *stochastic* that does not occur in either its oversold or overbought zones. In a similar fashion, the signals that occur in the middle ranges of the McClellan oscillator are best ignored without compelling other evidence of a technical nature.

Arms Index (TRIN)

Another popular stock market indicator is often described as the "TRIN" (TRading INdex). Its proper name is the "Arms Index," after technical analyst Richard Arms. The Arms Index brings in volume to its formula so is a *hybrid* indicator, with price and volume components. *TRIN* is a common *ticker symbol* for the Arms Index for the NYSE market, *NASTRIN* for the Nasdaq market. The Arms Index, while a widely followed technical indicator, does not mean that most stock market investors are aware of how this index is calculated. As with any other indicator that is popular with *trader* types, the Arms Index has proven to be useful in showing market buying extremes on a short-term basis, and this is enough knowledge for most.

The Arms Index indicates whether *volume* is flowing into *advancing* or *declining* stocks. Put another way, the index shows whether more of the total volume is advancing (up) volume or whether more of the total volume is declining (down) volume, for all stocks on that exchange. As mentioned, there is a version for both the NYSE and the Nasdaq, and the Arms Index number for any given day is fairly easy to find, especially from *live* or end-of-day data vendors. The cable business sites and certain investing-related web sites like the Wall Street Journal Online (WSJI) will often provide the Arms Index, or TRIN, reading for the current day. If more volume is associated with declining stocks on any given day, that day's Arms Index will wind up being *above* 1. If more volume is associated with advancing stocks than declining stocks, the Arms Index will register *under* 1, at the close— see Figures 7.42 and 7.43 for examples. The Arms Index is calculated over the course of the trading day, but the close is primarily what is of interest and the daily reading is displayed as a (close-only) *line* chart.

Extremes in the Arms Index have an *inverse* relationship to the market. An inverse relationship is one of opposite actions (e.g., if interest rates go up, bond prices go down and vice versa). *High* Arms Index readings, well above 1, indicate heavy selling pressure. If Arms Index closes above 1 in NYSE stocks (above 2 in the Nasdaq) persist over a few or more days, this is associated with a likelihood that the market is oversold, perhaps near a bottom, and might soon turn up—in this sense the Arms Index functions as a *contrary indicator*. This is the idea that if everyone is selling, it might be the time to buy. It depends on the circumstances, but when either buying or selling activity predominates, it gets over done, hence the terms overbought or oversold. Arms Index readings well under 1 in both the NYSE and Nasdaq markets, occurring for a number of days such as in a two-week period, has not been seen to be as

Figure 7.42

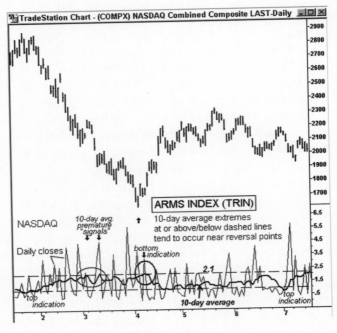

Figure 7.43

correlated to major market *tops*. I have noticed that 10-day averages around .95 seem to be associated with peaks and have preceded many downside reversals, but this doesn't appear to pinpoint market turning points as well as when the readings spike up for a while.

To better define the overall selling or buying pressure, use of a moving average of the daily Arms Index figure can be used for analysis and projections of the longer-term market trend. A meaningful market statistic for NYSE stocks comes from fellow technical analyst Peter Eliades and involves his study of the Arms Index over past years when the 10-day average has had at least a one-day reading above 1.50. When the 10-day NYSE Arms Index has gotten to this kind of extreme, the stock market has moved significantly higher in the months after it occurred. Eliades, who is an avid historian of market "cycles," has noted that in the 40 years prior to May 2001—there has been another instance since then, as of this writing—a 10-day NYSE daily Arms Index average above 1.50 occurred only 12 times and preceded major market bottoms. This is not to say that we could not see future exceptions to this past pattern, such as in a prolonged bear market, but the prior record suggests paying attention to this kind of heavy selling extreme.

It appears that a 10-day reading for the Nasdaq Arms index has to be slightly above 2 (e.g., 2.1) to suggest that the Nasdaq may be due for a good-sized rebound. As indicated, the 10-day average has been the most predictive for long-term trend changes and is therefore of the most potential interest to investors. More trading oriented individuals could experiment with a simple average of the prior 3–5 days.

CUSTOM INDICATORS—EQUITIES

Net A/D Oscillator

With charting software that allows *manual* entry of the daily net difference between advancing and declining stocks, applying a 10-day simple moving average to the resulting daily figure creates an oscillator-type indicator, useful in suggesting when the market is overbought or oversold, also in terms of breadth considerations. What I call the *net A/D oscillator* has been an excellent tool in predicting possible market turning points, as seen in Figures 7.44 and 7.45, which are calculated based on the Nasdaq composite stocks.

If 2,100 Nasdaq stocks advance and 1,700 stocks decline on the day, the net difference is + 400; if 1,700 advance and 2,100 decline, the net A/D

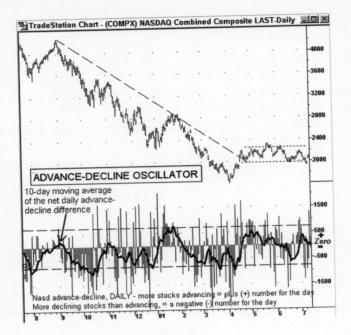

Figure 7.44

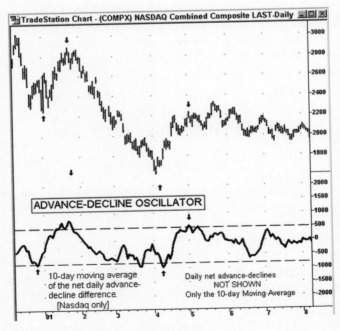

Figure 7.45

figure that day is − 400. The 10-day average of these daily figures needs only level lines placed so that they touch the area where price peaks and bottoms have been made in prior months—these become the oversold/overbought zones. Depending on the dominant trends, the levels that mark the extremes will change over time, like the other unbounded oscillators. Different market phases and cycles cause this model to shift in what could be considered to be overbought on the high end and what area tends to constitute oversold on the low end.

Credit goes to fellow technical analyst Helene Mistler for bringing this technical study to my attention in her technical analysis column for theStreet.com. This simple indicator, when it has reached extremes, has closely preceded many key secondary and primary market bottoms and tops. Due to the significant divergence in the two major market averages of recent years, the Nasdaq and NYSE, it is like mixing apples and oranges to combine the net A/D figures from the two exchanges, so one should be computed for each exchange.

Advancing Volume Indicator

Volume, as I've said before, will typically precede price. Before either major index gets to a price area that will be perceived as offering *value* after corrections occur, there will typically be a *contraction* of trading activity (volume) to a similar and reoccurring level. This occurrence will tend to occur at or near the starting point to most substantial and sustained market rallies.

The most significant volume figure, in my estimation, is *up* or *advancing* volume, a count of all shares bought on *up ticks*, or at a price higher than the preceding transaction. *Up volume* is a true test of buying interest as it reflects willingness to pay up for stocks. Shown in Figures 7.46 and 7.47, as the lower indicator, is a line measuring the 10-day moving average of *advancing volume* for Nasdaq, one of the two major U.S. equities exchanges. In the years shown, when the 10-day moving average of Nasdaq up volume shrank to between 500 and 575 million shares, and then turned up, market upturns followed or coincided with it. For any given similar period in terms of the type of bullish, bearish, or nontrending period, this 10-day average up volume number will tend to contract or drop to a particular baseline figure before the market index is in a position to turn up again. This *baseline* can be seen readily in Figures 7.46 and 7.47. The specific area will not be the same in every market cycle so it has to be viewed in terms of recent months to best determine what the extreme is.

Particular levels of *declining volume* on a 10-day average basis has not

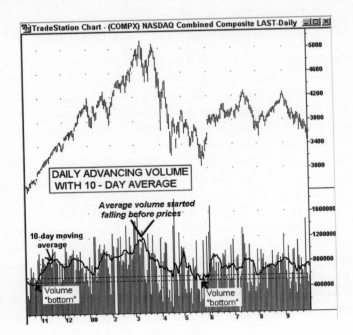

Figure 7.46

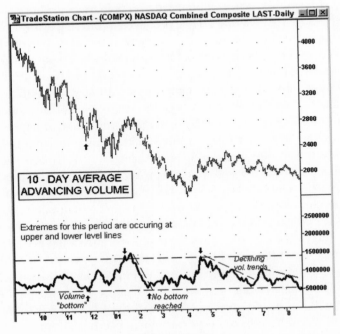

Figure 7.47

proven to be especially predictive for market tops, nor does the market appear to peak reliably at a particular level of up volume, contrary to the correlation to market bottoms. However, in Figure 7.47, you note the two market tops were similar in terms of their 10-day average up volume (at, or a bit above, 1.4 billion shares). At tops, when the 10-day advancing volume line turns down, whether from an area where it has peaked before, the downward trend of the line is a good secondary indication that prices will continue.

SENTIMENT

Charles Dow was the first observer we know about who correctly noted how *public* participation, mostly as buyers of stocks, is most pronounced at major tops. He also observed that the public was decidedly disinterested in stocks at market bottoms. The opposite role, of "buying stocks when no one wanted them and selling when everybody did," was primarily occupied by the most highly knowledgeable and well-capitalized market professionals. While the term "sentiment" was not employed then as a descriptive term for the "public's" bullish or bearish *bias*, this was what Dow was describing.

THEORY OF CONTRARY OPINION

The beginning of what became known as the *theory of contrary opinion* was born with Charles Dow with his idea that, characteristically, when the opinion of the most people involved in a market is predominantly one-sided (bullish or bearish), this extreme corresponds to major market reversals *opposite* to the prevailing opinion. There are now well-established polls of market professionals to gain a weekly (sometimes daily) idea of whether they are of a predominantly bullish, bearish, or neutral opinion (e.g., the Investor's Intelligence survey). When this professional group gets more than 60 percent bullish, it is at a level that has tended to precede market tops. The American Association of Individual Investors (AAII) also conducts a weekly survey of its members as to being bullish, bearish, or neutral. Overbought levels appear when the AAII bullish percentage is greater than 60 percent. This number tends to go a bit higher at market tops than the Investor's Intelligence figure, but otherwise it seems the market "pros" are not appreciably better at market forecasting as a group than are their public peers. On the other hand, those with bearish convictions have only to climb above 40 percent in both surveys to suggest a market bottom. Perhaps it's unfashionable to be bearish or convinced that stock prices will decline. We know that there is a generally optimistic attitude in the United States or people think that optimism, equated with bullishness, is a valued trait. Both the Investor's Intelligence and AAII survey numbers are quoted in some of the financial press (e.g., *Barron's*).

Call/Put Ratio and Sentiment "Extremes"

The opinion among many market professionals is that the "individual investor" as a collective body, is typically the most bearish at market bottoms and most bullish at market tops. Nowhere is this seen more accurately than in the options markets which have a preponderance of individuals who make bets, so to speak, on the future direction of the market by buying either calls or puts. This activity, if measured in a way to reflect extremes of over (or under) confidence most associated with major tops (or bottoms), has been remarkably accurate in preceding secondary reversal points in the stock market by anywhere from 1–5 days, at least as measured by what the S&P 500 Index does.

An overbought/oversold indicator can be based on this concept by measuring high levels of bullish optimism as reflected in call activity, or bearish pessimism as reflected in put option activity. Market reversals tend to occur not long after such extremes of collective opinion or sentiment. One method I've used to create a gauge of this trader *sentiment* is by a simple calculation of total daily call to put volumes, using the resulting ratio as a type of *sentiment* oscillator—one that shows extremes at major market tops (2.5 and above) and bottoms (a reading of around 1). These extremes happen repeatedly, not necessarily *often*, prior to many significant market reversals. The volume numbers used are the daily total of equities call volume versus the total equities put volume on the Chicago Board Options Exchange (CBOE), by far the biggest options exchange.

This indicator is a custom one and not the standard put to call (*put/call* reading) ratio widely reported. For example, a put/call reading of .50 is where total put volume represented 50 percent of that total day's options trading. This number is almost always a fraction, as call volume usually dwarfs put volume, and includes *stock index* options. In my variation, I divide the larger number, call volume, by the smaller put volume figure to arrive at a whole number, and index options volume is *excluded*. Excluding these volume numbers is based on the idea that use of individual stock options activity takes out some of hedging activity related to index options, or use of options as insurance against a general drop in stock values.

Activity in individual stock calls and puts tends to better reflect the speculative nonhedging use of options—although there is covered call writing going on also—and this is the activity I most want to isolate. Options trading reflects active conviction about the future direction of stock prices ("putting your money where your mouth is") and therefore has significant *conviction* attached to it, which is what market *sentiment* is all about.

There is no apparent need to average this daily number, as even a 1-day reading at an extreme has frequently *preceded* turning points on reversals in the market. Anytime an indicator extreme reliably predates, even by a few days, secondary lows and highs and, sometimes, primary tops and bottoms, it is an excellent predictive tool—examples are shown in Figures 7.48 and 7.49.

The *call/put* indicator described here, is one of three that I look for to be showing extremes, in order to signal an imminent market bottom—the other two being a low in a 10-day up volume average and an oversold reading in the net A/D 10-day average, both of which are explained previously in the custom indicator section. Tops are another story, in that the up

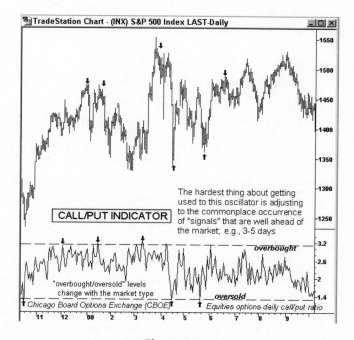

Figure 7.48

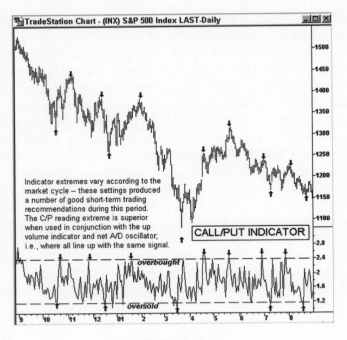

Figure 7.49

volume figure provides less guidance, although when it turns down from a high level, it is suggestive of a possible trend change.

Volatility Indexes and Marketing Turning Points

Besides the call/put readings, there is another useful indication for possible market extremes that is also based on stock options activity. Two options *volatility* indexes can also be correlated to possible trend changes and are watched by many professional traders, investors, and analysts. Use of these numbers for such predictions is similar to the overbought/oversold oscillators we have seen. When price volatility, as measured by these indexes, reaches extremes based on past trading patterns, such areas have often been associated with trend reversals of a short to intermediate nature (e.g., 1–4 weeks typically, at a minimum). I have not typically applied a moving average to the daily volatility numbers, and, like the call/put options readings, look for a 1-day extreme, or at most a cluster of a few such extremes.

A common way to measure the level of general market volatility is by use of the Chicago Board Options Exchange's (CBOE) Volatility Index, known as the VIX, which is also the *ticker* symbol used to obtain its last calculation. This index measures volatility in terms of the S&P 100 stock index options. Volatility is a measure of the fluctuation in the market price of an underlying security. Mathematically, volatility is the annualized standard deviation of returns. The VIX provides updates, during U.S. equities trading hours, of estimates of *expected volatility* over the upcoming 30-day period, by using real-time S&P 100 (OEX) index option bid/ask quotes. The VIX is calculated by taking a weighted average of the *implied volatilities* of eight OEX calls and puts. The CBOE Nasdaq Volatility Index or VXN, (ticker symbol VXN) is a benchmark of technology stock volatility based on the Nasdaq 100 Index (NDX) options and is calculated using the same methodology as the VIX.

With regard to stock prices and stock index levels, *volatility* is a measure of changes in price, expressed in percentage terms without regard to whether price direction is up or down. While volatility simply means the degree of price movement, there are different ways to describe volatility that we need not go into here.

As with the Arms Index, the volatility indexes have an *inverse* relationship to possible trend changes in the market. A *high* level for VIX (indicating high volatility) is associated with a strong trend and also with the increasing likelihood that it may be overdone. For examples, see Figures 7.50 and 7.51—Figure 7.50 being a chart of the S&P 500 (a virtual stand-in for the S&P 100) with the VIX plotted below it, and Figure 7.51 of the Nasdaq 100 Index price chart with VXN. Due to the more common condition of volatile declines, high volatility is more associated with market downswings. When very active selling activity creates wider and wider price movements (high volatility), certain such extremes often precede a market bottom. When everyone rushes to get out (of the market), this could be the time to get in—a high number is therefore a type of contrary indicator. The reverse is not always true, that is, low volatility preceding a market top, but it seems that relatively low readings in VIX around 20 sometimes precede market peaks. What constitutes an extreme in VIX is better defined, as this index has been published since 1986.

VXN is a more recent index (my historical data dates from early 2001 only) and there is less history to evaluate. VXN reflects the greater volatility of the Nasdaq and this index got close to 80 just prior to a significant Nasdaq low in early 2001. While the VXN is worth watching over time, the area that likely represents an oversold extreme, prior to an upside market reversal, is not well defined yet. And, with its very limited history, it appears that there is no particular level yet that we could say might be correlated to a market top with this index.

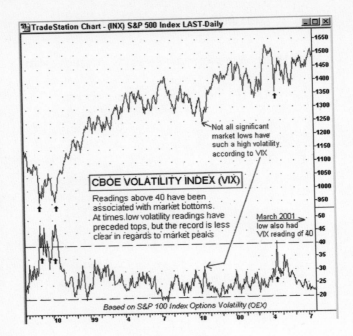

Figure 7.50

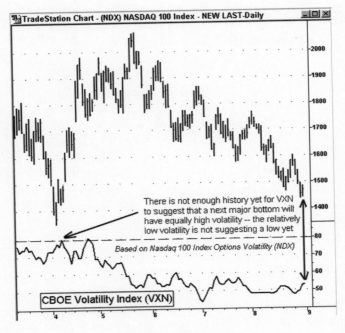

Figure 7.51

New Highs Versus New Lows as an Indicator

A year is an important time frame in the markets and there is a widely looked at daily compilation of either NYSE or Nasdaq traded stocks that are making new 52-week highs or new 52-week lows every day. The list of new highs and lows includes all varieties of a company's stock, so one company may account for more than one new high or low (e.g., both the common and a preferred stock make new lows together). Also many stocks on the list keep showing up day after day. For example, after a stock has an initial occurrence of a 52-week low and especially if it was a high flying stock that is now crashing, this same stock may keep making a new 52-week low repeatedly.

Plotting the difference between, for example, the number of Nasdaq new highs and new 52-week lows is an easy task. If the number of new (daily) highs equals 150 and the number of new lows equals 50, the net (NH-NL) number is 100. If the new lows were to equal 150 and new highs 50, the net figure is –100. When the number of stocks making new highs exceeds stocks making new lows and is a positive number, this is a bullish *coincidental* (occurring along with price changes) trend. When stocks making new lows exceed new highs and the difference is a negative value, this becomes a bearish confirmation of the price trend. The midpoint line is 0, where the new highs and new lows are either both zero (highly unlikely) or equal to each other.

Figure 7.52 shows examples of the new highs minus new lows average for Nasdaq as an indicator: +200 was associated with a peak level and –250 to –300, a low point, during this period. Used in this way, the indicator becomes similar to other *oscillators*. Another use of it is to just monitor the *trend* of the net difference—is it increasing in one direction slowly or rapidly—if the market is going up or down sharply, and the NH-NL trend is lagging this rate of increase, this lag suggests that the trend may lack staying power. Occasionally, the net difference will become a *leading* indicator by turning up or down while prices are still going in the opposite direction—as noted in Figure 7.52. This instance was an indication of a market rebound ahead and suggests that this indicator can both confirm and lead a market turn.

BELLWETHER STOCKS OR SECTORS

The concept of the *bellwether* stock or subindex is that there are certain companies, market *sectors* (e.g., semiconductor stocks), or indexes that by virtue of their size or relative importance will be virtual *stand-ins* for, or will

Figure 7.52

be closely linked to, the movement in a market index or average. The most famous and earliest example of a bellwether is the role the Dow Transportation average plays relative to the Dow Industrials. If one average or the other fails to also move to a new high or low, this is a bullish or bearish *divergence*.

As a bellwether goes, "so goes the market" is the operative role of these key stocks and related indexes. For example, in the megabull market of the late 1990s, Cisco Systems (CSCO) was a key stock to follow if you wanted to follow only one specific company's stock in the Nasdaq Composite index. Cisco, along with Nasdaq biggies, Microsoft Inc. (MSFT) and Intel Corporation (INTC), accounted for close to 25 percent of the entire value of the index during this period. But size is not the only criteria for assuming a bellwether status. As important, the bellwether must be a company that has had a stellar growth and represents the leading edge business that exemplifies that exchange. In the case of Nasdaq, the Internet and communications revolution was driving this exchange (besides the rapid high-tech growth in general) and Cisco was perceived as the leading company in supplying the required equipment to run it.

Besides a key individual stock like Cisco, a related stock index that is also a *bellwether* for Nasdaq is the Russell 2000 (symbol: RUT). The Semi-conductor Index (symbol: SOX), as calculated by the Philadelphia Options Exchange, is an index of stocks that provide a key underlying component of the high technology industry. Without the participation of the stocks making up the Semiconductor Index, the overall Nasdaq market will not likely be firing on all cylinders in terms of a strong trend.

The predictive value of a *bellwether* is when it changes direction or forms a reversal pattern ahead of the index in question—for example, the bellwether drops below a key moving average or forms a double bottom ahead of the index. Such action can provide an early indication that the in-dex may follow in the same direction. While the bellwether will most often have the *same* technical patterns or the index will sometimes *lead* the bell-wether index, it's the occasional instances where the bellwether leads or di-verges from the index that make them valuable to follow. The points where the bellwether is a leading indicator often occur at key junctures in the market trend. See Figures 7.53 and 7.54 for examples of this occasional, but key, role played by two of the Nasdaq bellwethers.

For the NYSE's Composite Index (common *ticker symbol*: NYA), as

Figure 7.53

Figure 7.54

well as the Dow 30 Average and the S&P 500 Index, a key bellwether stock in recent years has been General Electric (GE) as it has represented a force in major areas of the mainstream economy that is represented by these averages. (Symbols for market indexes vary among web sites and charting services, whereas individual stocks are standardized.) Comparison of GE's price and volume trends can be done in relation to the Dow Jones average, S&P 500 index, and the New York Composite Index. As well, overall market health is difficult to maintain without the participation of the financial sector, as can be represented overall by the bellwether NYSE Financial Stock Index. The trend in the Financial Index should concur in direction and strength with the broad market averages. If it does not, it should be taken as an alert for any other signs of an overall trend reversal. Conversely, the index should confirm the bellwether, or there is a *divergence* not unlike what has been seen when the Dow Industrials and Transports do not confirm each other in a new relative high or low. The concept of bullish and bearish divergences will be discussed in the next chapter more fully. Figures 7.55 and 7.56 provide a look at bellwethers that relate to the NYSE market and the S&P 500.

Figure 7.55

Figure 7.56

SUMMARY—USING INDICATORS
TO BUILD A TECHNICAL OUTLOOK

I began this chapter with an extensive look at moving averages, and they are worth spending this time and more on your own in the future, as they provide enormous help in knowing where things stand with the unfolding trends in the markets. Use of moving averages is complemented with volume as an indicator. Understanding how to use the various oscillators presented will then also provide you with the knowledge of specific ones you might most usefully employ relative to your market interests, as well as how to use them to gain further information on trend:

I *Direction*—up, down, or sideways

I Strength or *momentum*

I Overbought or oversold information—including a long-term view

Understanding indicators as a group, in terms of their effective use, completes our examination of the second major class of technical analysis tools and techniques. The first major component being, of course, pattern recognition and classical chart analysis. Further suggestions and guidelines about how to put together these various techniques, which range from chart markings like trend lines, moving averages, and more complex mathematical formulas like MACD, into one seamless study of market trends and how to profit from them, are summarized in the Putting It All Together chapter at the end of this book. Before that, there is a further step to take by reading the next chapter, in order to take advantage of the confirming and diverging links and relationships that develop between indicators and price action.

8

CONFIRMATION AND DIVERGENCE

INTRODUCTION

Various types of *confirmations* or *divergences* between price behavior and indicators develop in markets, both as a whole and with individual items, and these can be very valuable to help determine market strategy and action, such as when to

I Stay with an existing trend and let your profits "run."

I Exit a current position and take profits or cut losses.

I Establish a new position, including when it is opposite to a prior position.

Because of their relative importance for a profitable use of technical analysis, a good working knowledge of confirmations and divergences of all types is examined here as a separate topic and chapter. Generally, the concepts involved are covered only as a part of a discussion of *oscillators*. However, the subject of confirmation and divergences—a form of *nonconfirmation*—has roots in many techniques and tools of technical analysis.

Understanding divergences, such that you readily see them develop, is also a matter of seeing many examples, which are presented in this chapter. Moreover, this material pulls together a discussion of the variations of confirmations and divergences that are relevant to comparing different stock averages to other indexes or bellwethers, comparing prices to underlying moving averages, and comparing price action to oscillator patterns.

A number of examples of confirmations and divergences related to using oscillators or other technical tools, in one location, will help reinforce the ability to easily recognize the pattern. The other necessary ingredient to finding divergences is to be always looking for them. For example, you may find only 1 for every 20 stocks you are following in a 3-month period. That is a lot of *looking* to find one divergence, but that *one* may offer the most profitable trade or investment, relative to risk, that you will find in that entire period. Risk can be held to the smallest amount when you are early in a trend—when the appropriate stop is also very close to the entry point—and there is no earlier entry than during or soon after a trend reversal is first apparent. A very effective way of spotting reversals is when a divergence precedes it.

DIVERGENCES BETWEEN AVERAGES, OTHER INDEXES, AND KEY STOCKS

As described in Chapter 3, Charles Dow originated the concept that there were two key stock market averages because each consisted of companies that engaged in different types of basic economic activity. His Dow Industrial and Transportation averages, considered together, gave an accurate picture of overall economic conditions in the United States. The health of the economy would be reflected in these averages in different but complementary ways. The stocks comprising the Dow Jones Industrial average would constitute a barometer of the current and future state of *production* and the stocks comprising the Dow Jones Transportation average would be an ongoing indication of the level of *shipments* of those goods. Both averages together would indicate overall economic health, an overall corporate earnings trend, and hence current and future price *momentum* in the U.S. stock market.

According to Dow, only if the two averages *confirmed* each other's trend was there a green light to invest or stay in stocks. If one average *diverged* or went its own way, such as by not making a new high or new low along with the other, this was an indication of a potential upcoming trend reversal in the market. A new high in one average, unconfirmed by the other average, was a potential bearish situation that sounded an alert to watch developments in the nonconfirming average closely—to see if this average would also eventually go on to make a new high or would falter further. A new low in one average, not matched by a similar new low in the other, was a potential bullish *divergence*. For example, failure to make a new bear market low in the transportation average might well suggest that shipment of new orders had picked up, but was not yet reflected in new manufacturing because those shipments were first drawing down existing inventories rather than resulting in new manufacturing. A Dow theory confirmation, as well as notation of diverging trends in the averages, is highlighted in Figure 8.1.

We have also seen examples where other closely related indexes diverge, such as the Nasdaq Composite index relative to the Russell 2000 index (Figure 7.53), or the example provided by the NYSE Financial index diverging from the NYSE Composite index in Figure 7.55. Divergences can set up between a key individual stock—a *bellwether* issue—and an index or average of which the stock is a key component

Figure 8.1

per the examples of Figures 7.54 and 7.56. Such divergences can also be early alerts or warning signals of a trend change in the parent or the other index.

In the commodities markets, individual markets are often tracked relative to an index of commodity prices, such as the CRB Commodity Index. There are commodity subindices as well (e.g., the grains, meats, metals, oils, etc.). An individual cash commodity or commodity futures market will often be compared and charted relative to the subindex of which it is part. Traders are going to be alert for instances where the individual item lags or moves ahead—types of divergences—of the overall index or subindex of which it is part. Individual bonds and notes whether corporate or government may lag certain key fixed income subindexes. Traders are often on the outlook for such divergences and what causes them. If such a diverging trend is not strictly *technical*, in the sense of some situation that is related to some limitations or special feature of the item, there may be a trading opportunity to buy the component that is cheap and sell what is expensive. This assumes that the differential or *spread* would normally be expected to converge again. The reverse case, to buy the expensive and sell the cheap, would be done if the divergence could be expected to widen, also given normal market circumstances.

The concept of *confirmation* involving market averages, or the reverse circumstance of *divergence*, was later applied by technical analysts to situations where market *momentum*, as measured by the formulas or indicators we have examined, goes in a divergent or opposite direction from price. Momentum, which is the internal *force* or rate of change, can slow and start to decline, while prices keep going *higher*—but price will follow momentum at some point. Price movements are a function (dependent on) of momentum in the end. This situation is one reflecting a *bearish* divergence. This concept can be visualized as the coyote character in the *Roadrunner* cartoons, who would keep going in one direction for awhile after he ran off a cliff, but where gravity would eventually cause him to come crashing down. Conversely, the momentum trend as measured by the technical indicators we have seen, can turn *up* while prices continue to move *lower*. Eventually, a turn up in prices will reflect the changing upside momentum. This is the concept of a *bullish* divergence. Whether an indicator/price divergence is *bullish* (having *upside* potential) or *bearish* (having *downside* potential) is defined by what is anticipated for or what actually happens to, the *price* trend.

MOVING AVERAGE CONFIRMATIONS

Moving averages are primarily *confirming* indicators due to the fact that they lag current prices and a changing trend. We have already seen numerous examples of where prices achieve a bullish or bearish crossover of a moving average. When prices cross above any key moving average or a shorter average crosses above a longer average (a bullish *upside* crossover) in a downtrend or sideways consolidation, this can also be thought of as a type of *divergence* (i.e., prices are diverging from the trend direction previously indicated by the moving average). The reverse situation is a downside bearish crossover of prices relative to an upward trending moving average.

Generally in technical analysis terminology and usage, a price reversal that *violates* or crosses above or below a key moving average, is generally viewed as signaling a possible change in the direction of the trend. *Divergence* is a term more commonly in use with the study of *oscillators* or in the relationship of difference averages. Moving averages represent a bigger-picture view of a price trend so are thought of more as a confirming or lagging indication of a trend. In a strict sense, only such contrary price action is called a divergence. Trend change confirmation occurs when the moving average itself changes its up/down direction.

Use of moving averages is another method, besides the use of trend-lines, of monitoring the direction and strength of a trend. We certainly are also alerted to the possible *trend change* that may be underway when prices begin accelerating, such that they widen the gap between a moving average and the changing price level. Moving averages are also a type of trend line themselves—a curving one. In summary we can say that moving averages *confirm* the direction of a price trend *after* the actual trend change occurs. *Divergences* are an alert or imply a possible buy or sell signal *before* a change in the price trend occurs.

OSCILLATOR DIVERGENCES AS BUY OR SELL SIGNALS

Indicators, besides their usefulness in providing some idea of whether a market is overbought or oversold, will also generate occasional divergent buy or sell *signals*, on either an intraday, daily, weekly, or monthly chart basis. A classic example of a bullish divergence would be a *higher high* in an oscillator relative to what came before, in the same trading period when prices made a *lower low*. This situation suggests the possibility of an *upside reversal*. A classic example of a bearish divergence is a higher price peak, accompanied by a *lower low* in the oscillator reading, compared to its last extreme. This development suggests the possibility that a *downside reversal* could be developing. There is a third situation that comes up, which is not considered a classic divergence, where the indicator bottoms or tops in the same area—marking a double top or bottom—whereas prices go on to make a new high or low. This type of divergence is also valid in terms of suggesting that the market may have topped or bottomed. Such measurements of momentum based on an oscillator formula, suggest that the trend strength could be waning and that the item or financial instrument in question is vulnerable to a reversal.

In a trend that we are participating in by being long or short a stock or other financial instrument, we expect to see momentum indicators like RSI, stochastics, and MACD, generally making a new *relative high* or new *relative low* along with prices. Relative refers to new highs or new lows *within* the secondary or primary trend that is ongoing, not necessarily an all-time new high or low.

Figure 8.2 is a chart of the Nasdaq Composite stock index along with

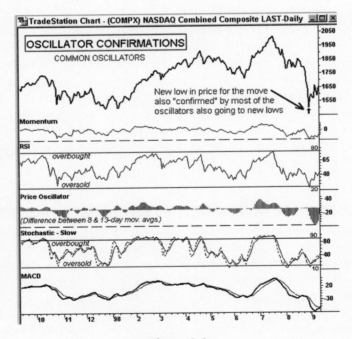

Figure 8.2

some of the more widely used oscillators applied to the chart, during a period when the Composite made its lowest low during the period shown, in the 1,500 area. Some oscillators have a dashed level line set so that it intersects the lowest low. The specific oscillators used with their settings (number of *bars*) are momentum (21), RSI (14), the price oscillator showing the difference of two moving averages (8, 13), the slow stochastic (14), and the MACD with its standard setting. These oscillators were *confirming* the price action—in this case, also registering new lows along with prices in the continued downtrend. The stochastics model has registered a low in the same approximate area as previously, whereas the other oscillators have clearly made lower relative lows. Reflecting a strong downtrend, the line that designates an oversold level has been adjusted downward on the RSI from 30 to 20 and from 20 to 10 for the oversold stochastics line. The oscillators here are confirming indicators, relative to price activity.

Figure 8.3 shows a chart with the same oscillators applied to a daily chart of the Nasdaq Composite as it advanced to the 4,200 area in the period shown, with the same oscillators mostly confirming this new high by also advancing to new peak levels. The horizontal dashed line seen on

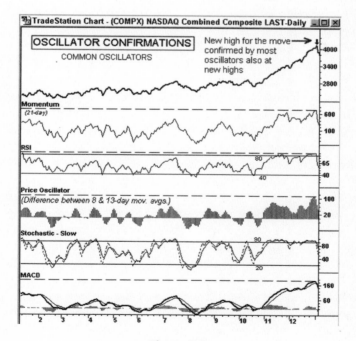

Figure 8.3

some of the oscillators indicates the high point of the oscillator. Reflecting the strong upward momentum during this major bull market trend, the *overbought* level has been adjusted upwards on the RSI and slow stochastic to 80 and 90, respectively. The *oversold* level on the RSI was also adjusted upward, to 40, whereas the stochastic oversold level line was left at 20. Even with these upward adjustments, this market is registering an overbought extreme.

The overbought extremes that are reached and then linger in Figure 8.2 in the RSI and stochastics—these oscillators don't go above a set level of 100—provide examples of not relying solely on overbought (or oversold) readings to decide that a top (or bottom) has been reached. Prolonged overbought/oversold periods often occur repeatedly in the late stages of a strong trend. This tendency for prolonged oscillator extremes creates an alert and forewarning of a possible trend reversal, as *over* or *under* valuations are characteristic of the final phases of bull or bear markets. For example, in a market that was this *overbought* on a long-term basis, we can predict that the *time* duration before a top is limited, while *price* objectives are far more elastic, as unusually strong momentum can carry prices considerable distances. It's best to make no hard assumption of how far, in point or dollar terms, the trend will propel prices, as final objectives are hard to pinpoint.

You'll note also in Figure 8.3 that the slow stochastic flattens out in such a strong trend, as it reaches the 96 area and stays around this level both before and during the highest high for the period shown. Since the high of the stochastics scale is 100, this oscillator is going to approach, but not quite equal, this limit. The stochastic is generally not as effective as the "unbounded" oscillators when there is a very strong *trend*, as this indicator is more likely to stay at extremes and less likely to show a divergence if prices go still higher but momentum slows. In a trend with more moderate momentum and back-and-forth price swings, the stochastic can be quite effective in highlighting reversal points. The RSI also has a maximum reading of 100 and it has the same tendency to *flatten* in very strong trends. However, the RSI will fall relatively quickly from its most extreme point as soon as a correction develops. When a rally resumes, the RSI will rise again with the advance, but may also give a more clear-cut divergent reading by not rising as far as previously if market momentum is not as strong on the next advance. RSI tends to be my oscillator of choice when I'm looking for divergences, although I don't stop examining the other ones. Sometimes, it is a different oscillator that highlights a particular bullish or bearish divergence.

The oscillators in Figures 8.2 and 8.3 provide confirming and complementary signals. When confirmation does not occur, the resulting divergence is an important alert for the possibility that this is signaling an upcoming reversal to the current trend. In a sense, divergences are *more* important than indicator confirmations as they can provide an excellent new buy or sell signal. If the signal is one that indicates a possible reversal to a trend that you are participating in, this is a valuable advance warning—one of the chief risks to potential gains is being caught in a trend reversal that you did not see coming and were not prepared for.

Figure 8.4 shows a later stage of the downtrend of Figure 8.2's chart, where the index has fallen to a new low. The new low is noted by an up arrow. At this latest low, a divergent buy signal has developed as price action is unconfirmed by several of the oscillators as they register higher lows than previously—in effect, momentum had turned up and prices would soon follow. The new up trend was confirmed when the advance exceeded the prior upswing high.

Figure 8.5 shows a later stage of Figure 8.3's uptrend, where the index has risen to a new relative high. Both the high seen in Figure 8.3 and

Figure 8.4

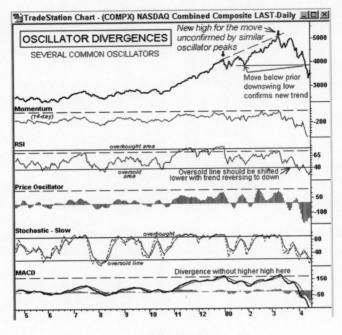

Figure 8.5

the new high are highlighted by the down arrows. At the new high, a divergent sell signal has developed as price action is unconfirmed by several of the oscillators as they either register a lower low than previously or made a top equal to their prior peak, such as is seen with the MACD signal line. The MACD representing the difference between two longer, smoothed moving averages, provides the least clear divergence—but even with this indicator it's apparent that the new rally high was not confirmed by the oscillator.

Figures 8.6 through 8.12 provide other examples of divergences involving one to two oscillators, to allow detailed examination. These examples of bullish and bearish divergences also include ones involving weekly charts.

There are often *multiple* divergences and some will be early and well before the actual occurrence of a trend shift. Instances of multiple divergences create a risk of premature trade entry one or more times if trade entry was based primarily on an *oscillator divergence*. There are some ways to avoid this situation in most markets (with point 4 pertaining to stocks only), as follows.

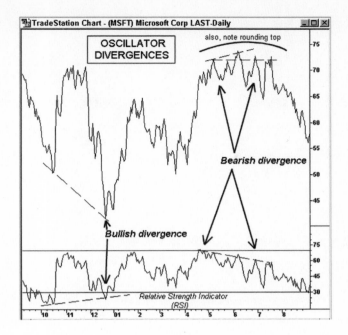

Figure 8.6

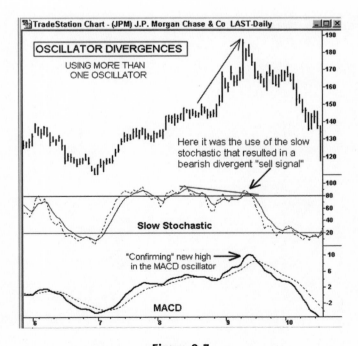

Figure 8.7

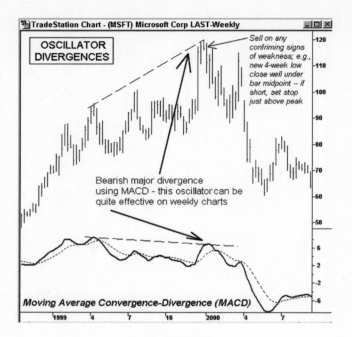

Figure 8.8

Figure 8.9

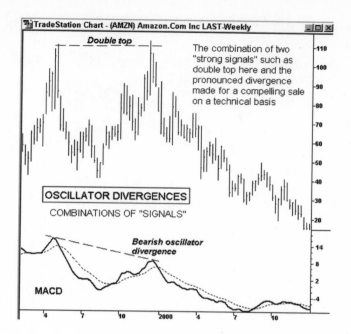

Figure 8.10

Figure 8.11

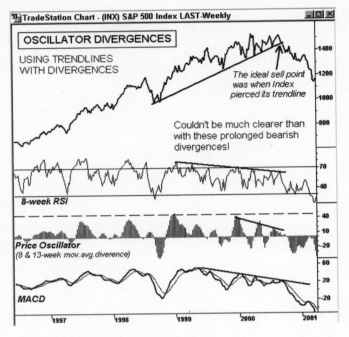

Figure 8.12

1. Give more weight to divergences that occur during or after over-bought or oversold oscillator extremes that have been adjusted to reflect the strength of the dominant trend (e.g., if in a very strong up or down trend, the appropriate RSI overbought-oversold levels may be 80 and above or 20 and below, rather than 70/30).

2. Look for confirming price (chart) patterns that are associated with trend reversals—especially trendline *breaks* or *breakouts*.

3. Examine any related *bellwether* index or other related financial in-struments for confirming signs of the same *type* of divergence or other signs of a reversal.

4. If you are concerned with individual stocks, also look at the key gen-eral stock market indicators for clues relating to any overbought or oversold extremes. This would include seeing how far prices are above or below the 21-, 50-, and 200-day moving averages and whether longer-term weekly oscillators like RSI or MACD are at overbought or oversold levels. Overall market extremes might also be found by recording the *net 10-day A/D figures*, 10-day up volume

numbers (for bottoms), the new highs–new lows (NH-NL) trend numbers, and the CBOE *call/put readings*. The first three of these figures should be calculated for Nasdaq *or* the NYSE or both, depending on the stocks being followed. If a stock trades on the NYSE, the appropriate indicators would be based on figures from this exchange. The call/put readings are best looked at in relation to the trend in the S&P 500 (SPX) or S&P 100 (OEX) index. However, extremes in the call/put ratio have fairly general pertinence to bullish or optimistic and bearish or pessimistic extremes of market *sentiment* in all or most segments and measures of the stock market.

VOLUME CONFIRMATION AND DIVERGENCES

Volume is an important secondary indicator that should be looked at relative to confirming moves in the direction of the trend. As stated previously regarding the role of trading activity, volume should in general *expand* in the direction of the trend and *contract* when there are price swings in the opposite direction to the dominant price trend (i.e., a countertrend move). Strong moves in the direction of the trend are often accompanied by substantial spikes in volume. Such volume *spikes* are examples of volume acting as a *confirming* indicator—see Figure 8.13. Trend *reversals* or market tops and bottoms are also often accompanied by a declining volume trend as in Figures 8.14 and 8.15. The volume levels act as a diverging secondary indication leading up to such price reversals. When the level of trading activity jumps when the trend changes direction, volume is then confirming the new trend.

When the volume trend diverges from price activity, contrary to the general rule of volume expanding in the direction of a dominant trend, the resulting volume–price divergence bears watching as a warning of a possible trend change. It is uncommon for this to happen without seeing other technical signs such as a price reversal *pattern*, trendline break/breakout, or via a moving average penetration. Sometimes the on balance volume (OBV) indicator might be the sole diverging secondary indicator as illustrated in Figures 8.14 and 8.15. When this happens, such a divergence is suggesting that the current trend may not be sustainable as less and less buying or selling is driving it, providing another example of waning *momentum*. Figure 4.19 in Chapter 4 also provides an excellent example of a diverging price and volume pattern that preceded a reversal of the existing trend.

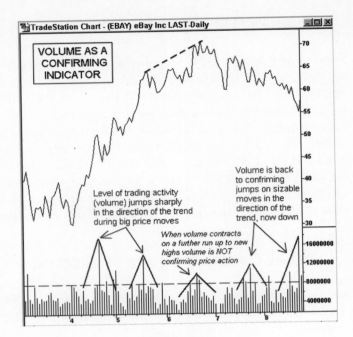

Figure 8.13

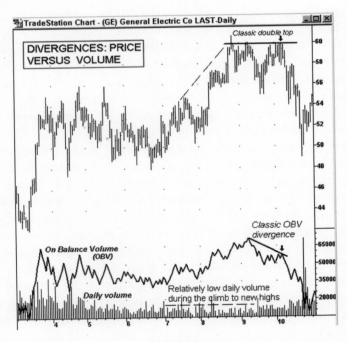

Figure 8.14

Figure 8.15

STRATEGY IMPLICATIONS AND CONSIDERATIONS OF DIVERGENCES

Bullish divergences that occur in a downtrend and bearish divergences that establish themselves in an uptrend are often used as an indication to liquidate an existing position and possibly establish an opposite position—for example, going from long to short. Changing positions, anticipates that the divergence will result in a trend reversal and that this will occur in the near-term. However, as we've seen, such divergences do not always result in a trend reversal as is the case of a signal failure. Or, there may be a considerable *lag* before the reversal occurs (e.g., prices carry a good bit higher or lower after the divergence). If you adhere to risk parameters, as is always recommended, time lags before a final trend reversal can create a significant problem with being *stopped out*, perhaps multiple times, before the reversal occurs. Divergences in an especially strong trend should best be viewed as an *alert*, which calls for watching the market more closely, rather than an automatic call to immediate market action.

Divergences should also be viewed as a call to adjust exiting *stops* to the point where the stop is the closest possible to current prices, while still being appropriate as the level, which, if pierced, would be the earliest warning of a possible trend reversal. Stops can also be used at varying levels to exit varying portions of an investment position (e.g., 300 shares, or 3 contracts, could have three levels of stop protection—one set relative to the minor trend, one that is below or above where the secondary trend would suggest a reversal, and finally where the major or primary trend would reverse according to technical criteria.

USE OTHER CONFIRMING TECHNICAL TOOLS AND TECHNIQUES

The best way to think of the relative importance or place of *oscillator divergences* is to understand that not all tops and bottoms that form, show indicator divergences beforehand. While many divergences do result in subsequent reversals, they are early warning signals to varying degrees. It is recommended to use some of the many other technical tools and techniques that also suggest or confirm a possible trend reversal such as

- An upside or downside break of the current trendline
- A volume *spike* or significant increase in the daily volume relative to prior days or weeks occurring on countertrend price swings
- A move below a significant prior low in an uptrend, or above a prior high in a downtrend
- A penetration above or below a 21-, 50-, or 200-day moving average
- *Key* or "spike" 1–2 day reversals
- A decisive upside or downside penetration above or below the high or low of the last week or the last five trading days
- A greater than 62 percent *retracement* of a prior major move

NEW TECHNOLOGIES AND HELP FOR MONITORING DIVERGENCES

Theoretically, by constant use and adjustment of exiting stop orders, it should be rare to incur any single huge loss due to sudden and sharp trend reversals. However, realistically in trading and investing, there are times when we are more alert to possible trend changes than others. Moreover, unless you are an investment or trading professional, the press of your own professional and personal life will not always allow you to be so in tune with unfolding technical patterns, that you are never caught unawares.

And attention lapses—the longer a bull or market trend goes on, the more complacency sets in—this is part of the human market dynamics that have been present since the advent of the public financial markets.

There are, however, some new developments and new technologies that allow easier and more effective monitoring of the technical developments in the markets and items of potential interest to you. There is now ready access to free public web sites that allow periodic monitoring, charting, and application of the most common technical indictors for any of the individual items in your portfolio—this didn't exist before the 1990s. There are even more potent tools available in the form of technical analysis software that allow setting of various automatic alerts, for example, when long and you want to be alerted to bearish technical developments as suggested by an indicator reversal, trendline penetration, or when there's a close under a particular moving average. In terms of searching for new trade entry, there is a comprehensive monitoring capability that can highlight, for any selected markets or individual items, instances of an indicator reversal to above an oversold line (e.g., RSI), by way of a bullish crossover (e.g., stochastics), an alert to a bullish moving average crossover or an upside penetration of a trendline that the *user* has drawn with the same software. Such alerts are typically collected in an *alert center* and notification is either visually (on the screen) or audibly during intraday price action in the case of a real-time data feed, or more commonly, after downloading end-of-day or closing market data. After collecting closing market data, alerts will then get generated according to any *preset* criteria and will then allow any appropriate market action to be taken the next trading day.

It is now also possible via the TradeStation technical analysis software application to have buy and sell orders, based on your entry criteria, automatically sent to a participating broker for execution. Exit criteria, both in terms of setting loss points or profit objectives, can then also be established and set up, so that these orders are also automatically generated and sent electronically so that they are in place. It always seemed to me to be a foregone conclusion that once there was the capability to automate trading signals and alerts based on technical criteria, that a similar and automatic means of order entry would be developed. We are now seeing the first services of this kind. There will be an introduction to "trading systems" in the next chapter.

SUMMARY

If the "trend is your friend," then tools and techniques that suggest that the trend is intact and continuing to unfold in a normal fashion, according to technical analysis criteria, is an ally. Conversely, when divergences set up, the resulting early warning of a possible trend reversal becomes a best friend. Such nonconfirmations can help preserve existing profits and/or investing capital and get you prepared for any trouble ahead.

Watching overall market indexes or related financial instruments for confirming or diverging price action, relative to what markets or items you are in, is a first basic. For example, you own a semiconductor stock, but the semiconductor index (SOX) falls under an important up trendline or moving average. Or you see clear signs of a major market top. It is highly likely that whatever mutual funds you own are not going to also be pulled down in a bear market.

Applying moving averages and moving average envelopes is a good next step to see if prices are narrowing, widening, or keeping the same relative distance to these measures of trend. Such daily or weekly checks will tend to prevent surprises when prices diverge radically from these moving averages. For example, a trend accelerates, such that the market or item in question gets to an unusual extreme relative to past periods. Volume should also be confirming what is going on with price activity. When prices keep going up, but volume lags, this is a possible early alert to a divergence between the level or volume of trading activity and the price action.

The importance of looking at oscillators like RSI, slow stochastics, or MACD on a regular basis provides one of the final checks for confirmations or divergences. It's useful to look at all of the above at times. A new high in a market, accompanied by a lower high in one of the key oscillators is a warning to watch trend developments closely—especially if the item in question is also, or has recently been, registering an extreme on the oscillator.

Much of the time either the market is not registering any divergences or simply may not be in a trending phase. According to studies relating to trending and non-trending markets, there is a definite directional movement only about 30 percent to 40 percent of the time. In nontrending markets or sideways consolidations and trading ranges, the tools and techniques useful for measuring the strength of an up or down trend are not going to yield as much useful information. Once there is definite trend, the same technical tools and techniques related to checking and rechecking trend direction and strength (momentum) comprise a significant part of what is predictive and useful in technical analysis. Besides the various technical indicators, the other major part of technical analysis consists of the tools and techniques of *pattern recognition*, which is useful all the time, in both trending and nontrending markets. One of these major components without the other is not half a loaf, but more like only half an engine.

9

SPECIALIZED FORMS OF ANALYSIS AND TRADING

INTRODUCTION

There are some specialized forms of technical analysis and trading methods that are not often covered in an introductory book such as this one. However, exposure to some of these topics is quite worthwhile as the methods involved provide some practical and useful market insights relative to market trends. These four topics include:

1. Seasonality in the markets
2. Basic market concepts of W.D. Gann
3. Elliott Wave analysis
4. Trading systems

That the contributions by Gann and R.N. Elliott are usually not covered in an introductory book on technical analysis is probably due to an unwillingness to provide only a precursory introduction to subjects that can easily be a specialized volume or volumes in themselves. However, having worked with the key concepts of these specialized methods in a basic way, I find them to be fairly straightforward and to add unique contributions to understanding market behavior. In more than two decades of involvement in market analysis, investing, and trading activities I've been struck by the tendency to make market analysis more complex than is necessary, perhaps due to the tendency to make an *ideology* out of methodology. The four topics listed previously complete an overview and study of the essential behavior of markets and trends.

Seasonality, especially in the stock market, is often overlooked, but can add to understanding what periods of the year have a historical tendency for price rises, declines, or sideways trends. Sometimes other technical approaches will not provide the same kind of insight and information. R.N. Elliott added significantly to Charles Dow's observations about the *phases* of bull and bear markets by observing that a key tendency of market moves was to unfold in three component parts or *waves*, although in uptrends two intervening down moves make for a total count of five. It is then also very useful to know that very often, the second upswing is the most powerful part of a bull market trend, and the third upswing is the least reliable in terms of its staying power. W.D. Gann pointed to the importance of examining the *time* duration of market trends. Use of trading systems to generate trade entry and exit signals is one of the modern trends enabling a more *objective* method of evaluating market entry and exit criteria—an approach helping to overcome the tendency to make mental mistakes and to have emotional factors work against the best execution of a technical trading strategy.

SEASONALITY

It is a well-known fact that commodity markets have pronounced seasonal tendencies, especially for ones that have growing seasons or have strong seasonal consumption patterns such as heating oil. Not as known or recognized is the pronounced tendency for a *seasonal trend* in the U.S. stock market. Even when the seasonal tendency is recognized, an actual strategy of being in the stock market only during the seasonally strong periods and then being in *cash* (invested in *money market* instruments like U.S. Treasury bills) during the rest of the year, works contrary to the common *buy and hold* strategy of equities. However, it is also a fact that investors often liquidate stocks when they decline against them by any appreciable amount. Risk protection principles, especially in placing stop–loss (liquidating) orders relative to purchases is another modification to investing tactics. If *market timing* is not good on price entry, such as is the case of entry well after a trend is underway and well before there is any significant countertrend reaction, stop liquidation orders will force some exits. This is even more prone to occur if investments are made during a seasonally weak period. The concept that money managers don't *trade* in and out of stocks anyway is somewhat suspect as there are studies that indicate that some of the best performing stock mutual funds have an annual turnover rate of 100 percent or more (i.e., the entire portfolio is turned over on average within a 12-month period). A 300 percent turnover rate indicates an average holding period of only 4 months. Some top funds have had rates like this in some of their best years.

Contrary to conventional wisdom that you cannot *time* the market, there is an example provided by at least one money manager who has improved his track record by doing just that. Due to a seasonally bullish tendency for stocks during the November to April period, investment in equities is oriented to this portion of each year. Fund manager Sy Harding has written extensively in *Barron's* magazine about his seasonal method of market timing, which employs an S&P 500 Index fund as the investment vehicle. He defines the optimum *average* seasonal pattern as being from the next to last trading day of October, through the fourth trading day of May. However, he also notes that the actual favorable season can range from 4 to 8 months. He has applied another key technical criterion for entry or exit from the market, in addition to being invested during the optimum seasonal time period. This modification also relies on a bullish crossover of the MACD. This must occur as the favorable seasonal period approaches, but with a latitude of several weeks—typically 4 to 6 weeks—before the seasonally favorable time period. This is an important refinement to a purely seasonal approach.

This method of yearly entries and exits, when back-tested from 1965 through the year 2000, resulted in returns that were approximately triple that of continuously holding the S&P 500 Index during the same time frame. This result should not be taken to mean that there was always a positive return in years when the Index was down, just that the negative returns were likely to be *less* on average, than losing years for the S&P 500 Index. It's also possible that an entire favorable seasonal period could be passed over if the MACD did not achieve a bullish crossover. His returns gets some boost from interest earned when not invested in the S&P 500 Index fund.

Figure 9.1, that of a weekly S&P chart that includes the MACD indicator, indicates periods (within the vertical lines) when the criteria used resulted in being invested. Any such period is marked as "in." Any other

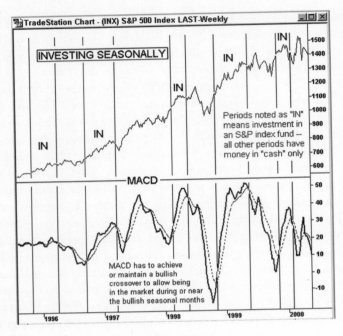

Figure 9.1

period between vertical lines, without notation, is a time span when the fund is earning interest only. Note that the years shown in Figure 9.1, using the seasonal tendency for gains to be achieved during or close to an optimum 6 months (November through April) out of 12 and provided the MACD was also in agreement, would not necessarily result in being in the market during every period when the Index advanced. However, several losing periods are avoided and the period shown was consistent with the better return this fund manager has documented with his *seasonal* method, relative to a buy and hold strategy.

While it is not my purpose to describe in detail the *fundamental* reasons for the U.S. stock market tendency for strength during certain months of the year, these factors are commonly noted:

I Extra investor cash coming from November and December capital gains distributions from mutual funds in up market years.

I More attention focused on the market before and after the summer vacation season.

I Third- and fourth-quarter dividend distributions from corporations.

I Employer's contributions to employee's 401k plans and pension plans, being made for the year.

I Year-end bonuses.

I Individual owners of businesses see what their profits are by early in the new year, and this money can be a source of funds that adds to an advance in the first quarter.

GANN TECHNIQUES AND MARKET PHILOSOPHY

W.D. Gann was a highly successful trader and investor in the stock and commodity markets, who was active in the first half of the 1900s. Gann became widely known and followed by virtue of the fact that he was both very successful in trading for himself and because of the unorthodox methods he wrote about and employed to determine his entry and exit into and out of individual stocks and commodities. He wrote several books on the markets, his trading methodology, and its rationale, beginning with *Truth of the Ticker* in 1923 and ending with *45 Years on Wall Street* in 1949, when he was 72. Since his time, many people have tried to duplicate his precision and trading capabilities. One of the problems in this endeavor was that, as with George Lindsay, Gann did not appear to have presented his methods to others in a way that revealed all aspects of them or his precise methodology. What he did reveal was not easy to employ in duplicating his success in market timing and decision making.

It is possible however to identify some of Gann's basic techniques and market observations that do provide some useful clues in finding possible future support and resistance areas and market turning points. Gann provided us with the concept that the laws governing trend strength and duration were identifiable to such a degree that it could allow advance identification of market *turning points*, such as when a trend would *reverse, slow down*, or *accelerate*. This approach is clearly in the realm of technical analysis as it says that market *fundamentals* apply an influence in line with principles that imply that any given trend has a certain natural duration and no more.

General Time and Trading Principles of W.D. Gann

When a market move takes place, the majority of the move in price will tend to occur in time periods of *three*, such as three months, weeks, or days. For example, in a bear market he noted a tendency for a rally to run its course by three weeks' duration and then resume its downward trend. This tends to also be true in an uptrend. An average decline will often run its course in three weeks. Sometimes, when this countertrend move is of an intermediate duration, it can stretch over three months, but the average often works out to three weeks or less. The great late 1990s tech bull market was essentially a three-year phenomena from March 1997 to March 2000.

Consolidation periods after up or down trends commonly take the form of a horizontal or sideways movement. The sideways trend is usually marked by at least two peaks and two low points—the third move to the area of the highs or lows is often decisive. However, failure to go through either the top or bottom will often result in a fast move in the other direction. In a series of upswing lows, it's common for the strongest move to begin from the third major low, if viewed on the weekly or monthly chart.

Tops in an overall market or in individual financial instruments, such as a stock, generally take time to form. More often than not there will be at least a second test of the high. Within the overall market, individual stocks can top ahead of the market, some will lag or tend to occur about the same time, especially in the bellwether issues. In a broad top after a sustained advance, you may see volatile sideways price swings form a top over 3 months or about 90 days, according to Gann. Spikes or V top formations are the obvious exception but this is more common in individual financial instruments.

Gann was the first person to talk about market cycles or trends in terms of there being a definite price and time distance that they travel. He was also the first to speak about watching not only the size of a price *retracement* in a correction, but to also make a careful note of how long the correction went on in terms of the number of days, weeks, or months, comparing this to the length of the trend that preceded it. For example, in a downtrend where a stock rallies not only further, but for a longer period of time, than its prior movement, the bigger price move *and* the longer duration, work together to suggest that this correction might be overdone or have what he called an *overbalance* of time and price. The idea of imbalance leads to the idea of *balance* in price and time. For example, look for buying opportunities when the price move and time duration are equal or greater than the last downtrend.

The opposite example is to look for selling opportunities when a rally has gone on as long and covered as much ground as the previous significant upswing within a bear trend. This in fact is what a *measured move* or *swing objective* is doing (for example, taking 100 percent of the prior range between low and high and adding that to the high on a breakout above that peak in an uptrend as a next objective. An additional element from Gann analysis is to measure the duration of a prior upswing. If it was 90 days and prices tack on both the prior gain and this move occurs over about 3 months, then pay attention to that as this financial item may be approaching the point where the trend will change yet again. This change in trend can be an acceleration, sideways consolidation, or reversal.

Figure 9.2 shows IBM's primary uptrend of late 1981 into its August 1987 high. This bull market was, in turn, followed by a primary downtrend into August 1993, followed by a primary uptrend until August 1999. Each major trend was of about 72 months' (6 years') duration. Sometimes major trends will have this close time symmetry, or trends that unfold over a similar number of months. This is often a multiple of 12 months or 1 year, a building block or *foundational* time duration for the longer trends.

Yearly Cycles and Gann

Gann would use the year as the *master cycle*. Rounding the year off to 360 days, the number of degrees in a circle, he considered that the important

Figure 9.2

time periods for market were 90, 180, 270, and 360 days. By extension, multiples or divisions of these numbers are important also (e.g., 15- and 30-day periods are important). A common default setting for the most common oscillators is 14, functionally the same as 15—this being also 3 trading weeks. A starting point in measuring the duration of price movements is to look for these numbers in terms of days or weeks. Gann divided important highs, or the distance between lows and highs, into eighths. One-half (four-eighths) of a prior upswing is an important retracement amount as we have seen. Gann held that 25 percent and 75 percent were other important points. As he equated trend duration as being coequal to price duration, he also divided 90 (one-fourth of 360), into eighths, or: 11, 22, 33, 45, 56, 67, and 90. These numbers were important day counts to make in terms of the minor trends. On weekly charts, divisions or multiples of 52 were considered important measuring milestones (e.g., 13, 26, 39, or 52 weeks). Gann noted that it was common to see the anniversary date of a prior important low or important high turn out to be another important turning point.

"Gann Charts," Angles, and Price "Squares"

The heart of the Gann work and its uniqueness is contained in a "Gann chart" or a *geometric* chart that is drawn, such that an identical distance represents both one *unit* of *time* and one *unit* of *price* (for example, a weekly chart where a $1 price change measures the same distance on the price scale as the measurement equal to 1 week). The equal price measurement does not have to be 1. One could assign a $2 value to each price increment for a stock trading over $100. The important thing is that measuring the width of 1 *bar* (e.g., day, week, or month) would equal the height of 1 unit (increment) of price on the price scale. This treatment follows the principle of *squaring* price and time that is central to Gann's view of market dynamics. The weekly and monthly charting is the most important to an investor and these are the time frames that Gann apparently felt would best show how time and price come into balance.

Effective use of geometric or what are called *square* charts, are made when prices break out above or below the top or bottom of a trading or *consolidation* price range. This is done by adding or subtracting the *width* of that move on the horizontal time scale, to the breakout point on the vertical price scale. The resulting price measurement with a chart constructed with equal proportions on the time and price scales, can yield estimates for a minimum upside or downside objective. This is similar to taking the horizontal distance on a *point and figure* chart in a sideways movement and measuring up or down on the price scale for a next objective. Figure 9.3 is an approximation of the *square* chart type. It is approximate, in that it was made without the special chart paper used for "Gann chart" construction or by use of a specialized charting product such as the *Ganntrader* application. It is difficult to achieve equal proportions in the horizontal price and vertical time scales in regular charting applications.

Angles

With the use of charts that have an *equal* time and price relationship, Gann discovered that certain fixed angles had a significant relationship to price swings. One-fourth of the degrees in a circle (360) or 90 degrees was his basic focus, with half of that, 45 degrees, being the most important angle related to the rate at which a trend ascends or descends—a 45-degree angle divides a square in half. The angles Gann used were derived from the circle. A 45-degree angle on a chart, with equal time and price unit proportions, will travel up or down at an equal rate in terms of the price and time

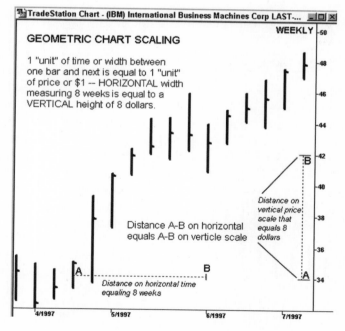

Figure 9.3

scale. One point up or down (price scale) on that line will equal one day, week, or month as in the chart in Figure 9.4. The common name for a line that measures a 45 percent rate of slope is the "1x1 or 1 by 1 angle." A "1x2 angle" is a rise of one point for every two *time periods* and is the next most important angle—and is used for the steeper rise that occurs in fast-moving trends. A "2x1" or 2 by 1 angle is the reverse situation, where there is a rise of two time periods for every one point in *price*.

Gann angles are drawn upward from important lows and downward from important highs. For example, once you have established a 45-degree (1x1) line up from an important low, it will often mark the area where the pullbacks in that upward trend will find support. If prices accelerate to the upside from the 45-degree rate of ascent, the upward price movement will often carry prices to the higher 1x2 line. This line could act as resistance, but a common situation, if prices move above this line, is that it becomes the support trendline. If the 45-degree line or 1x1 angle is broken on the downside, then prices will often carry to the still-lower "2x1" line. Figure 9.4 takes the same *square* chart of Figure 9.3 and draws from the point of a significant low (lower left of chart), the three principal angles that Gann

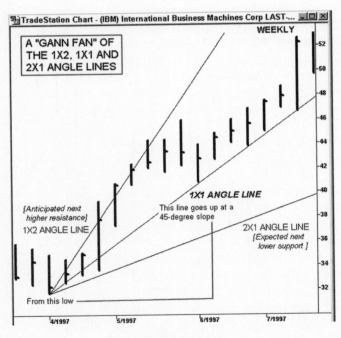

Figure 9.4

said marked most trend trajectories. Again, the usefulness of this technique is greatest when applied to a chart in the right proportions.

The important point about these fixed angular lines is that such angles can provide both a visual measurement of the type of momentum developing in a stock or other instrument and an idea of likely price support and resistance. What is especially interesting is the idea that trends tend to achieve certain rates of momentum, which are fairly well measured in the set of three angles.

Price "Squares"

Another unique and interesting method employed by Gann in his work was by using squares that begin from a major prior high or low, or from the difference between the same prior high and the prior low. Gann used the lows and highs for the entire period (daily, weekly, or monthly) being charted and not just the close, so relied on *bar* charts. Use is made of the "square of the high," the "square of the low," and the "square of the range." Squares drawn from measurements of high, low, and the range between a high and low, are cyclical in the sense that when prices get to the middle or end of the square, there is often a trend change. A trend change will tend to have two possibilities in terms of the type of change: change in the rate of price momentum—slowing down or *acceleration*—and a trend *reversal*. Acceleration is achieved when the relative steepness of an advance or decline increases—the idea also conveyed in the idea of a trendline angle becoming more or less steep. For example, XYZ stock's decline was from 100 to 80 (–20%), over a 10-month period, but then the stock drops a further 40 points (–50%) in only 2 months.

Figure 9.5 is an example of the *square of the range*, in terms of technique. The chart is not the exact price/time square chart type best achieved by use of a specialized software application. Nevertheless, the technique is adequately demonstrated. The monthly high for this period was $34.94, the later low was $10.16, 30 months later—this 2½ year price *range* was 24.78. Division of the highest high is typically by 8, but the most important divisions are to divide by 4 and draw a level line at what would be the 25, 50, and 70 percent retracements of the *price range* as seen in the second square in the figure. The measurement between high and low on the vertical price scale is one side of a square, and the same distance on the horizontal *time* scale is the other. A projection of the most likely time frame for a *trend change* is at the midpoint and end of the square on the horizontal time scale at bottom.

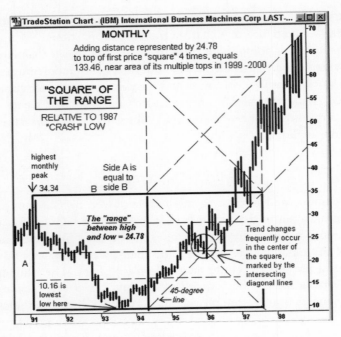

Figure 9.5

Even though Figure 9.5 does not have the exact Gann proportions, the chart nevertheless highlights the trend changes at the middle of this square and the sideways consolidation at the end of the square. The important 50 percent midpoint is easily found by drawing straight lines between the two sets of diagonal corners, which created this intersection. The principal support up trendline is the 45-degree angle line from the left-hand corner of the square. Interestingly, the square is 40 months wide and there was a high made for this stock in September 2000 (not shown), which is about 40 months after the end of the second price square.

Without using any special scaling we can calculate the important *price* retracements only. The distance between low and high of a past major move is a number that is the same regardless of price *scaling*. From this we can arrive at natural (according to Gann) future support or resistance areas by adding or subtracting 25 percent, 50 percent, 75 percent, and 100 percent of a prior major price range to either the high or low end of the range, according to the breakout direction. If the trend is up, a future high may be close to a distance that is equal to a prior price swing or range. This is how a measured move price objective is calculated. Adding squares of equal dimensions *multiple* times to the chart in Figure 9.5 produces the following relationship: The price range (24.78) rounded off is 25 and the prior high (34.94) is 35. This is the top line of the first level of price or Gann *squares*. When adding the 25 range figure 4 times–4 squares—to 35, we get the result 135, quite close to the 1999 bull market peak at $139, as well as equal to the 2000 top at $135.

Figure 9.6 is the *square of the high* in the Dow Industrial average prior to the 1987 *crash*. The peak price for the period shown is divided by 8. Horizontal lines below this top are drawn, at increments of 343 points. The lines that represent $1/4$ and $1/2$ of the topmost price will typically be the more significant levels. However, in this example, that of an average that is at an all-time multiyear high, the one-eighth levels all should be noted. In the chart of Figure 9.6, there was a rapid rebound after a weekly low was made just under one of our divisional lines, specifically at 1,716—five-eighths of the 2,746.70 top. The rapid rebound and weekly close well above this level was strong evidence, in Gann terms, for a bottom. The *square* shown in Figure 9.6 demonstrates expected *price support areas only*. Time cycle projections for possible future market *turning points* would be accurately done

Figure 9.6

only where the graph's time and price scales are such that the distance measuring a week is equal to a *unit* of price that does not change—for example, 50 points of the Dow Jones average. This is not the case with computer graphs, as scaling is according to *best fit* for screen dimensions depending on the time frame chosen (e.g., 6 months; 1–5 years).

Calculating squares based on the "square of the low" is a less-used technique, but the principal idea is to look for price objectives at levels that are 1.5 and 2 times (and higher such multiples) to the low. These areas are natural price objectives and resistance points. For example, the low of a stock is 13; a natural upside price target and expected future resistance would be 26.

SUMMARY OF GANN'S LEGACY

The foregoing attempts to convey some essence of the unique and unconventional measuring techniques employed by Gann can also be viewed as a way of looking at markets that gets us thinking *outside the box*, pun intended. The predictive ability that Gann could muster was quite extraordinary and he had some fame for being highly profitable in his investing and trading activities. A repeat of the market mastery he had may not be transferable, as Gann appears to have obscured his methods somewhat, which had an esoteric side anyway. It is fair to say that, among people who most closely follow his precepts—as closely as is possible, given the lack of a simple overall or unifying method—there have not been repeats of his financial success in the markets. Nevertheless, some quite good traders have profited from the use of Gann's *angle* and *price squares* ideas, particularly taking note to see if a current high is also a multiple of a prior price range and taking count of the *duration* of a trend (number of weeks or months) relative to an *acceleration* and extension (a new leg) of an existing trend or a *reversal* of the trend.

I particularly find the technique of taking the prior price *range*, or taking a major high and dividing by half, fourths, and eighths useful as a supplemental set of price targets or support/resistance possibilities. Sometimes one of these values will coincide to other techniques, and then I especially will take note of that. Moreover, the method of making the simple price divisions (of the high or the range) does not take any special graphing capabilities, so it is an easy one to apply from the various methods of forecasting associated with W.D. Gann. The essential idea from Gann is that price and time may be more intertwined than we realize, with strong links between price *and* time components—each moving until the point where momentum is spent or balance achieved, after which a new change (in trend) develops.

ELLIOTT WAVE THEORY

Not everyone examining the basics of technical analysis will agree that the Gann perspective can be put to practical use in terms of improving investing and trading success. Most will likely come to agree, if they try out the principles, that the *wave* theory of Ralph N. Elliott is something that can lead to an increase in profitable investment and trading decisions. A check of the price pattern will then come to include an evaluation of the basic wave structure *when* it is apparent or obvious. I emphasize this last point because I am a more casual Elliott wave practitioner, so to speak. That is, I have not joined the company of fellow investors and traders with a technical bent, who invest large amounts of time interpreting and re-interpreting detailed wave structures.

Ralph Nelson Elliott usually referred to as R.N. Elliott (1871–1948), was not quite an adult contemporary of Charles Dow, who was born in 1851 and lived to 1902, but was influenced by Dow's theories on the behavior of the stock market. Unlike W.D. Gann (active in the markets during 1900 to 1950), he was not a well-known and rich stock investor and shrewd *speculator* in stocks and commodities. However, the *Elliott wave principle*, is better known today than it ever was in Elliott's lifetime. This is not to say that R.N. Elliott didn't attract significant notice among some important market advisors and professional money managers. Elliott had an accounting background and worked with the railroads, including a stint in Central America where he contracted a severe illness in the late 1920s. The next several bedridden years gave his active mind ample time to turn to a study of the stock market. The buildup and crash of the U.S. market over the 1920s was something he knew well, being an avid follower of the stock market. Elliott was quite familiar with the work of Robert Rhea, who was the first to call and describe Dow's ideas in terms of a comprehensive *theory* of market behavior.

By 1934 and after, Elliott's own comprehensive theory of market behavior had become defined, and his predictions at times amazed some key market advisors and participants in terms of their forecasting accuracy. By 1945 Elliott was operating his investment advisory service from a Wall Street office. The *Wave Principle* based on his ideas, had been written already, but Elliott himself wrote a more comprehensive study called *Nature's Law*, which was only partly about the wave principle as applied to financial markets. I will, however, stick to the essence of the Elliott wave analysis regarding how market trends begin, unfold, and end.

Distilling what you need to remember about *Elliott wave* analysis is the idea (again) of there being three components to a trend. You will hear about "five" waves, because a bull market is said to consist of three up movements, interspaced by two corrective countertrend moves. The advancing waves or upswings of a bull market are called the three *impulse waves*. In a bear market, there are also three waves, comprised of two downswings and one corrective rebound. This pattern is "down-up-down" in terms of the direction of the trend. Often, but not all the time, such wave patterns are clearly and easily seen. When the wave structure is clearly and easily seen, it's possible to forecast much more accurately how a trend will unfold. The first impulse wave in a bull market trend is the weakest, but after the corrective downswing following it concludes, the next impulse wave—*wave three*—is usually the *money* wave. Wave three is the middle or *second* advance in a bull trend and is usually the most powerful. This insight might suggest, for example, going into a market more heavily in terms of participation, on the second big upswing.

An example of a three-wave would be, in my estimation, the 1997–1999 Nasdaq advance that carried prices to dizzying heights in the 1990s tech stock bull market. This is also an example of what I term a *megabull* market. However, even in a moderate bull market there will tend to be one, more lengthy advance, that carries further than the other secondary uptrends. The duration and intensity of this second advance, the three wave, will often see the biggest gains, in the most compressed time frame, for the entire bull market. In a bear market decline also, it is the second downswing that tends to carry the furthest. Accurate depiction of where we are in an unfolding price pattern that is *cyclical* in nature—having distinct components that comprise a *beginning*, *middle*, and *end*—is extremely valuable, especially when it helps accurately identify the early stages of a new trend.

"Wave" Structure of Common Bull and Bear Market Trends

Fellow Market Technician Association (MTA) member, Robert Prechter, is the best known of the market advisors and analysts that have made wave analysis popular from the 1970s into the new millennium. As Bob has pointed out, like the other theories of technical analysis, it is not even necessary to understand *why* the wave principle works as it does, as long as you can employ the technique to a profitable end.

In a major bull market trend of five waves, waves 1, 3, and 5 will be advances and are called impulse waves, with waves 2 and 4 being countertrend moves or corrective waves. The totality of the component moves of a bull market may be referred to as five waves "up." After the five waves of a major bull trend, a major bear trend will begin and consists of three down waves. These waves are actually not all down, but are described this way as they are all part of a down or bear market cycle. The three components together of such a bear market trend *correct* or are countertrend to the bull market that preceded it. These waves are given the letters A, B, and C, in capital letters, to distinguish between waves 1 to 5 that came before. The A and C waves are declines, with the intervening B wave being a *corrective* rebound that takes prices sideways to higher.

There is another way of using letter designations for waves—*a*, *b*, and *c* in lower case are used for the corrective price swings within *wave 2* and *wave 4* and in the countertrend rally of *wave B*, that is, any time the trend is *contrary* to the direction of the primary trend. When a market move or wave is in the same direction as the primary trend, including declining bear market waves A and C, these waves are broken down into smaller component parts that have five parts (1–5) and are waves of a smaller *degree*.

Figures 9.7 and 9.8 are examples of bull and bear market trends that unfold with the classic (Elliott) wave structure of a 5 up wave bull market and a 3 down wave bear trend. Moves in the direction of the primary trend break down further into a five-wave structure. Moves *against* the trend subdivide into the three-part *a-b-c* structure illustrated in Figure 9.9. This further subdivision of the larger wave structure is one of the ways that you know when a move may be in a final stage of completion. For example in Figure 9.9, it can be seen that the *third wave* or the second big advance is in a completion phase when the smaller fifth wave (wave 5 of a smaller degree) is underway. My wave interpretations are my own only and should not be considered as the only wave structure interpretation. Examples used are for demonstration purposes only and in an attempt to provide the basic concepts of how a trend is viewed in terms of the Elliott wave structure. I use ideas gleaned from the wave principle in patterns where the wave structure appears clear cut. The success of successfully identifying a *classic* wave structure will be whether it provided early recognition of a trend that led to a profitable investment or trade.

R.N. Elliott spent more of his time applying his wave analysis to the major market averages. He also found the same wave patterns in individual

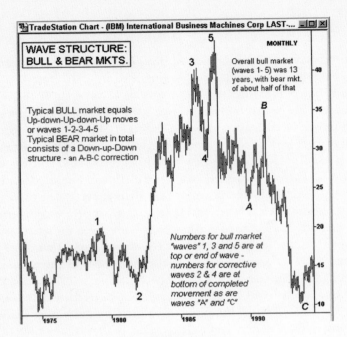

Figure 9.7

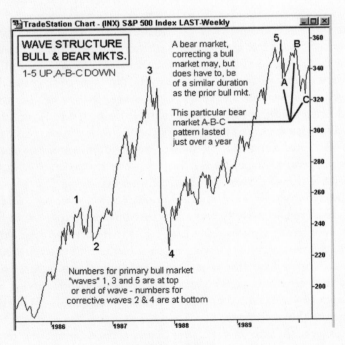

Figure 9.8

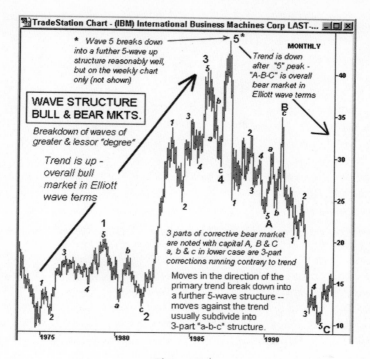

Figure 9.9

stocks, but specific stocks were less of a focus for him compared to defining the overall market trend. The bond and commodity markets are not different in terms of the underlying wave structure. However, the commodity markets will tend to see wave patterns unfold more quickly.

Elliott talked about *alternation* in wave duration and strength. While wave 3 is typically longer and stronger than wave 1, if it is of about equal length, wave 5 will tend to be the more prolonged advance. Conversely, major bear market down wave A is usually of shorter duration, but if prolonged, then Elliott would look for the down move C to be relatively shorter. As with other technical analysis techniques, a surge in average volume will help identify the strongest part of an overall move. Longer-term charts, such as weekly, are favored over daily charts in terms of seeing and defining the dominant wave patterns.

Longer-term trend definition in Elliott wave analysis is different from the way that a primary bull market is defined in Dow's interpretation. In Figure 9.7, up wave 1 could be considered to be a primary bull market, corrective wave 2 a primary bear market, up wave 3 a primary bull market, and so on. In terms of Elliott's viewpoint, the entire sequence of waves 1 to 5 constituted one complete bull market cycle. The entire sequence of the correction that follows wave 5, consisting of the large moves labeled A-B-C, is all part and parcel of a major bear market trend of many years (see Figure 9.7). Wave B would be a *bear market* rally, even though a year long and consisting of a big percentage rebound. Elliott defined different degrees of bull and bear markets by different terms than Dow's less complex descriptions of primary bull or bear markets. Elliott's descriptions of the type of bull or bear market also related to smaller or larger *degrees* of bull or bear markets. Elliott used modifications of *cycle* to describe some of them (e.g., a *supercycle*).

Employing Wave Analysis Along with Other Technical Factors

Using the same stock as seen charted on a monthly basis, that of IBM in Figures 9.7 and 9.9 (during the years shown, a market *bellwether*), Figure 9.10 is the weekly chart and Figure 9.11, the daily. In the monthly chart the interpretation made was that corrective wave 2 was completed. At this point good use can be made of the weekly chart (Figure 9.10) and refined with the daily chart (Figure 9.11), to arrive at an entry decision relative to the next expected advance (wave 3). For purposes of *timing* trade entry it can be valuable to use other technical analysis entry *signals*, such as a bullish moving average and oscillator crossover and/or a breakout above the dominant down trendline. I usually have higher confidence in these indicators when I can use them in conjunction with a fairly clear, well-defined wave pattern. Having confidence in your investing or trading decision is very important early in a trend. It is hardest to sit tight in the early stages of a trend, as the business and economic news, for the most part, rarely supports the side of the market chosen.

If I anticipate that the *a-b-c* pattern of a corrective *wave* has ended, I have a reasonable expectation that the next move is an *impulse* wave that will take the financial item in question well above where it went on the highest peak during the correction. However, as Dow said, early in any major bull market upswing there is limited bullish enthusiasm. In fact, the public may be decidedly *un*enthusiastic about the market, so it's hard to find public support for being long early. Of course, it is not enough to be early in a trend, as prices could always be heading into an unprofitable multiyear sideways pattern, such as seen with precious metals for most of the 1980s and 1990s. In stocks, this can also happen, as was the case for much of the 1960s and 1970s. However, if entry is made early in the trend and with an exit strategy, most of what price movement does develop can be captured.

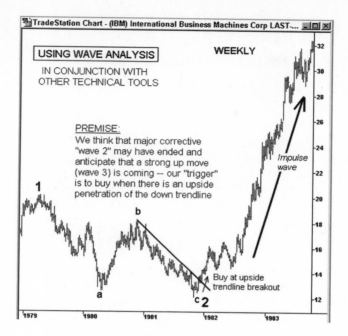

Figure 9.10

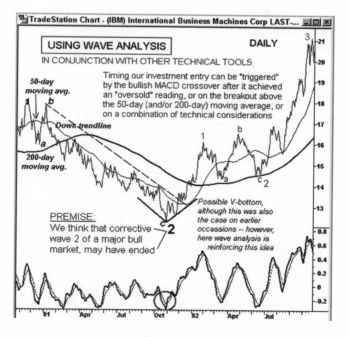

Figure 9.11

Wave Characteristics

R.N. Elliott, like Charles Dow, observed that there is progression of human emotions in the marketplace from pessimism to optimism and back again. This pattern tends to repeat in a *cyclical* fashion, such that the characteristics and price patterns of the *cycle* we are in can be recognized. The impulse waves, or the three up moves, of waves 1 through 5 that make up a typical bull market, behave differently from the two corrective downside moves of a bull market, or the larger corrective bear market waves that follow a bull market completion, labeled as A, B, and C. All the wave patterns from 1 through 5 and A through C have a characteristic *flavor*, as seen in Figures 9.12, 9.13, and 9.14 and described here:

1. First waves—Many of these are part of the basing process, and so the second wave that follows will sometimes retrace all of wave 1. This explains a double bottom in Elliott wave terms. If wave 1 follows a *big base* pattern, then its rise can be far stronger than this, however.

Figure 9.12

Figure 9.13

Figure 9.14

2. Second waves—With this corrective pattern, prices retrace some or all of the first advance. This corrective wave pattern will often produce bullish *divergences* as prices, a key average, or indicators don't decline as far as their prior lows.

3. Third waves—As discussed previously, this advance is what makes *believers* out of many investors, as it is a strong rally and often prolonged. In the stock market, this advance tends to have the broadest participation of stocks on each major exchange.

4. Fourth waves—This is another corrective wave. If the second wave, also corrective in nature, was relatively simple and short-lived, this wave will tend to be more complex and prolonged, according to Elliott's rule of *alternation*. Stocks that lagged the advance in wave 3, will dip the most and start to build tops.

5. Fifth waves—This advance will most often be less powerful and prolonged than up wave 3. Sometimes, this wave will extend, in time and price, relative to wave 3, especially if the third wave was relatively short-lived and carried prices less far than wave 1—rule of alternation. If so, wave 5 may look more like wave 1. If wave 1 was a good-sized advance, then this final (fifth wave) rally may be also. This upswing completes the bull market trend.

   ▮ A waves—This is the first decline of a bear market trend. As in the 2000 Nasdaq top, investors by this stage will tend to be convinced that this down move will be a short-lived decline. This wave is characterized, in terms of the psychology of investors, by continued faith in a longer-term buy and hold philosophy.

   ▮ B waves—A rally phase that typically has less volume and, in the stock market, fewer stocks that rebound strongly. Being a move *contrary* (i.e., up) to the dominant down trend, it typically has three parts—an *a-b-c* correction. But this pattern starts with a rally and therefore follows an up-down-up sequence, which is the reverse start and finish of the *a-b-c* (down-up-down) correction of waves 2 and 4. The B wave advance might carry to as high as the levels previously achieved by the market, but technical and volume indicators will tend not to confirm as much strength as previously. A double top, relative to the top of wave 5, is a possibility. It is during this rebound, that nonconfirmations will occur in the two Dow averages and/or in key bellwethers, such as related market averages or key market segments.

▌ C waves—This decline, in the reverse direction but with similar intensity to wave 3 on the upside, carries the market sharply lower. The C wave decline will often be of longer duration and carry prices significantly lower. A *Fibonacci* relationship to the first down move or A wave, suggests that this decline could carry 1.38, 1.5, or 1.62 times, or more, further than the first downswing. In stocks there are few sectors that offer much shelter to investors, as there is a broad decline. Fear and gloom tend to build. At the bottom of this move, investor sentiment becomes very bearish and as discussed by Dow, previous stock market investors don't want to own equities, no longer maintain much interest in the market, and are disillusioned with it.

Summary of Elliott Wave Theory

As with the theories of Charles Dow, the Elliott wave principles cannot be proven according to any statistical proofs—there are too many variables and interpretations to facilitate this effort. Unlike Dow's simple rule that holds that the averages must confirm each other's new highs or lows to maintain trend validity, Elliott wave analysis can be complex, and an unfolding price pattern can be open to differing but valid wave interpretations, according to wave principles. And, like Dow's nonconfirmation (of the two averages), correct identification of the wave pattern may occur only after a formation completes itself and too late to take defensive or appropriate action. That said, in its simplest terms and used when a wave pattern is well defined and fairly *obvious*, understanding Elliott's rules of market behavior can lead to some very profitable investments. And to the avoidance of key mistakes, like staying fully invested in the market long past the end of a bull market.

Use of Elliott wave principles has given me a useful tool in identifying the *structure* of an unfolding pattern, such as a bull market wave 3, when a knowledge of its strong trend greatly increases the likelihood of being invested in this phase when it gets underway. Conversely, being aware of a correction in an advancing trend that follows a threefold down-up-down pattern, allows an understanding of where the market is in terms of the unfolding of a corrective *cycle*. *Cycles* are trends that have a repetitive sequence depending on the type of cycle. Because the markets tend to repeat similar patterns (waves) in a similar sequence, recognition of the current point in this sequence often has a predictive value and hence a profitable value.

TRADING SYSTEMS

Technical trading systems are an outgrowth of the computer age, in that computer power is what has allowed what can be described as the *STAD* method for making market entry and exit decisions—for System Testing And Development. Trading systems are composed of a set of objective entry and exit conditions that can be defined to allow computerized entry and exit *signals*. These entry and exit conditions may then be *backtested* on historical market data to see how profitable these *trigger* conditions for entry and exit would have been in the past. Backtesting, in turn, allows refinement of the technical rules and is another key part of STAD. Without computer applications to handle this task, trading systems would not have evolved as a popular means for systematic investing and trading. Use of backtesting and picking the best entry/exit rules based on past market data, must be monitored to prevent a serious drawback of the *systems* approach—that of *curve fitting*. Curve fitting is finding a set of rules that worked perfectly with the benefit of hindsight and based on past market conditions, but that is not necessarily effective going forward into new types of market conditions and cycles.

I concentrate here on demonstrating some basics of trading systems and not on detailing the pitfalls and shortcomings of trading systems. There are strengths and weaknesses in the trading systems approach, but this discussion can be left to a specialized study, should you become interested in applying technical analysis in this manner. I would just note that the obvious appeal and a strength of trading systems very much relates to the common investing and trading pitfalls—lack of a plan or discipline in carrying out a plan which includes rigid risk management principles and the difficulties in taming negative emotions like fear, greed, and fantasy—seeing market conditions in a way that reflects our bullish or bearish biases rather than objectively.

Specialized computer applications are required to develop and use trading systems. The one I am familiar with is TradeStation. This application product is also probably the best known for systems testing and development, certainly for individual use, and that benefits from having many user groups who swap knowledge and ideas.

Trading systems can, in their most simple categorization, be broadly broken down into ones that use technical *indicators* or ones that use *chart patterns* or some combination of both methods. The validity of each approach stems from a basic principle of technical analysis—the knowledge that market cycles repeat and are identifiable. The sample systems I use as illustrations are *applied* to or tested on daily or weekly charts, but systems that employ intraday data are not materially different in construction.

Indicator-Based Trading Systems

One example of a popular oscillator type indicator is the relative strength index or RSI. In the past it has been hard to identify how well the RSI worked in terms of its use as a buy or sell signal. The systems language set up in the TradeStation application for a simple *rule-based* trading system using the RSI is shown in Figure 9.15. A common use of the RSI is to buy a market or individual item (a financial instrument) when the RSI is registering an oversold or overbought condition—for example, buying below 30 and selling above 70. However, because markets can stay at overbought or oversold readings for some time, the system shown in Figure 9.15 triggers a position only when the RSI crosses above 30 or below 70, when this oscillator is coming back from an extreme. Early exit may be desirable if the RSI moves back into those extreme readings. Such a move is an alternative exit signal and is also part of the way this system is written.

Figure 9.15

The resulting *RSI system* can then be applied to any chart or charts of whatever duration after values are put in as to the dollar amount that will be traded in the case of stocks, or the number of contracts in terms of futures contracts, and so on. It's also possible to enter stop-protection *exit* rules after trade entry, trailing stops, rules about pyramiding positions, and so on. Moreover, an *optimization* process can determine what RSI length, as well as overbought and oversold trigger levels, would have achieved the best results for individual markets for various *past* time frames. Optimization determines what set of values for the variable *input* rules will yield the best results for a prior time frame—for example, the most profitable overall results, but perhaps adjusted to take out trading parameters that have very large losses during losing periods. Designing an optimal system will present some traps for the novice user. For example, it's not desirable to just look at the percentage of winning trades generated. Expected *gain per trade* is a better standard. This formula is the percentage of winning trades times the average gain, minus the percentage of losing trades times the average loss per losing trade. It is desirable to increase the former and decrease the latter so that the gain per trade profit figure rises.

Pattern Recognition Systems

Many investors and traders who analyze charts based on technical analysis principles will tell you that they are looking for clues to future market direction based on particular patterns that they have found meaningful in the past, for example, identifying any period of a few days' duration, when a market begins making higher daily highs or lower daily lows. For example, you have observed that it's quite predictive for the early stage of an uptrend, when there are at least three days of higher highs. Establishing this as a trading system rule can be quite simple. First, we define the condition we are looking for: a high greater than (>) the high of one [1] bar ago, when that high (of 1 bar ago) is also greater than the high of two [2] bars ago and the high of 2 bars ago is also greater than all the highs of three [3] bars ago—all conditions must be true. The reverse situation applies to a series of lows less than (<) the three preceding bars.

The resulting *pattern* system based on successively higher highs, for whatever time period (e.g., hourly, daily, weekly), is easily established with rules written in a shorthand form for the TradeStation application. These rules might take the form

Condition1 = High > High[1] and High[1] > High[2] and High[2] > High[3];

Condition2 = Low < Low[1] and Low[1] < Low[2] and Low[2] < Low[3];

If Condition1 then buy this bar on close; If Condition2 then sell this bar on close;

Exit in the above system is triggered only by the reverse conditions and where the system is always "in" the market, at least absent the addition of a stop-loss *rule* or an addition of a set of conditions. There could also be a rule written to exit if long when there was a *key downside reversal* and exit short positions if there was a *key upside reversal*. Entire trading systems and very profitable ones also, are sometimes constructed as simply as the one described. The software application usually triggers an audible and visual alert when the entry or exit condition of a trading system, applied to any market or individual item, is triggered. This might occur after you download end-of-day data or it could be in real time if you have a *live* data feed.

Some Basics of Trading System Development

An exit is assumed if a position contrary to the original is triggered. If the *system* is long, and short conditions are met, selling triggers both an exit and a new short position alert in the systems management software.

An effective systems trading strategy should have components that at a minimum govern

1. Entering the market
2. Exiting the market while capturing profits
3. Exiting the market in order to minimize losses

These three components often involve three different rules and corresponding *signals* when the system rule or rules are met. For example, if you create a rule that enters the market based on a momentum indicator, you will likely also want to add a trailing stop signal that can retain or capture some portion of unrealized gains, in the event of a trend reversal.

Once there is a well defined set of rules to enter and exit positions, in order not to risk money with unproven strategies, it is then important to see how well the ideas comprising the system performed in various past market periods. Backtesting involves applying the system to as much price history as you can find (e.g., 5–10 years or more). *Optimization* of a rule-based system is often undertaken here. Optimization is a computerized test to determine *which* variables (e.g., which specific moving average or averages) resulted in the most profitable or the most consistent profits for the past period being examined. A technique known as *walk-forward* optimization can then mitigate the tendency to select only variables in indicator or pattern-recognition systems that fit past conditions. The walk-forward technique involves testing some period for the most profitable system inputs, then applying them for a later period and adjusting the values, then testing some further *forward* period again and so on.

Regardless of the rules and markets, one of the things that should be considered when studying results, is to examine why the losing trades were unprofitable? How were the losing trades different from the winning trades? It is important to scrutinize the losing trades and investigate what happened on each occasion. The software applications that have well-developed systems testing and development capabilities like TradeStation, have templates and tools that allow the study of all of these aspects of trading system results and scrutiny.

Analysis of the biggest losing trade is a starting point to see how a system *doesn't* work, so there are no holes in the system rules by which a trade would cause unacceptable losses, or more than the maximum you are willing to take. Trading strategy should be studied on two levels: as a system with profitable net results over time and at the *trade-by-trade* level to determine if the individual trades have acceptable results compared to one another and to the group. For this type of analysis to be correct, all trade results need to be comparable to one another. Since we are working in the financial world, this means that we should see all our results in terms of dollars (or monetary units). It is not correct to compare the return on investment of buying 100 shares of a 10-dollar stock with buying 100 shares of a 100-dollar stock. The comparison would only make sense if you were buying or selling some set dollar amount of each (e.g., $10,000).

Summary of the Trading System Approach

Regardless of whether you have any interest or inclination to use trading systems now or ever, it is an appropriate part of our study of technical analysis to know about the trading systems option to supplement (or substitute for) what is typically the more subjective methods we use to make market decisions. It is also worth noting that the more investing and trading experience one has, the easier it can be to define sound system rules that prove to be profitable. Moving from the stage of ideas that may be profitable to backtesting these rules is a fascinating and worthwhile process that serves as a market reality check. Often, through the results of backtesting, it becomes apparent that even with a promising system, merely slight changes can result in investing or trading rules that have significantly greater profit potential.

Systems testing and development may be an approach that is useful only after a lengthy experience in using technical analysis. This was the case with me and I thought I would never warm to the approach of devising *mechanical* systems. I became enthusiastic about this type of application when I saw that it could validate, or invalidate, long-held personal beliefs about what kinds of technical analysis techniques worked best as a basis for market action. Moreover, I found that the more I knew about technical analysis and the more months and years that I had observed the unfolding of many different chart patterns, the more I got out of the ability to create trading systems with the new software that appeared in the 1990s. This was quite the opposite result of what I expected. Systems testing and development is a natural continuation of applying technical analysis to trading and investing, especially for those who are more oriented to the use of computers and software.

10

PUTTING IT ALL TOGETHER

INTRODUCTION

To profitably employ technical analysis in the real world of market action, especially given the emotional or psychological pressures that develop at times in the financial markets, takes time and considerable perseverance. There can be many mistakes along the way to consistent favorable results based on technical analysis. You may make an investment decision based on an apparent long-term *double bottom* or base a trade on the formation of a *bull flag*, only to see the double bottom give way and the flag pattern fall apart. The purpose of controlling risk through the use of liquidating stop orders and diversification is to not erode investment or trading capital through a period of market entry decisions that did not work out. There are occasions when price chart patterns with technical significance in terms of a usual predictive outcome do not lead to the expected outcome. There is always the possibility of a pattern failure. More often than pattern failures is a mistake in identifying or correctly accessing all the key technical determinants. For example, there is a presumed *double bottom*, but without a confirming move above the last significant upswing high or on a subsequent rally after the presumed double bottom, the item fails to penetrate a key moving average like the 50-day, and this brings in renewed selling.

If consistently profitable investing or trading was an easy accomplishment, based on either technical *or* fundamental analysis, most stock market investors would have greater prior profits than is the case and would probably not rely on the expertise of professional money mangers as much as they do, as evidenced by the vast sums that are invested in managed mutual funds. However, *perseverance furthers* in this area—only a large number and variety of market experiences, including making decisions that are mistakes and taking losses, will typically result in an eventual expertise that pays off. Besides perseverance, use of a checklist to run through all relevant technical analysis considerations and tools is of considerable help.

TECHNICAL ANALYSIS CHECKLIST

The big-ten technical factors are:

1. *Background* information—major averages, *bellwethers*, and the market *sector*. If the item being considered is a stock, then it's important to also look at the technical picture for the average(s) of which it is part—if available, examine the market *sector* chart. Checking related indexes or stocks may be of use here. If a commodities market is involved, bellwethers might include the key futures market in that complex (e.g., for heating oil, this would be the crude oil chart). Here it would also be appropriate to focus on any obvious *wave* pattern.

2. *Looking at all time frames*—daily, weekly, monthly. Study longer-term charts, volume, and indicator patterns before making any decisions based on the daily charts. Look at the daily chart and indicators, if trading on an intraday basis.

3. *Trend* considerations—Examining whether there is a *trending* or *consolidation* pattern apparent on the chart(s). Basically, this is always having an eye as to whether the market is trending up or down, versus being in a sideways *consolidation* or *trading range*. If in a trading range, is it well-defined, wideranging or relatively narrow, and how long has it gone on? For example, is its duration as long as the prior trend in terms of weeks and months? When a consolidation has gone on as long or longer than a prior price movement of a similar nature, be alert for any trend change.

4. *Overbought/oversold* considerations—long- and short-term. As a further technical backdrop, it is recommended to be aware from

day to day or week to week, of the relative position of price momentum oscillators like RSI and MACD for daily, weekly, and monthly timeframes. Be aware if the market or instrument is approaching an overbought or oversold extreme, whether momentum up or down has been strong, or has slowed significantly. If an extreme reading is at hand or if momentum measured by these indicators has stalled, then it's important to follow the price and volume patterns closely for signs of a reversal, while keeping in mind that there are many consolidations along the way in a trend. A sideways trend bears watching in terms of protecting existing profits if the high of the price range already got near price objectives. It may be time to take profits or raise protective stops.

5. *Predictive patterns*—price and volume. Make a determination of what patterns, if any, are developing, such as rectangles, flags, triangles, double bottoms, double tops, and so on with a possible measurement of an associated minimum upside objective. Volume is (on balance volume also) something to look at, along with price, to determine if the volume pattern is confirming price action or not.

6. *Trendlines* and price channels. Construction of any relevant trendlines and price channels is very basic to effective technical analysis and a study of the trend—even if you merely use a straight edge to make more of a mental check of where trendlines are forming or get pierced. While not an everyday occurrence, a return to a previously broken trendline often offers a second opportunity for trade or investment entry.

7. *Retracement* calculations. For the markets and individual items you follow, calculations for any return or rebound of 38 percent, 50 percent, or 62 percent of a prior price swing is essential. A strong move that retraces more than 62 percent on up to two-thirds or 66 percent, often suggests that momentum will carry back to the prior high or low.

8. *Moving averages*. It is suggested that you keep track of some of the basic and key moving averages, such as 21, 50, and 200 days for stocks, and the 5-, 9-, and 18-day ones, and perhaps 21 days, for sometimes faster moving markets like commodities and FX.

9. *Oscillators*. Another frequent check is of the relative position of at least one of the popular oscillator-type indicators like RSI, slow stochastics, or MACD on both a daily and weekly or monthly chart basis. This is more than just seeing if they are at an extreme (over-

bought or oversold) as in point 4, as oscillators are a basic indicator of price momentum. On daily charts, I especially keep track of the RSI indicators with a length calculation of either 13 or 14 and 21 days as well. On weekly charts check the MACD oscillator.

10. *Divergences.* One of the great values of the oscillators, and volume indicators as well, is to highlight points when they diverge from price action, such as failing to accompany prices to a new relative high. This type of divergence is much more crucial when the market has been trending for a long period and is, or has been for some time previously, registering an extreme (e.g., below 25/30 and above 70/75 on a 14- or 26-day RSI. Such divergences are not, by themselves, indications to buy or sell usually, but alert you to a possible reversal. This situation should then cause you to check where key trendlines or moving averages would be violated. Surprise often is the enemy of quick market action, as there is initial *disbelief* in a *reversal*—preparedness is important. Ultimately, you rarely should be surprised when a market reverses in such a situation—the reasons why or the news explaining it, tend to be lagging events. Even when there is a fundamental surprise, such as an unexpected earnings shortfall, the reaction to this news is usually far more severe when there is an *overbought* situation and conversely, less so, when the market is *oversold*. If a stock is quite overbought and an important earnings announcement is due, this is exactly the time when you may want to exit some or all of a position.

Figure 10.1 is a daily chart of Intel Corporation (INTC), one of the major components of the Nasdaq Composite, during 1997 through October 1998. The daily chart for this period, by itself, suggests that the stock is in a trading range from $16.5–17 to 23–25—this is the dominant impression for this chart and does yield a trade or investment idea. However, by looking at other related charts and indicators for the same stock, Intel Corporation, as shown in Figures 10.2 through 10.4, a more comprehensive outlook is gained by looking at the technical factors on our checklist—the sum of which adds up to a quite bullish outlook and future trend forecast. Based on our checklist items, the stock appeared headed for another up *leg*, with the multimonth sideways trend playing the role of a bullish *consolidation*. While Figure 10.1, the daily chart of key Nasdaq component stock Intel Corporation, could be viewed possibly as that of a *top* formation. The Nasdaq Composite last weekly low seen in Figure 10.3 during the same period, suggested the third and *confirming* point of

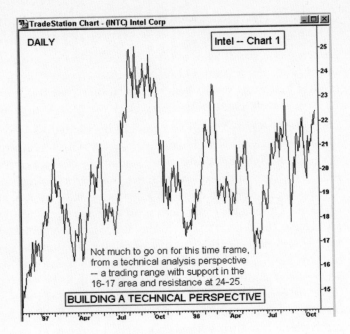

Figure 10.1

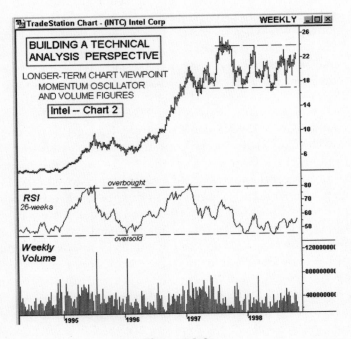

Figure 10.2

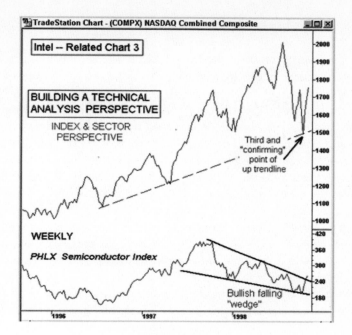

Figure 10.3

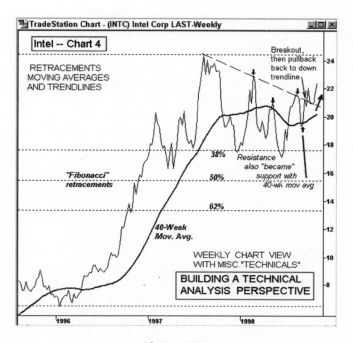

Figure 10.4

an up trendline. Moreover, the weekly chart of the Semiconductor Index (SOX) in the same figure appears to be breaking out on the upside from a bullish *falling wedge*.

Other bullish checklist items: Weekly *volume* for Intel tended to contract on declines and expand or surge on rallies. The long-term, 26-week *RSI* (Figure 10.2) indicates upward *momentum* after the indicator reached an *oversold* reading. The stock did not *retrace* more than a minimal Fibonacci 38 percent of the 1996–1997 advance (Figure 10.4) and held this price area on a second occasion, which was bullish. There was also an upside breakout above a weekly down trendline—with a minor subsequent pullback to this line, which acted as support, which was confirming for the breakout. Moreover, the weekly closes (Figure 10.4) traced out a *descending triangle*, with a subsequent *breakout* to the upside. Per the analysis of all the factors cited, the technical outlook for this stock, based on our checklist items, appears to be quite bullish. The stock should have been purchased on its last dip to the $17–18 area when it was seen to rebound from there, and again on the breakout above $22.

Figure 10.5 goes on to picture Intel's price action from October 1997 to March 2001. For long-term investors, purchases worked out well in the following 12 months, as the stock more than tripled from the $22 area, after prices achieved the aforementioned bullish upside breakout. Stops set to close below the prior lows between $18 and $20 could have been touched off or *elected* during a final downswing to the $16.50 area. If so, re-entry could have been made prior to the next rally, which occurred just after the stock again got *oversold* according to the RSI. If purchases were made in the $17 area, at the low end of the *consolidation* or *trading range*, a premature exit would not have been a factor—assuming a stop equal to a 10 percent risk relative to the purchase price.

A situation of a *rolling bottom* with a minor new low is fairly common. It also demonstrates the importance of entry near technical support as would be the case at the low end of a consolidation or in the early stages of a new or renewed trend, especially in terms of a *safe* stop-loss point. A safe or sheltered stop is placement where the stop will not be *hit* unless the trend is really going to go in that direction. Interestingly, that final bottom was made only after the consolidation had gone on at least as long (in fact, about eight weeks longer) as the prior uptrend, in the stock's first big upswing.

Figure 10.5 labels a five-part wave pattern of three component upswings or *impulse waves*, interspaced or punctuated by two *corrective* sideways to lower price movements or *corrective waves*. The fact that corrective wave 2 had a well-defined three part *a-b-c* (down-up-down)

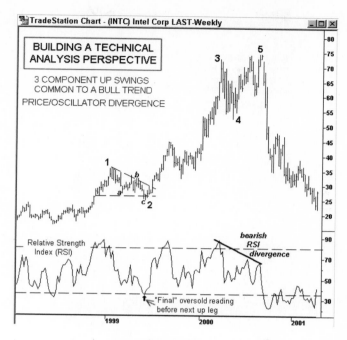

Figure 10.5

structure helped identify when the downward correction had run its course. There is nothing obvious in the weekly chart about wave 5 that tells us when it will end, except that the long advance in wave 3 would suggest a shorter last leg up in wave 5 (rule of alternation). The final up move in a bull market is most often accompanied by bearish divergences. In this case, it was apparent from the RSI action shown in Figure 10.5.

Figure 10.6 shows another weekly chart with some more of our checklist items. Some further technical sell indications were given when prices (1) fell below the low end of its uptrend channel, (2) broke its 40-week (200-day average equivalent), and then (3) fell below the prior swing low of major significance in the $53 area. There was a pronounced failure of on balance volume to confirm the last peak of the stock, as also noted in Figure 10.6.

PAGE TURNERS

To better simulate real-world study of unfolding market analysis, with subsequent favorable and unfavorable outcomes, some charts are presented

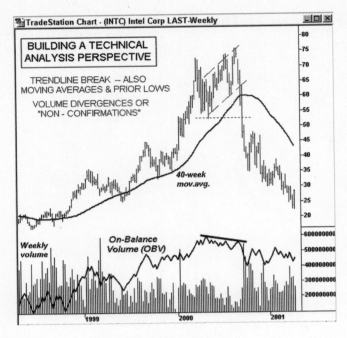

Figure 10.6

next with my technical outlook at the time, with the subsequent page presenting a chart that is a future continuation of the same chart for the same item. Such a treatment demonstrates not only how the price pattern unfolded after the original outlook, but also presents a further analysis and/or the lesson presented by the winning or losing trade—lessons from incorrect or losing choices being especially valuable.

I suggest that you study the chart, indicators, and the entry rationale presented to see first if you agree with the rationale and why or why not, before turning the page to see how things came out later. You may not have an opinion, but you could first go back to a prior chapter to study the chart pattern discussed or the indicator employed, with this earlier explanation to see how it fits with what could be anticipated next, pricewise—then come back and turn the page. Enjoy!

Figure 10.7

Suggested market action and rationale—Figure 10.7
Sell in $34 area with objective for a new low under $22

Stock is in a bear market trend as suggested by decline A to well under prior lows. Recovery or corrective rally from first down leg will often stall at about ½ of the prior downswing and intraday highs have stopped four times at the $34 level. Moreover, RSI has gone sideways to lower on the most recent rally, which is a slight bearish *divergence*. A next decline should make a lower low than previously. Place a stop just above $36, as prices are not expected to get back above the 200-day moving average.

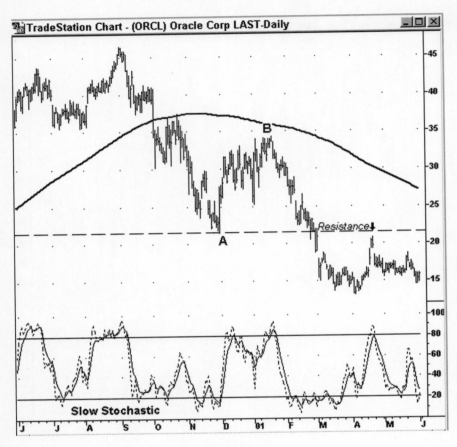

Figure 10.8

Outcome—Figure 10.8
Position bought back on the second decline to the $15 area

There was a further move down to the $11–12 area after the period shown in Figure 10.8. Buying was apparent around $15 as evidenced by the sideways trend. The *oversold* oscillator reading suggested that further downside potential might not be that great. Before this liquidation, the exiting stop was lowered to just above resistance implied by the prior low at A.

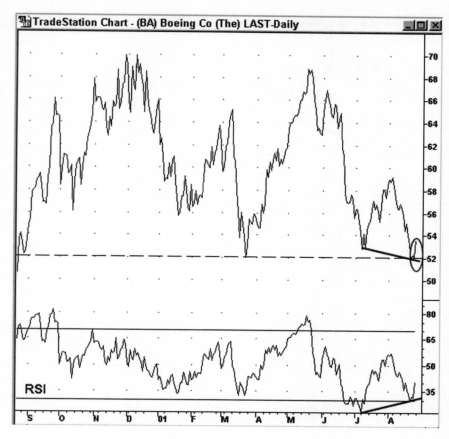

Figure 10.9

Suggested market action and rationale—Figure 10.9
Purchase was made in $53 area

This buy recommendation anticipated that a bottom has been made in
the area of the prior March low and based on the bullish RSI divergence—
also while this indicator was at an oversold reading—as the most recent
RSI low was above its prior low, contrary to price action. Stops should be
set at $51, not far below the assumed double bottom at $52.

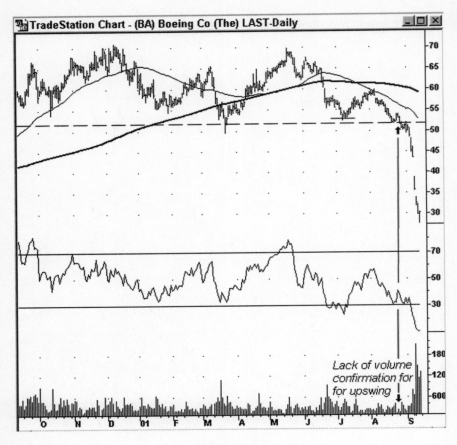

Figure 10.10

Outcome—Figure 10.10
Stop elected at an approximate $2 loss

This trade was a speculative one, as the trend remained down. There were some important lessons here: (1) The minor rebound to the $53 area did not see prices holding above the prior low. A better trading strategy would have been to wait to see if prices held this area on pullbacks (i.e., prior resistance, once exceeded, should become new support; (2) Volume did not surge on the advance and was very light, suggesting that the rally stemmed from short-covering and an absence of selling as prices got back to the low end of a broad trading range; (3) While the RSI had reached an oversold 30, this is no guarantee of price *support* being found; instead, this stock went on to get much *more* oversold.

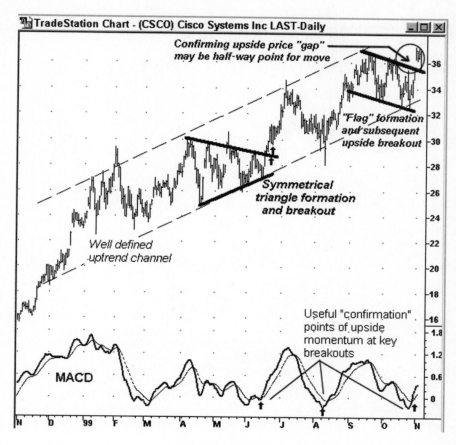

Figure 10.11

Suggested market action and rationale—Figure 10.11
Buy at $29 and again at $36

The first purchase was on the breakout from a *triangle*, and the second was on the bullish breakout above the downward sloping *flag* pattern. There is an uptrend *channel* that is traced out as the advance progresses. Since the lower (up) trend line is well defined, placement of a trailing stop (gradually moved higher with the trend) can be established under this line—or just below the key downswing lows made as the trend progresses. MACD confirms the upside *momentum* at key points.

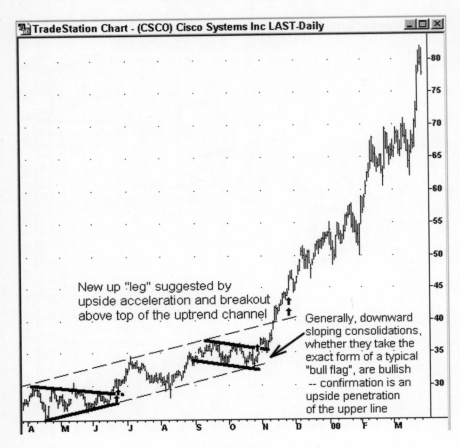

Figure 10.12

Outcome—Figure 10.12
Stay long with the trend

A discussion of what technical factors might trigger profit taking is discussed and shown in the next figure (Figure 10.13). One possibility for an upside objective for this trade would be suggested if the upside gap in the $36 area was a *measuring gap*, about midway in the total anticipated advance, and this scenario would then imply an upside price target to at least $72.

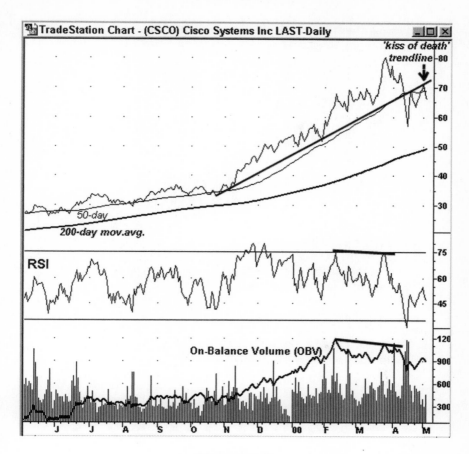

Figure 10.13

Suggested market action and rationale—Figure 10.13

*Take profits on earlier purchases (at $29 and $36) on the advance
    above $75*

Go short on the rebound to the $70 area

The last rally, before prices began coming off highs in the $80 area,
was accompanied by a failure of either RSI or OBV to confirm the new relative high, which warranted profit taking. The subsequent break of the up
trendline suggested a reversal of trend, as did the break below the 50-day
moving average. The rally back to the trendline, now expected resistance
(the "kiss of death" trendline) was a shorting opportunity, particularly after the bearish divergences.

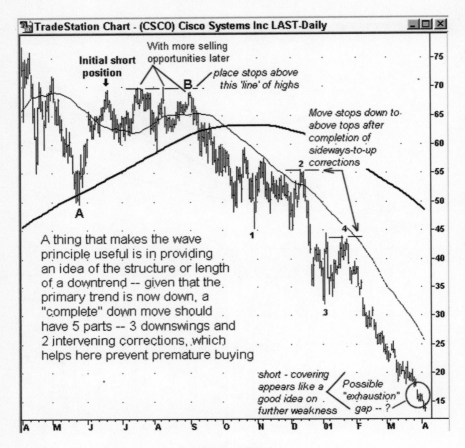

Figure 10.14

Outcome—**Figure 10.14**
Take profits on short positions at $15

The steep decline came after repeated rally failures at resistance in the $70 area, providing ample opportunities to sell the stock. The wave structure of the down move after the rebound to B would typically be that of three distinct downswings and the overall decline would typically be longer than the first decline to point A, which is how this bear trend unfolded. The downside price gap in the $17 area, after such a steep decline already, marked a possible *exhaustion gap* suggesting that prices were nearing a bottom.

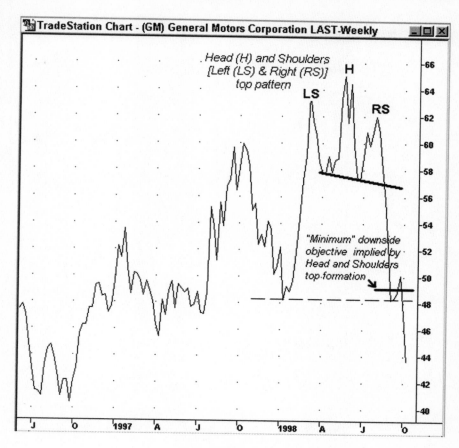

Figure 10.15

Suggested market action and rationale—Figure 10.15
Sell in $56.50 area

Sold on downside penetration of neckline of weekly head and shoulders top formation. While minimum downside objective for $49 was met, the penetration of the prior (early 1998) downswing low suggested a new primary downtrend, so the suggestion was to stay short, with a stop moved down to $50.50, just above the minor upswing high.

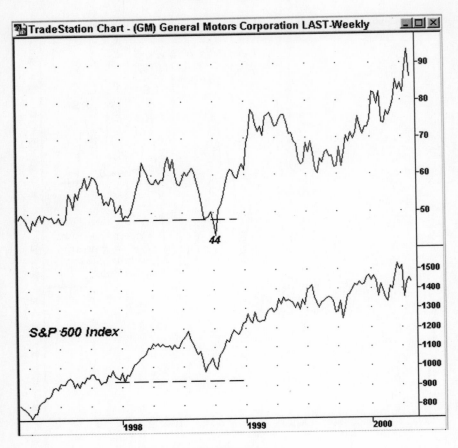

Figure 10.16

Outcome—Figure 10.16

Exited short positions on stop order at $50.50 for a profit of $6

The downtrend reversed in the $44 area, so the attempt to stay positioned for a further decline in the stock was unsuccessful. If the S&P 500 weekly chart had also been taken into account, it would have more likely suggested a buy in GM on dips, given the action of the bellwether S&P 500 Index as the S&P Index reversed well above its prior low.

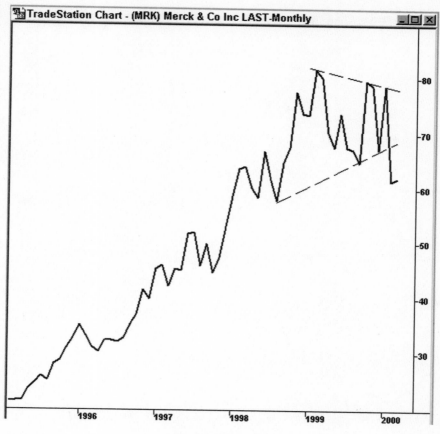

Figure 10.17

Suggested market action and rationale—Figure 10.17
Sell at $66.50

Prices on the monthly chart traced out a broad *triangle* pattern. The downside breakout below the lower triangle line, suggested that prices were headed still lower, suggesting a sale of the stock. Set stops just above the lower triangle line at $69.25.

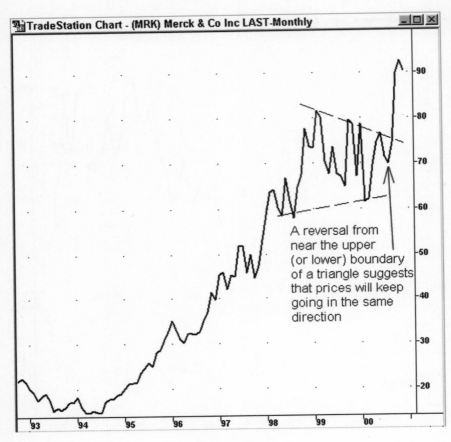

Figure 10.18

Outcome—Figure 10.18
Bought back short positions at $69.25 for a $2.75 loss

Prices reversed back to the upside and the point of reversal set up the outline of a new *triangle*. A subsequent upside breakout above this triangle's upper boundary led to the common result of such a breakout, that of a further upswing. Triangles, as well as *flag* consolidation patterns, often will change their shape as they evolve. In this case, what appeared to be a bearish pattern was only one more downswing that defined a different triangle, which implied a still ongoing consolidation rather than a downside *reversal*.

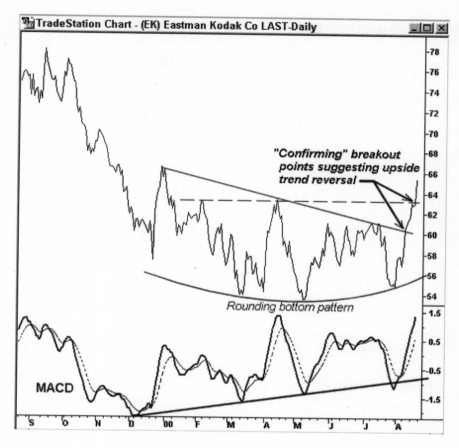

Figure 10.19

Suggested market action and rationale—Figure 10.19
Long at $60.70, with stop at $58.70

After the formation of a *rounding bottom* and series of higher relative lows made by the MACD oscillator, the stock appeared poised to reverse its downtrend. A first confirming price *reversal* action was a rebound to above the down trendline then, secondly, a further extension of this advance to above the two prior tops at the dashed line. Liquidating sell stop set under the first *breakout* point, as a pullback to under the trendline, would negate the bullish pattern.

Figure 10.20

Outcome—Figure 10.20
Stopped out of long position at $58.50

Fortunately, the liquidating stop order was elected *prior* to a sizable gap lower opening on 9/26 at $50.75 versus the prior day's close at $59.00, offering a good example of the value of adhering to initial stops. The *rounding bottom* is one of the more reliable patterns, but nothing works all the time and it was a relatively short-term formation. The only technical forewarning about this bottom was the low, and declining, volume trend according to OBV—expected at the last low would have been *more* volume. The breakout above the triangle was bullish initially. However, as soon as prices fell back below the topmost trendline, this was a *failure* of that pattern.

SUMMARY

The choices of what to focus on among the myriad of possible technical analysis tools, techniques, and interpretations are a matter of individual preference and choice. There are some analytical tools that I don't use, for example, the Commodity Channel Index (CCI), a common indicator presented on charting applications and financial web sites that provide such technical studies. To take this example, the CCI is a fairly complex formula that makes an assessment of whether the particular item's chart this study is applied to, is *trending* or not. I find that the study of the chart itself presents ample visual evidence for whether the item in question is in a trend, either up or down, or is undergoing a sideways move. My personal experience has led me to this conclusion. However, someone else could find the same indicator to be worthwhile and will employ it.

For the most part however, the tools and techniques I present are the key or basic ones of technical analysis. The intent is to distill from the broad array of technical analysis, the *essence* of technical analysis and to focus on what in my experience works best. However, my selections and choices are not the only ones, and others may employ some methods that I don't. My intent and goal is to provide the most useful and practical techniques that could increase the profitability of your investing and trading activities based on my experience and knowledge. From this start, you can begin your own study and application of technical analysis to see what works for you.

My orientation to technical analysis and this book need not be construed in a way that would prevent a study of fundamentals involving the economy, a market, or individual financial instrument whether that item is a stock, fixed income securities, crude oil futures, or the eurodollar. In stocks for example, I like the technology area for many fundamental reasons. However, my approach to investment and trade *entry and exit* is *technical*. Your approach may differ in what specific technical tools you find most useful or in the mix or blend of the two approaches or disciplines, fundamental and technical.

The tools and analysis presented are also offered in the hope that they assist you in making your own discoveries. You will also find that it is one thing to calculate, for example, that a *double bottom* has developed and make a purchase accordingly and quite another thing to sit tight through the days or weeks before a meaningful trend develops and you actually have any gain to consider. During the period after entry, it can also be a battle, with yourself usually, to adhere to the stop order that, hopefully, you entered at the time of trade entry. My encouragement and best wishes in making good choices in this process as you join the many other people who are attracted to the challenge and reward potential in the financial markets.

RECOMMENDED READING LIST AND OTHER RESOURCES

RECOMMENDED READING LIST

Advanced Technical Analysis

Technical Analysis for the Trading Professional, by Connie Brown. Advanced strategies and exploration of technical analysis techniques.

Basic Technical Analysis

Getting Started in Technical Analysis, by Jack Schwager. A basic guide to technical analysis, with an introduction to technical trading systems.
The Visual Investor: How to Spot Market Trends, by John Murphy. An introduction and guide to technical analysis.

Classical Chart Analysis and Trading Systems

Schwager on Futures: Technical Analysis, by Jack Schwager. An in-depth overview of classical chart analysis, with explanations and exploration of the structure and design of technical trading systems.

Comprehensive Guide to Technical Analysis

Technical Analysis of the Futures Markets: A Comprehensive Guide to Trading Methods and Applications, by John Murphy. Complete guide to all aspects of technical analysis.

Elliott Wave

The Major Works of R.N. Elliott, edited by Robert Prechter. R.N. Elliott's best-known student presents and organizes Elliott's own explanations on the workings of the market.

Gann

Gann Simplified, by Cliff Drake. Basic foundations of Gann theory and methods.

General Investment Interest

Battle for Investment Survival, by Gerald Loeb. A classic on general stock market strategy and the dynamics of investing.

Extraordinary Popular Delusions and the Madness of Crowds, by Charles Mackay and *Confusion de Confusiones*, by Joseph de la Vega. Two classic works in one book, about crowd delusions and the extremes of financial manias.

How to Make Money in Stocks, by William O'Neil. A blend of technical and fundamental approaches by someone who has been a successful market investor and the publisher of *Investor's Business Daily*.

Intermarket Technical Analysis: Trading Strategies for the Global Stock, Bond, Commodity and Currency Markets, by John Murphy. Complete guide to intermarket analysis.

References in Technical Analysis

Elliott Wave Principle: Key to Stock Market Profits, by Frost and Prechter. A classic explanation and interpretation of R.N. Elliott's wave principles.

Encyclopedia of Chart Patterns, by Thomas Bulkowski. A definitive and detailed explanation of chart patterns, with extensive research on each pattern's reliability.

Japanese Candlestick Charting Techniques, by Steve Nison. The basics of candlestick charts and discussions of candlestick patterns.

Technical Analysis from A to Z, by Steven Achelis. Brief explanations and summaries of most of the technical trading tools and indicators.

Technical Analysis of the Stock Market

Technical Analysis of Stock Trends, Eighth Edition, by Edwards and Magee. The bible of technical analysis and a long-time classic and reference work.

Trading Systems

Breaking the Black Box: Learn How to Design, Test and Apply Mechanical Trading Systems Using Profitable Examples, by Martin Pring. A course—listen, watch, read, and learn how to design, test, and implement your own trading systems.

Trading and Technical Analysis Sources

Traders Library; www.traderslibrary.com and (800) 272-2855—Online availability of a wide range of trading and investment-related books. Catalog available by mail.

Traders Press, Inc.; www.traderspress.com and (800) 927-8222—Online ordering and information on trading and investment-oriented books. Catalog available.

Charting and Technical Analysis Web Sites

www.bigcharts.com
www.clearstation.com
www.sixer.com
www.bullchart.com

Technical Analysis and Systems Testing and Development Applications

TradeStation 2000i, from Omega Research; www.tradestation.com and (800) 556-2022.

Charting Software

MetaStock, Equis International; www.equis.com and (800) 882-3040.
TC 2000, Worden Brothers, Inc; www.TC2000.com and (800) 776-4940.

Data Vendors

Each charting/technical analysis software provider will provide information on their most widely used market data vendors for end-of-day, real-time, and historical market data, compatible with their products. Most such applications will work with a wide choice of data sources.

GLOSSARY

accumulation Purchase of stocks, especially over time and often implying steady and significant buying in a particular price zone, which is perceived to offer value. A stock is said to be under accumulation when it is being bought in such a fashion—the opposite of *distribution*. The formation of large *base* patterns is often the effect of accumulation.

advance/decline line The advance/decline, or *A/D*, line, is a measure of market *breadth*, which is the number of stocks that are advancing relative to those that are declining on a daily or weekly basis on either the NYSE or Nasdaq exchanges. Wherever this cumulative total begins, the starting value is zero. Thereafter, whichever total is greater, advancing or declining stocks, the net A/D figure that day is either a plus number or a negative number, respectively, and is added or subtracted from the running total. The A/D difference, plotted as a line, will tend to have either an upward or downward slope. This line can then be compared to the chart of the relevant index. The directional movement should be the same as the index to confirm the trend. An A/D line that is trending in the opposite direction to price is a *divergence* and possible forewarning of an eventual trend reversal.

Arms Index A ratio of the average volume of declining stocks divided by the average volume of advancing ones. This index also goes by the term *TRIN* (from *trading index*) and was developed by Richard Arms. A reading above 1.0 means more volume is going into advancing stocks, whereas below 1.0 means trading activity predominates in declining issues. A 10-day average of the Arms Index that is above 1.2 suggests a market that is oversold and may be due for a correction, whereas a reading below .80 is considered to be overbought. Oversold readings are considered more reliable than ones suggesting the market is overbought.

arithmetic Arithmetic or linear scaling means that equal price moves on the vertical price scale or axis, are the same, as opposed to a semi-logarithmic scale where only equal percentage moves are measured equally. For example, a move from 10 to 20, a 100 percent price increase, is the same distance on the arithmetic price scale as an advance from 50 to 60, equal to a 20 percent gain.

arc pattern A strong price rise that goes up at a steeper and steeper rate, tracing out a circular pattern below the lows that can reach an angle of ascent that is almost straight up. When such an arc goes vertical like this, especially on a weekly and monthly chart basis, it often signals a major trend reversal to come that will involve an equally steep collapse of prices.

ascending triangle The type of triangle that can be traced out on a chart when the lower trendline goes up at an angle, representing a pattern of higher upswing lows, whereas the upper triangle boundary is a flat or horizontal line, as the highs are stopping in the same area repeatedly. This type of triangle, usually suggests a bullish outcome as buyers are willing to purchase (and start rallies) at increasingly higher price levels. As with all triangles however, the direction of the price breakout is the key predictive event.

backtesting   The rules of a trading mechanical system that trigger trade entry and exit and then are applied to historical data with a subsequent report of the trades that would have been entered and exited according to these system rules, with a tally of hypothetical profits and losses.

bar chart   A chart type that shows each trading day as a vertical line known as a *bar*. Relative to the price scale, the low (L) of this line is equal to the low of the period and the high (H) of the line is equal to the high of the period being measured (e.g., daily). The opening (O) price, if shown, is represented by a horizontal slash mark on the left of the line and the close (C) is marked on the right side of the line. Sometimes, charting applications present OHLC as the bar chart display option, unless the Open is omitted, in which case this variation is listed as a HLC chart.

base/base patterns   The duration of a sideways trend in the same approximate price zone, equals the extent of a market or individual financial item's *base*. The longer the time duration, the bigger the resulting base pattern, with a correspondingly higher upside potential later.

bearish   *See* **bullish/bearish.**

bear trap   A significant new low and downward price thrust, which is immediately or closely followed by an upside price reversal. Such price action springs a trap for those bearish.

bellwethers   A stock, related index, or subindex that tends to move in the same direction at the same time, or to move in advance of, a broad average or index. When a bellwether fails to at least move in the same direction as the broad index and/or, for example, to also go to a new relative high or low, this sets up a divergence and warning of a possible trend reversal.

Bollinger bands   An indicator invented by John Bollinger that begins with a moving average of the close that is usually 20 periods in length. An upper and lower line is then plotted that is two standard deviations below and above the moving average. The upper and lower lines, respectively, suggest areas of possible price resistance or support. The upper and lower lines contract or expand according to whether price swings are limited and narrow in scope or are wide-ranging and volatile.

breadth   The degree to which there is participation of stocks in a rally or decline. Positive or bullish market breadth is where a majority or most stocks participate in a rising trend in terms of the major averages. Negative or bearish market breadth is where a minority of all stocks are participating (moving in the same direction) in an uptrend. Such a situation indicates that fewer and fewer stocks are pulling up the market averages or index.

breakaway gap   A price gap on a bar chart—a space between one period's low or high and the next period's high or low—that forms early in a price move, such as when there is a trend reversal from down to up or vice versa, or on a price breakout above or below a trading range.

breakout   A price swing or movement that moves above or below an area of prior or perceived resistance or support. This area could be the high or low end of a *trading range*, or support or resistance implied by a chart pattern marked by one or more trendlines.

broadening bottoms/broadening tops   Reversal patterns where price *volatility* increases in a series of higher highs and lower lows. The *broadening bottom* is where the prior trend has been down, and a sideways series of price swings develop that form a series of higher upswing highs and lower downswing lows, making one upward and one downward sloping trendline that have opposite sloping angles, thereby assuming a megaphone shape. When the preceding trend is up, the same pattern is assumed to be *a broadening top*.

bullish/bearish   The current trend direction, as well as the outlook or expectation for the future direction of a trend can be described as *bullish* when prices are rising or expected to rise and *bearish* when prices are falling or expected to fall. The term "bull," or someone who thinks prices will rise, comes from the charging (ahead) characteristic of a bull. The term bear, applied to someone who thinks prices will fall, stems from the falling asleep characteristic of a bear in hibernation—also, from the bear's ability to maul or do damage.

bull trap   A new high for a price swing or move that is immediately or closely followed by a downside price reversal. Such price action springs a trap for those bullish.

call/put ratio   A ratio of the total daily volume in call options, divided by the total volume of put option volume. As the trading activity in calls almost always exceeds put volume, the resulting call/put ratio will most often be a whole number (e.g., 2 or twice as much call volume). This is a custom way of calculating this ratio, as the standard method is to divide put by call volume—the *put/call* ratio—resulting in a fraction, e.g., .5. The call/put ratio is a *contrary* type indicator. When a bearish market outlook results in put buying nearly equal to, or more than call volume, it suggests that a rally may be coming as there are few sellers left. The reverse situation is when call volume approaches or exceeds three times put volume; a selloff may be near.

candlestick chart   A chart type that displays the same OHLC information as a bar chart for each period, except that displaying the open is not optional for candlesticks, as there is an emphasis on where a market closes relative to the open. A wide, real body, with a solid color, usually black, for a down period and a dark outline with a filled-in white background for an up close, represents the price difference between the open and close. The lower line of the solid-color body is the close, whereas the close is at the upper line of the solid white body. The high and low is given distinctly less emphasis by a thin (shadow) line above/below the wide, real body. The visual depiction of color and body width allows some key aspects of price action to be grasped quickly.

channels   A *channel line* may be initially drawn through any first upswing peak by drawing a straight line parallel to an uptrend line formed by two to three higher lows. Further rally highs then allow redrawing the upper parallel channel line for a best fit and defines likely minor resistance. The resulting two parallel lines then constitute an uptrend channel, which often then defines the future price boundaries (support and resistance) of an up trend. In a decline, a parallel line drawn through one, two, or more, reaction lows and below a down trendline, forms a downtrend channel.

close-only chart   A chart type that plots the closing values only, without reference to the highs and lows for the time period being charted. This chart is more commonly known as a line chart.

compression   The process where a price range narrows, such as when prices are near the apex of a triangle formation, or near the end of a rising or falling wedge. This event signifies that bullish and bearish forces are more and more in balance, at least temporarily. However, when there is a breakout out of this narrower and narrower range, the resulting move or follow-through can be explosive, as money pours into the winning side of the price swing and out the losing side.

confirmation   A condition that occurs when a secondary or related indicator, index, or event strengthens the validity of a technical pattern relating, most commonly, to the price trend. A common example is when trading activity, as measured by contract or share volume, increases or dips in lockstep with price activity with an increase in average daily or weekly volume occurring on days or weeks when prices move in the same direction as the dominant trend. Price patterns can confirm trend direction also (e.g., several higher price *gaps* occur after prices reverse direction from a declining trend to a rally phase).

congestion   Usually used as a term for a price zone or range where there has been significant prior trading activity, but where buying and selling have also been sufficiently in balance to prevent either an uptrend or downtrend from developing.

continuation pattern   A chart or price formation, such as the sideways move of a rectangle pattern, that implies a pause or consolidation for a limited duration, prior to the resumption of the dominant trend's up or downward direction. Other common types of continuation patterns are *triangles* and *flags*.

consolidation   A movement counter to the prior trend that retraces some portion of this price swing, after which the trend continues in the same direction as previously. This countertrend move is viewed as having a consolidating function relative to the prior price swing.

contrary opinion   A theory that suggests that when an overwhelming majority of traders and market analysts are either bullish or bearish, an opposite (contrary) trend will develop. This is because most participants have taken a position in the market already and there are few buyers left to take prices much higher on rallies, or sellers to take prices lower on declines. The resulting scarcity of buyers or sellers makes a trend reversal more likely.

correction   A countertrend movement. If the trend is up, a correction or corrective move is a downswing that retraces some portion of the prior advance, which is often in a range of 38 percent to 62 percent of that up move. If the trend is down, the correction or countertrend move is up.

crossover moving averages   When two moving averages of a shorter and longer duration are plotted, one will cross above or below the other whenever a price trend reverses direction long enough so that the shorter average crosses above or below the longer moving average. An upside crossover generates a buy indication or signal; a downside crossover generates a sell signal.

cycle The time duration of a complete move in a market—for example, the duration of a major or secondary uptrend. Standard time cycles involve a search for any tendency for a market to top or bottom at set intervals (e.g., every 13 weeks). Gann work considers a *natural* market cycle to be 52 weeks, with attention paid to market activity 1 year after a major low or high.

descending triangle The type of triangle in which a series of lower upswing highs trace out a downward sloping line, while lows in the same area form a flat or horizontal line comprising the bottom side of the triangle. This type of triangle often has a bearish resolution, as the pattern stems from rallies that reverse at successively lower levels, suggesting that selling pressure predominates. However, as with all other triangles, the breakout direction is the key predictor.

distribution Sale of a stock or stocks, especially over time and often implying steady and significant selling in a particular price zone, which is perceived as fairly valued or overvalued. A stock or stocks in general are described as being distributed, especially when sold by market professionals to the investing public—the opposite of *accumulation*. The formation of sizable top patterns can be seen as an effect of distribution.

divergence A situation where a secondary or related indicator, index, or event is opposite to or does not confirm the validity of a technical pattern relating to the price trend. A divergence is the opposite of a technical *confirmation* and is sometimes also referred to as a nonconfirmation. For example, prices move to a significant new high, but an indicator like OBV (on balance volume) or an oscillator like RSI does not follow suit relative to its prior history.

double bottom/double top A double bottom is a chart pattern formed when prices make a low in the same area where there was a prior price low, usually one considered to be significant. The two lows, if they are not subsequently penetrated, form a double bottom. A double top is a price pattern where prices make a high in the same area as a prior significant peak. The two highs, if not exceeded, comprise a double top.

Dow theory Predictions of market and economic behavior made by Charles Dow in the late 1900s. This theory says that the market and economic trend is sound as long as both the Dow Industrial and Transportation averages (first formulated by Dow), confirm each other by both going to a new relative high, after this event occurs with either average. If the other average does not follow suit, the resulting divergence suggests an end to an existing bull market. Conversely, if there is a new low in one average, but not the other, this is also suggestive of an eventual reversal—to the upside.

Elliott wave principle Based on the theories and writings of R.N. Elliott, the wave principle looks at a bull or bear market cycle in terms of three component moves in the direction of the trend. In the case of a bull market, there are three *impulse waves* higher, interspaced with two downswings that retrace some portion of the preceding upswing, resulting in a five-wave structure. In a bear market, there are two down moves, interspaced with a corrective upswing that retraces some or all of the first downswing for a three-part bear market trend. The relationship of these waves to each other often can be expressed in *Fibonacci* ratios.

envelopes   Lines that track a moving average and are found by adding or subtracting some percentage value above and below a moving average. An example is a 21-day moving average of closing prices, with envelope lines equal to three percent above and below this moving average. Upper and lower envelope lines may also be set at different percentage values (e.g., 3% and 5%).

exhaustion gap   A price gap that occurs at or near the end of a significant trend, representing a possible sign of an approaching trend reversal and a last gasp of bull or bear market influences.

exponential smoothing   A moving average that gives greater weight to the most recent close and also uses all prior market data.

failed pattern/pattern failure   A chart pattern that often or normally predicts a certain future price movement, trend duration, or reversal, that does *not* lead to the expected result. This event sometimes leads to a strong move in the opposite direction of what was expected. For example, an apparent *double top* is exceeded and a sizable and strong advance develops.

Fibonacci numbers   The Fibonacci number sequence, named after the mathematician who described it, is the number series that is arrived at by adding the first two numbers to arrive at the third one, beginning with 1: 1, 2, 3, 5, 8, 13, 21, and so on. The ratio of any number to the next larger one is 62 percent, a common retracement amount for a countertrend move relative to a preceding price swing. The inverse of 62 percent is 38 percent, also a common retracement. The other common retracement, 50 percent, equals the ratio of the first (1) to the second number (2) in the series.

filter   A modifying rule for a trade entry rule or set of criteria that seeks to increase the likelihood that the trade or investment selected will result in a successful or profitable market entry. For example, entry into a market based on a breakout above or below a trendline has an additional rule or filter that the penetration above/below the line be by an amount of at least five percent.

flag   A short-term chart formation seen on bar or candlestick charts that display highs and lows, which is a common continuation pattern. The components to this pattern are usually an initial strong *thrust* up or down, followed by a shorter back and forth price movement bounded by two parallel lines, followed by a further breakout in the direction of the first thrust.

fundamental analysis   Study of the external and internal supply and demand factors that influence the economy, a market, or a specific financial instrument. In a stock, fundamental analysis will concern itself with the current and future prospects for corporate earnings and perhaps will make price projections for the stock price based on these considerations.

Gann principles   A body of market theory devised by W. D. Gann that uses specialized charting methods to attempt to pinpoint (1) the beginning, middle, and end of a market trend cycle; (2) the *price* and *time* points where trends are likely to falter, reverse, or accelerate; and (3) a method of finding support and resistance. *Gann charts* and *angles* are specialized tools for this form of analysis. This work holds that market trends have predictable time and price durations and objectives.

gaps A price area where no trading occurred from one period to the next, as happens if the daily open of a market is above the prior day's high and the subsequent low for that period remains above the prior day's high. Any distance between one day's high and the next day's low creates an *upside* price *gap*. The reverse situation, of a *downside gap*, comes about when one period's high is lower than the preceding period's low. An upside gap, particularly one that is pronounced, is often a sign of market strength and a strong uptrend. A downside gap provides a technical indication of the reverse or a bearish trend. Gaps can be further categorized by the position they occupy in a trend: *breakaway*, *runaway* (or *measuring*), and *exhaustion* types.

Good-Til-Canceled (GTC): An order that is held by a market broker on behalf of an investor or trader to buy or sell, which is in effect until it is canceled or for some set time duration (e.g., six weeks) after which it can be renewed. A GTC designation is often used for liquidating stop orders.

head and shoulders pattern A three-part reversal pattern. The middle high or "head" is above or below the secondary highs or lows formed before and after the head. The two secondary highs or lows form the "shoulders" in this pattern. The middle low (the head) of a head and shoulders (H&S) bottom is below the two secondary lows that form the two shoulders with the H&S top having a head that is above them. A line drawn between the top or bottommost extreme of the two shoulders forms a "neckline." When this line is penetrated there is a measuring implication for a further move equal to at least the distance between the top of the head and neckline, subtracted from (for an H&S top) or added to (an H&S bottom) the neckline.

histogram A way of plotting a data series where each value is at the top or bottom point of a bar that extends above or below a zero line. If the value is positive, for example 190, the top of the bar will be plotted at that level on the right-hand point scale above zero. If the value is −190, the bottom of the bar will intersect at that figure on the right-hand point scale below the zero line.

indicator A price, or volume, based mathematical formula that evaluates a market in various ways. Broadly speaking, indicator types are (1) moving averages, which measure and confirm trend direction and (2) oscillators, which measure *momentum*, and calculate the rate or speed of price changes. Another term sometimes used for a technical indicator is a technical *study*.

internal trendline A trendline that is drawn as a "best fit" through the most number of highs or lows in a price trend and that may bisect or cut through one or more bars of a HLC chart or through one or more closes on a line chart. The conventional method of trendline construction is to connect only the extreme highs and lows.

island bottom A bar chart pattern involving price *gaps*, occurring when prices gap lower, usually after a lengthy downtrend and over a few or more subsequent periods, trade under this gap, leaving the gap "open." This is then followed by a gap higher. The resulting bottom pattern has a "body" of bars at the lows that are isolated, similar to an island surrounded by a body of water. This is a *reversal* type formation.

island top A bar chart pattern involving price gaps, occurring when prices gap higher, usually after a lengthy uptrend and over a few or more subsequent periods trade above this gap, leaving it "open"—this is followed by a gap lower that takes prices below the gap area. The resulting top pattern has a "body" of isolated bars at the top, similar to an island surrounded by water. An island top is a *reversal* pattern.

item/instrument   A convenient way of referring to an individual financial security in a general or *generic* way when one is discussing technical analysis principles, and that generally pertain (unless otherwise specified) to any traded security: a stock, futures contract, bond, foreign exchange (FX) transaction in the interbank currency market, and so on.

key reversals   A pattern occurring when, during a downtrend, prices make a new low but *close* above the prior bar's close (i.e., a key upside reversal or key reversal up). Conversely, in an uptrend, a key downside reversal or key reversal down occurs when prices make a new high, but during the same trading period fall such that the *close* is below the prior bar's close. A more restrictive definition for a key upside reversal up requires that the close is above the prior day's *high* and a key downside reversal down requires a close below the *low* of the prior period.

line chart   A chart that plots the closing price only, ignoring the high and low for the period.

line formation   A sideways move that occurs after an uptrend or downtrend and that is typically a consolidation of the preceding movement. The line formation is functionally the same as the *rectangle* pattern or sideways trading range. Charles Dow said that a line formation could serve in lieu of an actual retracement of the prior price swing, that is, a strictly lateral move can serve the same "corrective" function as does a move that is opposite or counter to the preceding trend.

logarithmic scaling   The type of price scale where equal *percentage* moves are measured equally. For example, a move from 10 to 20, representing a gain of 100 percent, will be 5 times as long on the logarithmic price scale as a move from 50 to 60, a gain of 20 percent. This is quite different from the arithmetic price scale, where both those price moves would be equal on that price scale. *Semi-logarithmic* is the proper term for the formula variation used in financial chart scaling. Also sometimes labeled "log" or "semi-log" in charting application scaling choices.

MACD (moving average convergence–divergence)   A moving average indicator that gives more weight to the most recent price changes as the moving averages are exponentially smoothed, and which also generates trading "signals" as two averages are used, producing crossover buy and sell signals. The first MACD line is most commonly the difference between 2 exponential moving averages of 12 and 26 periods. The second line is typically a 9-period exponentially smoothed average of the first line and is called the *signal line*, and is the line that will cross above or below the MACD line. An added MACD component is simply a histogram with a bar that plots the difference between the signal line and the MACD line, allowing a distinct view of the difference.

McClellan oscillator   An indicator that is the difference between two 19-day and 39-day exponentially smoothed moving averages of the daily net advance/decline figures in the U.S. stock market. Crossings above the zero line are positive and below the line, negative. Readings above +100 are considered *overbought*, below −100, *oversold*.

measured move   A calculation for the extent of an advance or a decline based on the distance traveled in a prior price swing. For example, a stock has an advance from 30 to 50, followed by a pullback to 40. A measured move objective for a next rally from 40 is at least equal to the first advance of 20 points, or to 60. A measured move objective should be thought of as a minimum price target only, as a second advance can, of course, be more prolonged than the first.

measuring gap (runaway gap)   A price gap occurring at the approximate midpoint of either an uptrend or downtrend. The tendency for a price gap or gaps to appear about midway in a move, as bullish or bearish influences build, allows an approximate measurement of the ultimate low or high for the price swing in question. As such gaps occur when the trend is seen to accelerate or "run away" from the gradual unfolding of the emerging trend, they're also called *runaway gaps*.

momentum   The rate or speed of price change. Technical *oscillators* plot momentum visually.

momentum oscillator   This indicator measures price differences over x number of periods, which is a variable input. If the value of 10 is used and the period choice is daily, the close of 10 days ago is subtracted from the latest price. Each period's resulting positive or negative value is then plotted above or below a zero line.

moving average   In its simplest form, a calculation adding some number of closes for a time period (e.g., hourly, daily, or weekly). Division by the number of periods of the moving average then results in a *simple* moving average. An average is said to "move" because, after each close the division is done anew, the result is a "moving" figure. Besides the simple type, there are *weighted* and *exponentially smoothed* moving averages. In practice a buy indication is signaled when prices cross above a moving average, a sell when prices cross below it. If two moving averages are used (*crossover moving averages*), a trade entry signal is generated when the shorter average crosses above or below the longer moving average.

on balance volume (OBV) indicator   A formula that creates a running total of volume. The total day's volume is added to the total of days when the item has an up close and the day's volume is subtracted from days when the instrument has a down close. Because the OBV number is zero on the date calculations are begun, which can be at any time, the absolute number is unimportant, only the directional movement, which should "confirm" the price trend. If prices are trending higher, but the OBV is moving sideways to lower, this is a bearish *divergence*.

optimization   A procedure done by computer, where all the parameters of a trading system, at least within the specified range, are tested for the best results (e.g., most winning trades). A common test of a parameter or variable is to check all moving average lengths for the best one.

oscillators   Indicators that move with the trend and measure price momentum in various ways. Many will move above or below a horizontal axis representing a neutral momentum. Oscillators are best known for their use in measuring potential market extremes either in a strong uptrend or downtrend. These extremes are defined as *overbought* or *oversold*, respectively. A common use of this information is to look for shorting opportunities in a rising trend and buying opportunities in a falling trend, which can be especially useful in countertrend trading. Common oscillators are the MACD, RSI, and stochastics. Another important use is when there is failure by the oscillator to also move, along with prices to a new high or low, suggesting a possible future trend *reversal*.

overbought   An extreme in a market when prices have risen strongly in a short, or for a prolonged, period of time, such that there is an increasing likelihood for a pullback or downside correction. An overbought condition is usually suggested by an oscillator reading at either a predefined point or area, such as above 70 in the RSI or—in an "unbounded" (no set range from 1–100) oscillator like MACD—when there is a reading in an area where the particular market or item formed a top previously. Strong bull markets can stay overbought for long periods.

oversold   An extreme in a market when prices have fallen sharply in a short, or for a prolonged, period of time, such that there is an increasing likelihood for a rebound or an upside correction. An oversold condition is usually suggested by an oscillator reading at either a predefined point or area, such as below 30 in the RSI or—in an "unbounded" (no set range from 1–100) oscillator like MACD—when there is a reading in an area where the particular market or item, formed a bottom previously. Major bear markets can stay oversold for a lengthy period.

parabolic arc pattern   A steep rise or fall in a market, the outline of which takes the form of a circular arc. In the late phases of such a steep uptrend, this chart pattern can go from an arc or circular shape to a nearly straight-up vertical move. Such a straight-up move marks the final cumulative "blow-off" phase, before a collapse in prices, which is the typical outcome.

parameter   A variable input in an indicator or trading system. In a moving average or in an oscillator, the number of periods set (e.g., days) is a parameter. Informally, any expected variable: e.g., an expectation for a stock to trade between 20 and 30, or within those parameters.

patterns   The tracing out of certain types of formations on a chart, by prices, by an indicator, or by volume, where the resulting formation is generally viewed as having predictive value related to future price direction. For example, in an uptrend, rally failures in the same price area as one in which there was a prior significant top, especially when separated by a period of time, such as a few or more weeks (or months), are predictive for a significant downside trend reversal (i.e., a *double top* pattern).

pattern recognition system   A trading system that is based on a particular chart or price pattern and not based on a trend following or moving average system. This type of trading system measures trend direction and duration. The trigger for market action is based on the formation of the pattern itself (e.g., a key reversal) and can be triggered rather quickly, rather than relying on a longer past period and averaging considerations.

pennant   A variation of a flag consolidation. Some consider all such consolidation patterns as flags but the triangular pennant shape also gives it a distinct identity. The primary distinguishing characteristic is that price action traces out both downward and upward sloping trend lines, forming converging upper and lower boundaries, like a *symmetrical triangle*. On a daily chart, time duration of formation of the flag is usually 1–3 weeks. As prices converge, or *compress*, near the narrow end of the pennant, a breakout usually occurs in the prior trend direction and travels a distance equal to the vertical side of the pennant.

point and figure chart A chart that shows all trading as a single stream of price activity, using a series of Xs and Os in vertical columns, without regard for when a price occurred. Each X is set to equal a price move of a preset amount, called the *box size*. A new X is added when, and only when, there is a high achieved that is this amount above the prior box (e.g., $3). However, if prices decline by an amount equal to or greater than a variable amount set as the *reversal size*, which is usually some multiple of the box size (e.g., three times it), a new column of Os begins in a column one over to the right from the last columns of Xs. Os continue as long as there is a new low that carries at least the box size distance under the preceding O, or until there is a reversal equal to the reversal size, in which case a new column of Xs begins one to the right.

primary trend The primary or *major* price trend in the stock market, as first defined by Charles Dow, is one lasting a year or more, up to several years. There are countertrends, or movements in the opposite direction of the primary trend, which Dow called *secondary* trends and which he considered unimportant to investors, as they should be primarily concerned with the major trend.

price swing Any segment of a price movement in a market that can be identified as a distinct and separate uptrend or downtrend. A price swing can be any of the different components of a trend. For example, an overall uptrend may consist of five price swings: an initial advance, a countertrend *reaction*, second advance, second reaction, and a final advance. A "swing" is another term for a price move with a beginning, middle, and end. At the end of a swing, momentum tends to reach a peak, slow, and then move in an opposite or sideways direction. A *swing objective* is a calculation for the extent of a price move. A *swing failure* is the failure to reach that price target.

put/call ratio A ratio of the total daily volume in put options, divided by the total volume of call options. As the trading activity in calls almost always exceeds put volume, the resulting put/call ratio will most often be a fractional number (e.g., .5, or put volume $\frac{1}{2}$ that of call volume). The put/call ratio is a *contrary* type indicator. When an extreme bearish view, reflected in speculative put buying nearly equal to, or exceeding, call volume (ratio is 1 or above), it suggests that a rally may be coming, as there are few sellers left. When call volume gets to, or near, 3 times that of put volume (ratio is .33 or less), a selloff may be near.

random walk The theory, attributed to the economist Paul Samuelson, that in an "informationally efficient" market, price changes are not capable of being forecast as they already fully incorporate the expectations and information of all market participants. This theory implies that the market cannot be *timed* in terms of predicting when fluctuations will occur. Due to this view, it's recommended to utilize only a long-term buy and hold strategy. Random walk theory implies that the more efficient the market, the more random are price changes. This runs counter to the tenets of technical analysis, which holds that price changes are not random events. Charles Dow observed that there was a long process in bull markets before all potential participants got fully invested. This occurs near the end phase of this trend and close to a trend reversal, which is predictable as to its eventual outcome.

range The price difference from low to high in any given time period. The hourly range is the difference between the hourly high and low; the daily range is the difference between that day's high and low, and so on. The price range can also be referenced relative to any period (e.g., 5 or 50 days).

rate of change (ROC) oscillator A price ratio that involves dividing the most recent close by the close of x number of days ago (e.g., 10). The resulting value is either a positive number above 100 or a negative one plotted below 100. The ROC oscillator is an unbounded oscillator, not having *normalized* values between 1 and 100, so *overbought* or *oversold* levels are evaluated and determined by the levels seen at past tops or bottoms.

reaction A countertrend move, relative to the trend that has preceded it. The term derives from the concept in the physical sciences, that for every action there is a reaction. In a trend, there are usually, if not always, participants with a market viewpoint that is contrary to an ongoing price move that *react* to the trend underway with contrary market action.

rectangle A sideways trading range that forms after either an uptrend or downtrend that most often is a consolidation of the prior trend before a further move in the same direction as this trend. The name comes from the shape of the pattern, which requires a sideways trend that goes on long enough that the pattern's width is longer than the consolidation trading range is high. Sometimes, a rectangle will form a *top* or *bottom* pattern. The key is the direction of a breakout move above or below the top or bottom lines drawn across the range's highs or lows.

relative high A daily high that is greater than any recent high or a high for the price move that is ongoing. This distinguishes a high that is a new high for the move or for some number of days or weeks, but not an *absolute* high or highest all-time peak reached by the stock or other item.

relative low A daily low that is less than any recent low or a low for the current move. This distinguishes a low that is a new low for the price swing that is underway, but not necessarily a new all-time low or a low that was part of an earlier secondary or major trend.

relative strength index (RSI) An oscillator which is a ratio of an average of up closes relative to down closes, over some number of periods such as 9 or 14. The RSI is plotted on a scale of 0 to 100, so has the set boundaries of a *normalized* indicator. This allows establishment of particular *overbought* or *oversold* levels, most commonly at 70 and 30, respectively. Besides being an indicator that is used in countertrend trading, for example, by selling into possible overbought extremes, the RSI has great value in warning of a possible future trend reversal when it does not follow prices to a new relative high or low.

resistance A price level, area, or zone, where selling comes in sufficiently in force to push prices back down. There can be current and expected resistance. Expected or anticipated resistance is based on past price history; if selling was sufficient to turn prices lower before, it can be anticipated to be an area where there will again be active selling. This must be judged for each situation; momentum may be so strong as to expect prior resistance to be overcome.

retracement The percentage amount of a price move in the opposite direction from the preceding trend, relative to that prior price swing—from low to high (an advance) or high to low (a decline). For example, a 50 percent retracement of an advance that carried prices from 50 to 100 would mean that prices fell back to 75.

reversal patterns Price action that traces out a formation usually indicating that the current trend will be coming to an end at some point either quite soon or on an intermediate-term basis, to be followed by a move in the opposite direction. Well-known reversal patterns include *double tops* or *bottoms* and the *head and shoulders* formation.

rounding bottom/rounding top A series of lows or highs that trace out a relatively smooth curved shape, rather than having a series of distinct highs and lows more jagged in appearance. Thus, a rounding bottom would have gradually lower lows on the left side, followed by gradually higher lows on the right side of a saucer-shaped bottom; also called a "saucer" bottom (or top).

runaway gap A price gap occurring, often at the approximate midpoint of either an uptrend or downtrend, when the trend is seen to accelerate or "run away" from the more gradual unfolding of the trend that came before. The tendency for these price gaps to appear about midway in a move, as bullish or bearish influences build, allows an approximate measurement of the ultimate low or high for the price swing in question. Thus, such gaps are also called *measuring gaps*.

sentiment indicators Investors, advisors, or traders (or collectively) dominate point of view about the market: *bullish*, *bearish*, or neutral (expects little change). This opinion or *sentiment* about the prospects for the future trend direction can be measured by actual surveys of market participants on their market outlook, or indirectly by the level of activity in call options, betting on rising prices, versus the volume in call options, where profit potential stems from falling prices—the *put/call* (or call/put) *ratio*. Such measures of market sentiment are used as *contrary* indicators. When there are extremes of either bullish or bearish sentiment, the market is often near a peak or a bottom. This is another way of assessing whether a market is overbought or oversold.

simple moving average A moving average with equal weight given to each day's price data. Other types of moving averages are *weighted* and *exponentially smoothed* moving averages.

signal line A moving average of an indicator calculation that generates buy and sell indications or "signals," when this average crosses above or below the indicator line (the *plot* of the indicator value). Such oscillator type indicators as MACD and stochastics have signal lines.

spike high/spike low A spike high is one that is sharply above the high of the preceding and following periods, such as on a daily chart. A spike low is one that is sharply below the low of the preceding and following periods. Typically, the term "spike" is used where there is little subsequent follow-through by the close. Therefore, a spike high is often followed by a close near the low, and a spike low by a close nearer the high than the low.

stochastics An oscillator type indicator that measures price momentum. Stochastics uses two lines—%K and its three-day moving average, %D. The three-day moving average is the signal line. Stochastics is a normalized indicator using a 0 to 100 scale, with readings above 80 usually defined as *overbought* and below 20, *oversold*. Stochastics measures the current close relative to the highest high and lowest low of either a 9- or 14-period duration typically. There are two stochastics versions: fast and slow. Slow stochastics is the one in common use and uses a smoothing factor to slow down the fluctuations, which has proven to be the most useful. Signals are taken when the crossover occurs in either overbought or oversold zones.

supply Stock that is for sale in a certain price area. To say that prices are into an area of supply or there is a supply overhang, means that there is the expectation that there is an abundant amount for sale if and when prices advance into the specified area. Supply is another way of defining resistance.

support A specific price, or price area, below current levels, where there is expectation that there is sufficient buying interest to halt a decline. A prior downswing low that led to a rebound, is commonly a point or area of anticipated support or a support "floor."

symmetrical triangle A sideways price move and a common form of price consolidation after an uptrend or downtrend. A series of lower upswing highs and higher downswing lows form downward and upward sloping trendlines of the same angle (i.e., they are symmetrical) and which converge over time. If the two angles are extended out, they form an apex or third point of the triangle. This narrowing *range* suggests *compression* or an even balance between buyers and sellers. When prices break out in either direction, there is often a strong move in the direction of the breakout. The direction of the breakout is most often the same direction as the trend prior to the triangle formation.

technical analysis The study of *price* and *volume* trends alone, or market action itself, in order to determine the future direction of prices for a stock, bond, commodity, or any other financial market. *Open interest*, or the number of matched long and short positions, is another possible component of technical analysis in commodities futures. The technical approach is in contrast to *fundamental analysis*, which studies supply and demand influences, rather than price action itself, to make forecasts about the future direction and objectives for prices.

thrust day A day that closes either under the low of the previous day—a *downthrust* day—or above the high of the previous session—an *upthrust* day. A series of days with this pattern in the same direction suggests a strong trend.

top pattern A price formation that develops in a similar way, with similar characteristics and, based on past outcomes, is predictive for being an end of the current move. A top pattern also implies that a declining trend will develop at a future time, usually within a few days to a few weeks.

trading range A period where prices move sideways or in a lateral direction and where a series of highs peak in the same area and a series of lows bottom around the same levels. Parallel straight lines can then be drawn through the high and low ends of this price range.

trailing stop A stop order to liquidate a position placed either above (buy stop) or below the market (sell stop) and that is periodically adjusted upward or downward to best keep the stop protection in lockstep with a rising or falling trendline, or some measure of the unfolding trend. The purpose of a trailing stop is to lock in profits.

trend A condition where prices are rising or falling, on balance, and where there is a definite up or down direction to a price move. Successively higher highs and higher reaction lows define an *uptrend*. Successively lower lows and lower reaction highs define a *downtrend*. A sideways price movement, with a series of highs and lows forming in the same areas, defines a *trading range*; sometimes also defined as a sideways or *lateral* price *trend*. Trends are also classified as to duration, ranging from *minor* (a month or less), *secondary* or *intermediate* (less than 6–8 months), and *major* or *primary* (6–8 months to several years).

trendline A straight line connecting two to several *reaction* lows (an uptrend) or two to several reaction highs (a downtrend). A trendline is traditionally drawn such that the line touches a series of the highest highs or lowest lows on a bar or line chart and does not bisect or cut through any lines. An *internal trendline* is drawn connecting the greatest number of highs and greatest number of lows and can cut across isolated extreme highs or lows; an internal trendline is drawn with an eye to what represents the best fit or the line that best represents the rate of price change occurring.

trend channel A parallel line drawn above or below an uptrend or down trend-line, respectively, and that touches one or more swing highs or lows, thereby enclosing a trend.

trend following system A trading system that waits for a price move to develop of a certain duration and strength and then initiates a position in the market in the same direction.

triangles Sideways consolidation patterns in which prices fluctuate within converging trendlines. Triangles are common *continuation* patterns, but can sometimes form at tops and bottoms. Types of triangles based on their shape, are *symmetrical*, *ascending*, and *descending*.

triple top/triple bottom Similar to a double top or double bottom, only there is an additional one price peak or one downswing low that forms in the same approximate area as the prior two.

volume The level of trading activity in a stock, option, futures contract, or any other financial instrument. For example, volume in a stock is expressed in the number of shares traded, such as in the thousands, tens, or hundreds of thousands of shares on a daily or weekly basis. Expanding or increasing volume, when price movement is in the same direction as the dominant trend, is a *confirmation* of that trend—otherwise, there is a price/volume *divergence*, suggesting that market momentum may be slowing and the trend could reverse direction.

volatility The degree to which, or amount that, a market exhibits back and forth price swings or price instability. A market that exhibits wide-ranging price fluctuations is one of high volatility.

V top/V bottom   A situation where a top or bottom forms in a single thrust to a peak or trough, then moves quickly away from this point. There is a rally to a peak, or decline to a bottom, followed by a quick reversal, without the greater abundance of technical evidence for a top or bottom formation.

wedges   A formation in which prices move steadily lower as in a falling or declining (bullish) wedge, or steadily higher—a rising (bearish) wedge—in a converging pattern of narrowing price swings. Wedges typically form over a period of a few weeks to a few months.

weighted average   A moving average uses a specific number of periods like a simple moving average, but counts recent price data more heavily. For example, a greater percentage value is assigned to the closes for each of the past three days; thereby giving reduced weighting to days further back. The practical effect is to make a weighted moving average follow current prices more closely, with less of a lag than a regular simple moving average.

whipsaw   A situation arising when there are repeated and abrupt trend reversals, which can cause trend-following methods involving indicators, such as moving averages, to generate repeated buy and sell signals that don't lead to profitable results. The term "whipsaw" thus comes from instances of whip-like or choppy price action.

zero line   On the momentum and rate of change oscillators, a middle line is called the *zero* or *equilibrium* line. Values above the line are positive numbers, suggesting a bullish or positive rate of change. Values below the zero or midpoint line imply a bearish or declining momentum.

INDEX